Adieu My Youth

And Montreal's Rachel Street Market

Roman Susel

Copyright @ 2018 Roman Susel
All rights reserved
ISBN - 10 1775258815
ISBN - 13 978-1-7752588-1-0

DEDICATION

This book is dedicated to the memory of a city block in Montreal and the many hard working people who shared my neighbourhood during my youth. Their friendship, hospitality, knowledge and wisdom enlightened me, helping me to grow up. Their ambition, dreams and perseverance inspired me to keep on trying, not to give up and to learn from each attempt.

Also by Roman Susel

 In Search of Snow

Adieu My Youth

And Montreal's Rachel Street Market

**Anyone can count the seeds in an apple,
No one can count the apples in a seed.**

DISCLAIMER

This is a work of creative non-fiction. Everything here is true, but it is not entirely factual. Names, characters, and occupations have been changed and incidents have been compressed or recreated for literary effect and are products of the author's imagination used fictitiously to protect the privacy of the people involved. The conversations in the book are retold in a way that evokes the feeling and the essence of camaraderie reflecting my recollections of experiences that took place over time. Historical facts have not been verified but were taken note of in trust. The opinions of the characters involved should not be confused with the author's. Any resemblance to actual persons, living or dead, is entirely coincidental.

CONTENTS

	Salute to the Neighbourhood, It's People and The Rachel Street Market	1
1.	Early Memories	3
2.	The Wonderful People	35
3.	Dark Clouds of War	59
4.	Home Front Activities	85
5.	Daily Living	115
6.	Historic Beginnings	143
7.	Early Development	165
8.	Time Marches On	185

ACKNOWLEDGEMENTS

I thank my loving and very supportive wife, Wanda for reading my early drafts, for giving me advice and guidance on the content and helping me in so many countless ways to write this story. I am also very grateful to our four sons, Roman J, Timothy, Christopher, Theodore, and their significant others for encouraging me to write about my youthful journey. A special thank you as well to all of my old time friends, neighbours and school teachers who taught me that nothing worth having comes easy; to be thankful for what I do have and to work hard for what I don't have. I may not be there yet, but I am closer than I was yesterday.

A Salute to the Neighbourhood
It's People and The Rachel Street Market

Is Anything Meant to Stay?

Life reminds us that we are in transit, a stopping place,
And even where we settle can disappear without a trace.
We all follow different journeys and paths along the way,
But we must never forget that we shared a yesterday.
Je me souviens the goodwill and harmony we enjoyed,
Which today seems that it has all been sadly destroyed.

These recorded memories hope to refresh the joy we knew,
As together we bid one another a warm and fond adieu.
First they silenced the sound of the church bells peeling,
Our church moved further away making the trip unappealing.
Next they closed the local S. S. Kresge five and dime,
Then the Rachel street market was torn down in time.

The farmers and chicken pluckers no longer came,
And Vallieres Square was given a new name.
The Mount Royal elementary school was sold off too,
Then the sale of the High School we hoped was not true.
Neighbours moved and synagogues ran out of people,
The Main and our neighbourhood witnessed quite an upheaval.

Old neighbours, friends, my parents passed on, as well,
Even family members bid us a sorrowful farewell.
We wondered if anything was meant to stay?
Or if this is just a resting place along the way.
Remember to keep the neighbourhood in your heart,
Even though life has ripped the intertwined fabric apart.

We were there, journeyed together right to the path's end,
Everyone worked hard and on each other we could depend.
Our neighbours were upright, honest stalwart people,
Now our memories of them is the only means of retrieval.
So we say shalom, adieu, trzymaj się, arrivederci, so long,
Wishing each other good health, we collectively say be strong.

Farewell to our youth and the place we called home,
Is anything meant to stay as the years have flown?
In the shadow of the market we met, haggled and played,
While merciless time marched on making memories fade.
Adieu to my youth, however this story had to be told,
Isn't this what happens when you get too old?

Omnia mutantur, nos et mutamur in illis
All things change and we change with them,

Thank God for dirty dishes; they have a story to tell.
While other folks go hungry, we're eating pretty well.
With happy home and good health, we can't make a fuss;
Because this stack of dishes says, God's very good to us.

Chapter 1 - Early Memories

Some of the earliest memories we have are of the places that we grew up in. We fondly remember the neighbourhood and some of the closest relationships that we had with our friends and neighbours. We never stop loving them – even though years have passed, neighbourhoods have disappeared and the people are no longer there. As we grow older, our experiences help us better empathize with the unique challenges and achievements of bygone days and the efforts that these individuals made. We appreciate their caring words and generosity and continue to share in their laughter and their heartaches. The compassion that we feel by remembering seems to grow stronger and somehow makes us feel closer, even if but for that one moment in time. This story is real and cherishes the memories of a historic magically harmonious district in Montreal and the hard working people who lived there during a tumultuous period of post depression, World War II and two decades or so thereafter. Only very faint footprints remain of the physical location and even more faded are those of its people. The place and people were there, they were very much alive and we still feel a connection which is important and demands to be shared with future generations. Recalling the physical attributes of the location at that moment of time and the interests, beliefs, events, history and the diverse personalities involved is a way to commemorate them. A way to recognize the sincerity, perseverance and tenacity of the people, the way of life in the 1940s through the 1970s, to share in their struggles, joy and pride of their achievements. Recording these moments spent together keeps precious memories alive before they fade into the shadows of antiquity.

The structures, monuments and relics of this period are vanishing memories of them are disappearing into eternity. Our neighbourhood in the borough of Le Plateau Mont-Royal in Montreal was a transitional area, a gateway; a point of arrival for many generations of immigrants. For them leaving the neighbourhood associated with their first impoverished years in their newly adopted country was their primary goal. What made the neighbourhood a unique place was the cohabitation of a variety of ethnic groups speaking various languages, belonging to different social classes and diverse religious traditions getting along well with one another. It was a place of social and cultural mixing, between Roman Catholic French-Canadian districts to the east and the Anglo-Protestant west. Montreal was renowned for its churches and had long been nicknamed "la ville aux cent clochers" (the city of a hundred steeples). We had several Roman Catholic churches whose bells pealed loudly matching strength with one another at different times of the day. Our local parish church was the Saint-Jean-Baptiste

Church located on Rachel Street between Drolet Street and Henri-Julien Avenue. Our street was also blessed with several synagogues in close proximity. At one end of our city block was the Beth Matityahu Synagogue and at the other end was the Chevra Mishnaysis Debeth Yehudah and the Kerem Israel Hebrew School and Synagogue. Around the corner on St Lawrence St. was the Zeirey Daath Vedath Synagogue.

The Saint-Jean-Baptiste Church that courageously stands on Rachel Street is the third largest church in Montreal after Notre-Dame Basilica and Saint Joseph's Oratory. The church built between 1912 to 1914 is actually the third church built on the site; the first two were destroyed by fire. The present church includes the same stone walls of the former church that were spared by the fire. The cut and bumpy stone exterior facade is adorned on the ground floor by a portico formed by eight twin columns that support a cornice topped off by a triangular pediment. On the facade, seven stone statues greet the faithful. At the top of the portico, there is a statue of Jesus surrounded by four evangelists. Statues of St. Peter and St. Paul are installed in the two lateral alcoves or niches. On the gallery, Corinthian pilasters surround high vaulted curved bays. The two octagonal towers crowned with a copper dome shelter five bells from the former church which also were spared by the fire.

The interior of the church is richly decorated with modern floral motifs and a beautiful set of brightly coloured stained-glass windows which illuminate the walls of the nave. The church pews can accommodate 2,200 persons and the side galleries surrounding the sanctuary can accommodate 1,000 more. The Carrara marble main altar is overhung by a baldachin embellished with gold symbols, resting on four columns. There are six secondary altars, numerous marble statues and the Stations of the Cross. The communion rail, balustrades, paneling, pulpit, pews and confessionals are beautifully crafted in cherry wood with a beautiful red varnish finish. The church houses a large 61-stop (opus 615) Casavant organ with 4 keyboards and pedal and a 15-stop choir Casavant Freres organ (Opus 616). Adjacent to the church, with a facade on Drolet street is the Saint-Louis chapel referred to as the "chapel of marriages" with beautiful stained glass windows dedicated to St. Louis-de-Gonzague (1568-1591). The St. Louis name of the chapel was selected placing the chapel under the protection of St. Louis the patron saint of the young and as a memorial for the work of the Jesuits in the parish. A two keyboard, 9-stop Casavant organ (opus 656) with two keyboards resides in the chapel.

Waking up on warm early sunny summer mornings in 1940 you heard the sound of birds singing, horses hooves clip clopping over the cobble stoned street. I listened to the clinking of milk bottles as the milkmen did their deliveries and the sound of doors opening and closing. The milkmen delivered milk and cream (sweet and sour) in glass bottles with cardboard bottle tops and picked up empty bottles. Our windows were open but our wooden louvered shutters remained closed. The sun's rays peeked through the shutters and created little circles of sunlight on the walls and ceiling of the bedroom creating a magical fairyland. Some circles were magnified on their perimeter with the colours of the rainbow. As the sun rose higher on the horizon, the pattern of these sun circles changed position until they finally disappeared. The sound of church bells from several Roman Catholic churches competed with one another calling the faithful to prayer at different times of the day. First the church bells peeling in the distance were heard soon followed by those from another, then another; sometime they would peel together. The loudest church bells came from the Saint-Jean-Baptiste Church which was the closest. Other churches in close proximity were L'église Saint-Enfant-Jésus de Montréal located on Saint-Dominique Street near the intersection of Saint-Joseph Blvd. and Saint Lawrence Blvd.; Le Sanctuaire du Saint-Sacrement on Mont-Royal Avenue; L'église Saint-Stanislas de Kostka located on Saint-Joseph Blvd. East and L'église de L'Immaculée Conception at the corner of Rachel and Papineau streets. The early morning sounds seemed to resonate best because there was less noise from the usual hustle and bustle of the street. Occasionally you would hear a person walking by or some activity outdoors; of people retrieving the bottles of milk from their doorsteps. How pleasant those sounds were as the cool early morning breeze came through the shutters, cooling the bed sheets.

Our shutters were painted green and were hinged on each side of the window frame and were easy to swing open or closed as necessary. The louvers on the shutters allowed for greater control of light and ventilation. They shed rain, allowed air transfer, filtered direct sunlight and provided privacy. Peeking through the shutters I could see a horse bedecked with the obligatory blinkers covering its eyes to filter out peripheral distractions, pulling a J.J Joubert or a Borden's milk wagon. The milk man and his horse drawn wagon delivered milk in glass quart sized milk bottles and cream in smaller glass bottles with cardboard bottle tops. Milk had to be delivered to houses daily since the lack of good refrigeration meant it would quickly spoil. These deliveries always occurred in the early morning and it was not uncommon for milkmen to deliver products other than milk such as eggs, buttermilk, cheese and butter. We had several dairy company delivery men pass by including Bordens, JJ Joubert, Cousins and the Guaranteed Pure Milk company. Jacques Janvier Joubert, the founder of one of Montreal's oldest and largest dairies, was the first milkman in the British Empire to deliver bottled milk. The Ferme St-Michel was J. J. Joubert's family farm in the parish of St. Léonard de Port Maurice. Joubert began his career delivering milk to people living in our neighbourhood, the Plateau Mont Royal. The Joubert dairy was one of the first in Canada to offer pasteurized milk to its customers in 1908. Montreal had implemented compulsory milk pasteurization in 1926 which restructured the dairy industry and modernized milk-processing plants. J.J. Joubert dairy was acquired by Borden in 1976 after which Mr. Joubert together with his sons Jean and Maurice, concentrated on their food canning factory in Saint- Vincent de Paul.

We bought Borden's milk more often, probably because of the advertising. Borden's had introduced Elsie the cow as their mascot in 1936 and during World War II Elsie helped to raise ten million dollars in war bonds. To the public Elsie was a time-honored symbol of taste, trust and tradition; she stood for excellence in the dairy business. Peeking through the shutters on several mornings right after the delivery man was out of sight you could see some women going door to door opening milk bottles and skimming off the cream into a jar. They very quickly filled the open milk bottle with water from another bottle they had and resealed the milk bottle with the cardboard bottle top. They innocently moved on with their bottles or jars in their arms. The cream skimming process was incentive enough for people to get up early to retrieve their milk as soon as the milkman had delivered it.

Horses were used extensively in the 1940s not only by milkmen and bread men but by all delivery men to deliver wood and coal to homes, by vegetable pedlars, by ice men delivering ice for ice boxes, and by rag men and scrap pickers. Rag men in horse drawn wagons accepted scrap metal of all kinds for the war effort. People who had home gardens in their backyards and those who enjoyed growing plants on their balconies and window boxes benefited by getting their fertilizer (horse manure) fresh from the street. The Montreal police came by on day patrol regularly on horseback. We referred to them as the cavalry. The horse unit had been created in 1885 with stables located on the corner of Rachel and Christophe-Colomb and at that time had six police officers. We often saw the police on horseback patrolling at Mont-Royal park, Fletcher's Field, Lafontaine park and St Helen's Island. In the late 1940s with more motor vehicles on the road some officers on horseback were assigned downtown to control traffic. In 1950 the cavalry had about 45 horses. In 1962, stables were built on Mount Royal

My city block is just a short walk away from the east side of Mount Royal (the mountain) in Montreal; a Canadian city founded in 1642. The mountain is part of the Monteregian Hills situated between the Laurentians and the Appalachian Mountains. The mountain has three peaks. The northeastern one, called Colline de la Croix (Hill of the Cross) stands at an elevation of 233 m (764 ft) above sea level; another called Colline d'Outremont (Hill of Outremont or Mount Murray) is at 211 m (692 ft) above sea level and the third called the Westmount Summit is at 201 m (659 ft) above sea level. The Colline de la Croix peak is crowned with a steel cross weighing 26 tons. It is usually illuminated at night in white but can be in any colour. The cross stands 252 metres above the St. Lawrence River and is 31.4 metres (103 ft) tall and its arms span 11 metres wide. Because of its location on the summit of Mount Royal it reaches an altitude of about 251 meters (823 ft) above sea level. On a clear day it is visible from eighty kilometers (50 miles) away. The first Mount Royal Cross was placed on the mountain in 1643 by Paul Chomedey de Maisonneuve, the founder of the city, in fulfillment of a vow he made to the Virgin Mary when praying to her to stop a disastrous flood. The cross atop Mount Royal is an iconic monument, a tribute to 1642, and an inseparable symbol of Montreal; emblematic of the Christian motives and principles which governed the founders of the city. It faces the east side of the city as a tribute to the city's francophone population.

My city block is bordered on the west by St Lawrence Boulevard, on the east by St Dominique street; on the south by Rachel street and on the north by Marie Anne street.

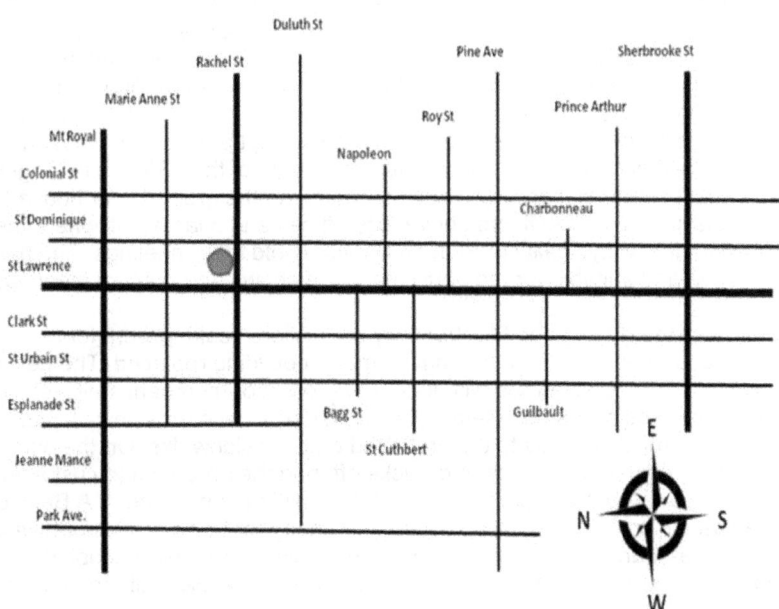

Location of the Rachel Street Market (Marché St Jean Baptiste)

It was once in the Municipality of Saint -Jean Baptiste which was created in 1861. The Municipality was delimited by Duluth street to the south, Mount Royal mountain to the west, Mont-Royal avenue to the north and Papineau street to the east. At that time the Municipality of Saint-Jean-Baptiste was outside the city limits of Montreal and residents did not have to abide by Montreal's bylaws, which restricted construction of wooden structures and prohibited offensive and nauseating odours from tanneries and barns. Imposing few taxes, the municipal council of Saint-Jean-Baptiste did not have the means to build an aqueduct and a sewer. Without running water, firefighters struggled to put out fires, which became more frequent as more people moved into the area. The few policemen barely managed to maintain order when fights broke out. Over run by the stables of the Montreal Street Railway, slaughterhouses and lime kilns, the population of Saint-Jean-Baptiste demanded more sanitation and gained access to municipal services and stricter regulations when the municipality was annexed to Montreal in 1886.

My city block had the Rachel Street farmer's market at one end, a fire station and a park called Vallieres Square, at the other end and was intersected by two streets, namely; Lozeau street and Vallieres Square street. The Marché Saint-Jean-Baptiste more often referred to as the Rachel street market at the north east corner of the intersection at Rachel and St. Lawrence was the heart of the community and a meeting place for our neighbourhood. Built in 1871 on a 21,000 square foot lot; land given to the municipality with the condition that it be kept as a market in perpetuity, by Côme-Séraphin Cherrier (July 22, 1798 - April 10, 1885) a lawyer, politician, and businessman. He who belonged to the powerful network of the Viger, Papineau, Lartigue, and Dessaulles families. One of his aunts had married Joseph Papineau, the father of Louis-Joseph, and another aunt had married Denis Viger, the father of Denis-Benjamin. Following his mother's death in 1801, Côme-Séraphin was brought up by the Viger family. After attending the Petit Séminaire de Montréal from 1806 to 1816, he studied law under Denis-Benjamin Viger and was called to the bar of Lower Canada on August 23, 1822 and practised law until the beginning of the 1860s. The original market was a commercial and civic building which on the ground floor housed merchant stalls, and on the floors above, city offices and a large hall where the city council of the Municipality of St Jean Baptiste held their meetings. The hall was spacious and suitable for the performance of shows and political meetings.

In the midst of the depression Montreal city councillors seeking work for the thousands of unemployed had the original market building replaced. The new art deco inspired two-storey edifice with indoor and outdoor merchant stalls, straight lines and floral motifs was completed in 1931. It had a covered sidewalk and shops all around with access to the protected outdoor sidewalks. On the outside farmers could align their wagons and trucks offering their produce to customers. In the interior it had butcher stalls and a fish market in the basement. A Bank of Montreal branch was strategically located and handy for trade at the northwest corner of Lozeau and St Lawrence Streets on the site previously occupied by the Merchants' Bank of Canada, which was taken over by the Bank of Montreal in 1922.

We had fire station number 14 on our city block where a ladder truck, a hose truck and a salvage truck were stationed. From a very early age, even before starting kindergarten it seems like all of my friends and I were being asked what we wanted to be when we grew up. Initially we wanted to be firemen probably because of the red fire trucks frequently zooming up our street. In the summer the firemen frequently attached a hose to the fire hydrant outside the station and sprayed water for the children to play in and to cool off. Having the fire station on our street made everyone feel safer and the firemen always came on the run to help whenever someone needed first aid or whatever. The firemen were housed on the second floor of the fire station. When an alarm was sounded they slid down the brass poles, dressed quickly, jumped in their vehicles and rushed to the scene of the fire by racing up the street loudly clanging their bell and sounding their sirens. First came the salvage truck, then the hose truck followed by the long ladder truck with a fireman seated on top of the back steering the rear of the truck. If the bell or the sound of the siren stopped very soon or if we could see smoke in the sky my neighbours and I abandoned our doorsteps and ran to watch the firefighters battle the blaze. Fires always attracted large crowds. We all watched the courageous activities that our firefighters performed, unrolling hoses, connecting them to the fire hydrants, mounting aerial ladders and some walking on the rooftops, pouring water on the fire. We often saw open flames with lots of smoke, buildings being destroyed and businesses laid to waste. Watching one of the fires I overheard one man telling another that three years ago he had insured his establishment for a hundred thousand dollars just in case. Overhearing the conversation, an elderly woman standing nearby asked, ""So Nu, what did you do with the money?" The suspicion was always there that the fires had been deliberately set to collect the insurance money.

Greene Bros. Signs Limited, manufacturers of neon signs and displays had their shop near the fire station on St. Dominique Street. On various days, trucks unloaded loads of hollow glass tubes, sheets of metal and tanks of gas and hauled away empty gas tanks. Frequently they left their wide front garage doors open enabling us to see the men inside wearing goggles and gloves, hard at work with brightly lit torches attached to gas tanks shaping glass tubes. After the shaping, they evacuated the air inside the tube creating a vacuum. Neon gas was then pumped into the tube and the glass tube was sealed off ready for an electrical charge to be applied making the tube glow. Neon gas glowed with a characteristic orange / red light. Every color other than red was produced using argon, mercury, phosphor, helium, and xenon. For a light blue color, mercury was used instead of neon. For a bold yellow glow, argon was mixed with phosphor. Carbon dioxide was used for white "neon" signs. Helium provided a bold gold glow. All of these gases were intermixed to produce as many as 150 colors. Businesses used neon signs to promote their products because neon signs were so eye-catching. Taverns and snack bar owners hung tons of neon signs, not only to catch the attention of passersby, but also because the glow of neon was almost expected in a bar atmosphere.

At the other end of the city block was an equal sized block of land to that of the market which Côme-Séraphin Cherrier had given to the municipality to serve as a park. It was known as Square Cherrier until April 4, 1899 when the city of Montreal renamed the square to Vallières Square in honour of one of its aldermen. During the 1940s and 1950s, Vallières Square park on St. Laurent Blvd. and Marie Anne street was a vibrant, lively place. It had park benches and some sparse patches of grass closer to St. Laurent Blvd. On the grassed in areas children played while their mothers sat on the benches knitting, gossiping and watching them. The park was packed on Sundays with men who traded gold watches, or swapped all types of goods, played checkers, smoked up clouds of smoke with their pipes and cigars or those who sat there and simply relaxed on the park benches. Chewing tobacco was very much in vogue as was pipe smoking. Half of the park toward St Dominique St. had no grass and was used by my friends and me to play baseball or touch football (ragball). In the 1940s there was a public water fountain on the St Dominique Street side of the Square where people could stop and have a drink of water. There was also a sandbox which was used in the winter to sand the sidewalk. On summer mornings we would often see a homeless person waking up from sleeping in the sandbox.

This was the same park where we built snowmen and snow fortresses for our snowball fights in the winter. When the snow was just right, my friends and I chose sides, built forts, and had epic snowball battles. Building opposing snow forts east and west separated them by a greater distance but proved to be problematic. Fueled by adrenalin our snowballs missing their intended targets landing instead on streetcars. Unfortunately some of these badly aimed snowballs were sent crashing inside the streetcar packed with people going home, just before the doors closed and the streetcar started northward. We could almost imagine the pandemonium one of those could cause by hitting someone in the head and spraying wet snow on everyone around. Conductors sat at their elevated post at the rear of the streetcar collecting fares surrounded by passengers in the crowded car. All conductors were in the habit of eating their supper (usually sardines and bread) at their post, while the passengers watched them chew. What if the snowball was added to the menu crashing the sardine can? Worse still if it sent the lunch flying along with the wet snow spraying everyone. These thoughts kept us focused on the opposing team as our target and may have improved our aim. Building forts north and south were even more problematic as the shorter distance put passing people at risk as well as placing panes of window glass in direct line of fire. In the summer we played ragball (touch football) north and south. In 1975 the square was renamed Parc du Portugal (Portugal Park) recognizing the new Portuguese community and Vallieres Square has since been transformed into a beautiful park with grass and flower beds.

Dominated by the Saint Jean Baptiste Church at the corner of Rachel and Drolet and the Saint Jean Baptiste market at the corner of Rachel and the Main (St Lawrence Boulevard) the working class area was densely populated with people living in duplexes and triplexes. Generally the landlords lived on the ground floor and the units above them were rented out. The majority of these rental units were cold flats with no running hot water, no bathtubs and with toilets tucked into closet enclosures. The only source to water was the kitchen sink. Our neighbourhood was an oasis of immigrant families from a variety of ethnic backgrounds; Jewish, Polish, Ukrainian, Romanian, Hungarian, Irish, Lithuanian, Slovakian mixed with English and French residents between two giant solitudes; namely, English to the west and French to the east with the overall majority being fervent and pious Catholic inhabitants. To the English we were foreigners and to the French we were Maudite Juifs (even if we were not Jewish). Antisemitism or anti-Jewish sentiment was rampant in Canada and in the province of Quebec. In 1939, Canada turned away the MS St. Louis, a German ocean liner with 908 Jewish refugees aboard. Captain, Gustav Schröder, tried to find homes for the Jewish refugees from Germany. Due to immigration policies, rather than humanitarian grounds, they were denied entry to Cuba, the United States, and Canada. Forced to return to Europe, the refugees were finally accepted in various European countries, including Belgium, the Netherlands, the UK, and France. Approximately a quarter of them died in death camps during World War II. Canada only accepted 5,000 Jewish refugees during the 1930s and 1940s in a climate of widespread anti-Semitism. In Quebec there was the traditional biblical Catholic condemnations of Judaism as killers of Christ. There were denunciations of the Jews by Catholic clergy and French Canadian journalists and politicians. French Canadians looked upon the English as being unwelcomed and upon the Jews, as a threat to their way of life. They resisted the influences of both. The English worried that the immigrants would deprive them of something. There were frequent outspoken French Canadian agitators against the English and Jewish invasion of what they felt was their French Canadian domain. On occasion Jewish businesses and synagogues were vandalized and individual Jews were assaulted.

Maurice Duplessis was elected premier of Quebec from 1936 to 1939 and again from 1944 to 1959. He held power without serious opposition and was known simply as le Chef ("the boss"). Duplessis and his Union Nationale party dominated the province with some calling his tenure in office as the La Grande Noirceur ("Great Darkness"). They championed rural areas, provincial rights, anti-Communism and were opposed to military conscription. The Duplessis years were ones of close church-state relations with traditional Catholic morality and Church doctrine defining many aspects of daily life. Catholic schools and hospitals were Church-controlled. Divorce was not fully legalized in Quebec until 1968, abortion was illegal and periodic outbursts of anti semitism in the French press were common. During the 1930s and into 1942 various French Canadian organizations, including Le Devoir, L'Action Catholique, L'Action Populaire and the Société St-Jean Baptiste, attempted to get French Canadians to promise never to buy from a Jew. The proposed boycott of Jewish shops and businesses in Québec complete with slogan "Achat chez nous" was intended to make Jews leave the province. The boycotting of Jewish stores however were largely ignored by French Canadians.

Often the political leadership in Québec added fuel to the fire of anti-Jewish sentiment. A striking example was the appeal made by Maurice Duplessis for the August 8, 1944 Quebec election. This was the first Quebec provincial election in which women were allowed to vote, having been granted suffrage at the provincial level in 1940 and at the federal level in 1919. Duplessis won the election by appealing to anti-Semitic prejudices in Quebec by making the false claim in a violently anti-Semitic speech that the Federal government together with his opponent, the Godbout government had made a secret deal with the "International Zionist Brotherhood" to settle 100,000 Jewish refugees left homeless by the Holocaust in Quebec after the war in exchange for Jewish campaign contributions to both the federal and provincial Liberal parties. By contrast, Duplessis claimed that he was not taking any money from the Jews, and if he were elected Premier, he would stop this plan to bring Jewish refugees to Quebec. To further get the message across, his party, the Union Nationale, handed out campaign pamphlets with a cartoon of a stereotypical Jew handing out bags of money, warning about the alleged plan. Through Duplessis's story was entirely false, his story was widely believed in Quebec and ensured that he won the election. The anti Jewish public opinion fueled by the political leadership in Quebec was sanctioned by the Catholic Church and echoed by the French Canadian press with accusations that the war was really a "Jewish war" started by Jews for the benefit of Jews. This nonsensical expression being allowed to grow during a time when reports of mass killings were leaking out of Europe, with Canadian soldiers dying in battle, and with millions of Jews being brutally murdered was hard to understand. The antisemitism set off campaigns within the French Canadian community including those promoted by the Société St-Jean Baptiste against Jewish immigration throughout the period in which Jewish refugees fleeing the Holocaust sought refuge in Canada. Rowdy anti-Communist riots and protests over the issue of conscription for overseas service also took place with outbreaks of commonplace antisemitic slogans.

Premier Maurice Duplessis had the Quebec legislature enact the "padlock law", which prohibited printing or publishing any document including pamphlets and newspapers that promoted communism. There was no process for appealing to the courts. The Act did not define communism and as a result Duplessis could order the closing of any premises that was suspected and Duplessis could use it against anyone who criticized him. French Canadian political figures even attempted to portray Jews as communists. The law was widely used against both leftist unions and political groups, and even cultural events by communist-linked groups like the United Jewish People's Order attracted attention from police. In this atmosphere of great suspicion, even labour organizations, like the International Ladies Garment Workers Union, which were decidedly anti-communist in their politics, had their activities in Québec placed under suspicion and were perceived as a plot by "international Jewry". All of these gave Jews in Montreal reasons to believe that their situation could deteriorate. Not only were my Jewish neighbours traumatized by their own experience in their former countries and their re settlement in Canada but they were also burdened by the extra guilt of having to be quiet while fellow Jews in Europe were being slaughtered by the millions.

On the northeast corner of Rachel and Saint-Laurent Streets was the Rachel Street Market (the Saint-Jean-Baptiste Market today's Parc des Ameriques) and on the south west corner was Labows Drug store. On the northwest corner was Richstone Bakeries and on the southeast corner was Wimpey's coffee shop which served hamburgers, sandwiches and coffee. Next door to Wimpey's was the Hollywood Tavern with wild west swinging doors at both entrances; one on Rachel street and another on St Lawrence. The intersection was a busy one and the tavern was a very popular destination where after a very busy day the farmers paused for a drink before heading back to the farm. Further south on St Lawrence Street was a hardware store, a linen store and a wonderfully aromatic spice and coffee store which also sold candy and biscuits, called Confiserie Oscar. The store had very large windows and large glass panes in the front door. The window frames and panels were painted a rich brown. As you opened the front door of the Confiserie Oscar store, a tingling bell announced your presence and you were overwhelmed with the aromas of ground coffees, teas and spices. The store had machines with large wheels all painted red. My mother said that they were coffee bean roasters and grinders. The store had large percolators, coffee presses, pepper grinders and was always well stocked with whatever spices you desired; all kept in glass jars which were stacked on shelves from floor to ceiling. This very large store also had a great selection of tea pots.

Down the middle of the store were boxes of soda crackers, various cookies and chocolate biscuits in bulk containers. Occasionally they had chocolate covered graham wafers and chocolate biscuits with jam inside. I preferred the regular "David" chocolate biscuits with no jam. My mother and I purchased pickling spice and bay leaves at the shop for marinating herring and for preparing dill pickles. The store carried sugar crystals and sugar cubes, icing sugar, brown sugar, flour, cornmeal, oatmeal in large sacks, coffee and tea. There were no tea bags in those days; loose tea was used or the tea was placed in a little silver ball with holes in it through which the tea released its flavour. The store carried green tea, Darjeeling, orange pekoe and many other varieties. The tea containers were very colourful with many pictures of far away exotic places. Proceeding further south on St Lawrence street was the Sinclair Radio and Appliance store which sold furniture, radio sets, vacuum radio tubes and vinyl phonograph records. Further south on the main below Duluth Street was Warshaw's Fruit Market that had been opened in 1935 by a Polish Jew, M. Florkivitch, a vendor who previously had sold his fruit and vegetables from a cart on the street. The store had wooden display areas stacked with mounds of oranges, grapefruit, pineapples, tomatoes, cabbage, lettuce and various vegetables. On the floor were crates and bushels of apples, and celery, carrots, etc. Oranges, pears and grapefruit were packed in wooden crates and were individually wrapped in orange, white and yellow tissue wrappers. The store keepers were very glad when people scooped up these wrappers that covered the center aisle floor in the store and took them home using them as toilet tissues. In 1964 the fruit store was expanded into a supermarket.

Labows Cut Rate Drug Store had a scale where people weighed themselves for a penny and received a printed fortune. The penny scale gave people an opportunity to weigh themselves without going to a doctor. It was the only public scale for blocks around and stood watch like a sentry outside the entrance to the store reminding everyone to watch their weight and keep healthy. Other than Labows there were three other pharmacies in the area; Bellman's Drug Store at the corner of St Lawrence and Duluth; the Arena Drug Store on Mount Royal Avenue west of the main; and Bussieres Pharmacy on Mount Royal Avenue east of the main. The Labow brothers were very well respected in the community helping to solve health problems quickly. This was the store where my mother bought cod liver oil, a tonic for me along with a very tasty laxative called Castoria; and where we bought Bromo Seltzer and Capsoline for digestion and aches and pains respectively.

Physicians began using cod liver oil in their practices as early as the 1800s to help treat patients with rheumatism, to heal wounds, reduce joint pain, to fight colds and as a treatment for rickets. In the 1940s children of all ages were forced to swallow spoonfuls of the foul nauseating and bitter-tasting cod-liver oil, one of the best natural sources of vitamins A and D. Doctors recommended it as a vitamin supplement, especially for those who might be suffering from a vitamin deficiency. Children were to take one to two teaspoons of cod-liver oil a day, while adults were to take two teaspoons. if accidentally dripped on a person's clothes the smell of rancid fish oil as it oxidized during the day was very offensive. Mothers who visited the city health clinics and milk dispensaries were given free samples of the precious oil for their infants. Every aspect of childhood, particularly dietary deficiencies and excesses as well as behaviour habits were the subject of critical examination by the medical profession. The addition of vitamins to certain basic foods, such as milk, and the development of vitamin supplements in the form of pills or capsules eventually supplanted cod-liver oil.

The Rachel Street Market had the St Lawrence streetcar (number 55) run along one side and the Rachel St (number 9) streetcar run along the other side. The St Lawrence St streetcar began its journey at the Craig St terminus near the Old Port (the waterfront), continuing northwards through China Town, past the Jewish quarters, the garment district and had stops at Pine Avenue, Duluth street, Rachel street by the Rachel St Market, Marie Anne St. just in front of Vallières Square, then Mount Royal, Laurier and Little Italy at Jean Talon, all the way up to the Terminus near Jarry St. In the later 1950's and early 1960's the garment district had moved north to Chabanel Street (north of Jean Talon). The passengers that came on and got off the streetcar came from diverse backgrounds; as they boarded the 55, their voices and languages intermingled. Women embarked with bags loaded with fresh produce, meats and occasionally with live chickens. There was always a commotion when a chicken got loose with people trying to catch it before it got out the windows or doors of the tramway. It was really funny to see this poor bird flapping its wings, loudly squawking, hopping all over the place with people trying to get a hold of it and then seeing the bird actually escape into the street accompanied by lots of shouting for the conductor to stop the streetcar so that the owner could chase after the freedom seeking chicken.

Farmers arrived at the Rachel St Market daily except on Sunday and surrounded the perimeter of the Rachel street market with their wagons in their assigned spaces, their carts rubbing shoulders with the crowded streetcars. Each had bought a permit for the season from the market custodian in order to occupy the stall. Vendors with indoor stores and meat stalls stayed open year round. My friend Jacques was the son of the superintendent of the Rachel street market. The farmer's horses were kept in stables on St Urbain street during the day. In the mid 1950s the horses were replaced by trucks and more fruit and vegetable stores were opened in the district in competition with the outdoor farmers of the Rachel Street market. The tramways were replaced by auto buses in the late 1960s and all of the steel rails were removed.

There was something thrilling and amusing about walking along St Lawrence street with the procession of people that passed all day. We became conscious of the procession mostly when we were in a hurry. It was as though we were one of a moving crowd that never began and would never end. As we walked we listened to the sound of voices from the wayside speaking in languages that we didn't understand. Idly we glimpsed faces that passed us in the procession. We saw faces with a thousand anxious wrinkles. We passed them and never knew the struggle, joy or tragedy that may have had or were having behind their brave smiles. We passed a man on the ground with his crutches beside him offering his pencils. We heard a newsboy, his voice almost hoarse, yelling "Star, La Presse" standing near a stack of newspapers at the corner. In front of the furniture store, a man and a lady were absorbed pondering deeply some detail of their soon to be purchased item. Workmen, their feet sore from standing all day were glad to be going home after work. Hearing an occasional aeroplane humming its way overhead we gave it an upward glance and wondered whether we would ever venture in one of them. In front of some stores people walked very fast with eyes straight ahead. It took a strong will to pass by some of these without spending any money. Perhaps it was better not to have any money at all than to be tempted to hold on to it. There was everything in the world displayed in the windows on the Main. There wasn't a phase of human activity that wasn't represented. Here were drugs, taverns, restaurants, snack bars with signs "Eggs any style", corsets, religion, fish, statuary, cemetery monuments, barbershops, shoe repair stores, paint and varnish, lumber, tailors, shoe stores with signs "Shoes Drastically Reduced", cigars, bakeries and choice European meats all in a row. There were people gazing in a photographer's window to discover if there was a photo of someone they knew. We passed a crowd around a dress shop window. Some at the back standing on tip-toes to see the latest style garments being displayed on the mannequins. It was fascinating to experience the spirit of Main street.

The market was a very busy and noisy place, particularly the outdoor stalls with people standing two or three rows deep holding heavy cloth shopping bags waiting to be served. At times it was difficult to pass from one vendor to another as women haggled and attempted to bid down the farmer's price for chicken looking for bargains. Often it was easier to cross the street and continue on the other side rather than try to get through the crowd in front of the farmers.
Once a deal was made the farmer tied the chicken's feet together and the lady stuffed the chicken into a cloth shopping bag or she simply carried it home holding the chicken upside down by the feet. Many times a chicken got free and took off. It was fun to watch as everyone got into the act trying to catch the bird. Live chickens were frequently bought and brought home by these women giving their husbands the task of slitting the chicken's throat over a bucket in the shed or struggling with their chickens in the backyards. The women then poured boiling hot water on the bird and plucked off all of the feathers. It was a smelly process.

The Rachel street market had stores numbered 1, 3, 5, 7, and 11 fronting on Rachel street and stores numbered 2, 4, 6, 8, 10 and 12 fronting on Lozeau street. On the Rachel street side of the market Lou Tucker, the largest live chicken vendor occupied three of the stores where customers picked their chicken and took it home live or had the store kill and pluck the chicken and even dress (eviscerate) them for an extra fee. The other two stores were occupied at various times by Duval H., Goodman Poultry, Weinrauch I & Son, Spungin H., Agulnik M. and Amster M. Poultry. On the Lozeau street side there were some fruit and poultry vendors such as Israel Steinberg, S. Attis, NDG Poultry Market,

Adelard Poultry Market, Poultry Slaughterers Inc., Poulton Poultry Slaughterers, Anctil M., Victory Fruit Market, Victor Poultry Co. and in the 1950s by Max Carpman, Herbert Kahn, Richter J. Poultry, D. Wolfe D. Rachel Farm Poultry and Berger Fruit Market.

On the St Dominique street side closest to Rachel street, was the entrance to public washrooms located in the basement. Closest to Lozeau street was the entrance to the basement premises of Portland Fish Co. Ltd., a fish market selling fresh cod fillets, salmon, carp, pike, sole, halibut, seafood and whitefish. Carp and pike were particularly popular for the preparation of gefilte fish, a favourite dish of European Jewish origin. Portland Fish occupied their premises from the start of the market right up to its end. Portland's largest competitor Waldman's Fish Market, a very popular Jewish fish store was located on Roy street between St Lawrence and Debullion streets and there were several other smaller fish markets on the Main.

In the 1940 and 50's, people frequented the poultry stores in the Rachel St. market and the outdoor farmers. Buying freshly laid eggs and a live chicken that they could choose and handle was easy in those days. Frequently these farmers were asked by ladies wearing colourful head kerchiefs to get a particular chicken from the farmer's crate. The woman then took the chicken and examined it and on many occasions turned the hen around and blew air at the hen's backside. Wondering why they did that, I was told that they wanted to make sure that the chicken that they were buying also had an egg ready for delivery. Once they had made a choice they had the farmer tie the chicken's feet together. They paid for and bought the chicken putting it in their cloth shopping bag. It was similar to what the women did inside the poultry stores where they could take the live chicken or have the store kill and pluck the chicken.

A visit to one of the poultry stores in the market was memorable. They were always crowded and amongst the clamour of loud voices in different languages was the well orchestrated sound of squawking chickens as they were being handled. The mothers of many of my friends as well as my mother bought chicken from Lou Tucker's store on the Rachel street side of the market. Rather than buy a live chicken and be faced with killing it, it sure was easier to have Lou Tucker do the job. The Tucker store offered a wide selection of chickens, (hens, roosters, capons), geese and ducks. Store workers wearing white coats and aprons hustled about trying to service the customers. During the day their aprons got more and more chicken droppings and blood on them. The store was packed with live quacking poultry kept in metal cages and women kept the employees busy picking out their chicken. The ladies haggled with the workers over the price, freshness, size or whatever. There was lots of activity and noise, with feathers flying in the air while chicken examinations were being performed. Once selected the chickens were carried through the crowded store with feathers flying in the air to the staircase and were sent downstairs with the shout "Kill em, pluck em" and if requested they could be eviscerated and dressed. The ladies waited five or ten minutes to get the cleanly plucked chicken wrapped to go. They could also have the chicken "koshered". Those who wanted their chicken koshered gave their name which the men then tagged the chicken with and they usually had to come back for the prepared chicken in about two hours. These chickens were picked up by a man wearing a black skullcap known in Hebrew as a kippah or in Yiddish as a yarmulke. I was told that they had to be orthodox Jews and that they were the only ones authorized to tend to koshered chickens. The men disappeared with the tagged chickens downstairs. Eviscerated, cleaned chicken was wrapped up, money changed hands and people moved about coming and going.

All of this pandemonium was transpiring in a relatively small store packed with crates of chickens. The stink in the place was awesomely disgusting; a mix of hot wet feathers and chicken manure; a stench that just permeated the entire store and lingered in one's nose and even remained fresh many years later. Saw dust was used to absorb some of the mess but it did not help much. The store had several sticky fly paper ribbons hanging from the ceiling to keep the flies at bay. There were two huge exhaust fans mounted above the doorways desperately trying to exhaust the smelly foul air to the outdoors and to bring in some fresh air in exchange. The poultry store keepers worked hard to maintain very high cleanliness standards, and the stores were thoroughly cleaned each day after each load of chickens were sold. Late afternoons you could see the workers sitting outside the store pausing for a smoke or just resting and watching the activities among the farmers and shoppers outside their store. These men wore bloodstained white aprons, some wore rubber boots and you could see that the store floor was all washed and was still wet but drying in spots.

Mornings were always frantic as everyone rushed to have everything ready for the rush of shoppers. Early every morning the store was packed with fresh cackling chicken by the clean white cloaked men who worked there, and daily a lot of chickens got sold. These black skullcap wearing men had long beards and peyes which is what they called their side locks and long sideburns. I later learned from my Jewish friends that the poultry butcher with the black skullcap was called a shochet. Rabbis usually required the shochet or slaughterer to be a pious Jew of good character and an observer of the Shabbat. Shabbat observance entailed refraining from work activities on the day of rest (the seventh day of the week) and is ushered in by lighting candles and reciting a blessing. Shabbat is observed from a few minutes before sunset on Friday evening until the appearance of three stars in the sky on Saturday night. In small communities, the shochet was often the town rabbi, or a rabbi from a local synagogue. A shochet was someone who had studied and was specially trained and appropriately certified to slaughter animals in a kosher manner. Larger stores and slaughterhouses normally employed a full-time shochet if they intended to sell kosher meat. Much knowledge and skill was required to practice kosher slaughter of animals clinically proven to be the most humane way of killing an animal for food.

In the case of chicken, the centuries-old technique spares the chicken from excess suffering. In addition to killing the chicken by making only one incision in its neck, the shochet inspects the bird's internal organs to ensure that the bird is not diseased. The warm water used to remove feathers in non kosher chicken cannot be used in the kosher process. The kosher process demands that the chickens be soaked in tap water for 30 minutes before the shochet brines the carcass in salt for an hour ensuring that the chicken's blood is completely extracted. The chickens are then triple rinsed. Only then can the chicken be certified as kosher.

The entrance to the market was on St Lawrence Street and near the entrance as you walked in were several brass spittoons (cuspidors) for spitting into by tobacco chewing men. Many places had passed laws against spitting in public other than into a spittoon. Use of spittoons was considered an advance of public manners and health, intended to replace previously common spitting on floors, streets, and sidewalks. Flat-bottomed, often weighted to minimize tipping over, and often with an interior "lip" to make spilling less likely if they did tip were a very common feature of public places.

Inside the market was a public washroom, the market custodian's office and ten butcher stalls that accommodated individual meat vendors who employed several butchers to serve the public. They sold meat of every description, beef, pork chicken, duck, geese, and even rabbit. The long tenured butcher shops were Walter's Meat Market, Marche Geoffrion H, and Kossy A. Regd. In 1939 Walter's Meat Market was in stall number 3; they moved to stall number 1 in 1942; changed their name to Marche Walter in 1947 and in 1961 expanded to occupy stall 1, 3 and 6. Marche Geoffrion H. occupied stall number 2 from 1939 until 1953 at which time Gold's Meat Market took over the stall until 1963. Kossy A. Regd. occupied stall number 7 from 1939 until 1964. There were a few others who occupied stalls for a short time. Udashkin B & Son in stall 6 from 1939 to 1945. Stall number 6 was then occupied by Mindel Sam until 1958; then Marche P M C in 1959. Stall number 9 was occupied by Lewis S Regd. from 1939 until 1945; then by Issie's Meat Market Regd. in 1946; then by Lazure P. H. until 1964. At times there were several vacant stalls as well.

Walter's Meat Market specialized in selling capons which were roosters that had been castrated enabling them to grow larger and provide tastier meat. Caponization is performed before the rooster matures, as a rule, from six weeks to three months old, by surgically removing the rooster's testes so that further development can occur without the influence of sex hormones. Capons develop a smaller head, comb and wattle than those of a normal rooster and reduces their aggressiveness preventing them from fighting. This makes them easier to handle allowing them to be kept together with other capons. Capon meat is more moist, tender and flavorful than that of a hen or rooster, which is due not only to the hormonal differences during the capon's development but also because capons are not as active as roosters, making their meat more tender and fatty. The ancient Romans are credited with inventing the capon. According to the 'Lex Faunia' of 162 BC, to save on precious grain, Romans were forbidden from fattening hens. To get around this the Romans castrated roosters, which resulted in much larger roosters.

Sitting in a snack bar I had the opportunity to ask a chicken farmer who had just delivered a truck load of crated chickens to the market about the caponizing process. He explained that it was quite a delicate surgery that chicken farmers had to perform. First they had to tie down the rooster and then pull out some feathers from the chick's side just in front of the thigh and below the back. Then they cleaned the spot and with their index finger of the left hand they located the space between the last two ribs and made an incision, pulling back the skin and tissue to reveal the testicle which they then twisted and extracted. They had to do this on both sides of the rooster. The testicle itself is a long, yellow, bean-like body of a very light color but no longer than the tip of your small finger. After the operation they stitched the cut closed on both sides using an ordinary large sewing needle and black thread. The threads did not need to be removed. They then fed the chicks soft light food for two days after which they were allowed to run. Since I was so interested he informed me that many chicken farmers needed the services of someone who could perform the delicate task. Further he told me that Sears, Roebuck & Co. even offered an "Easy-On" Caponizing set complete with tissue spreader, forceps, an elevator instrument and a scalpel with a detailed Sears Caponizing Kit instruction booklet which I could get and then to call him. What a career choice that would have been! Imagine filling out a form and stating occupation as a "caponizer" and if asked to explain saying, I castrate roosters!

Many years later my wife and I while shopping at Walter's Meat Market were confronted by one of the butcher's who boasted about the wonderfully large inventory and therefore the great selection of capons that they offered. Wondering about the process and thinking how bull's testicles known as Rocky Mountain oysters served in a rich brown sauce, are considered such a great delicacy in parts of the American West and Western Canada where cattle ranching is prevalent, I kept asking the butcher more and more questions. Finally I asked him if I could have a jar of what they had cut off from all of those young roosters. He admitted that he didn't have any and that he was not the one who did the job and did not know where I could get some. He may even have promised to get some for me, a promise which I knew that he could not keep. I finally told him about the process and owned up to having fun pulling his leg. On many subsequent visits we both laughed about getting a jar full of the rooster cutoffs.

Depending on the season, the farmers in the outdoor stalls sold potatoes, radishes, carrots, beans, parsnips, parsley, cauliflowers, cabbages, onions, sorrel, string beans, spinach, shallots, raspberries, strawberries, gooseberries, currants, blackberries, choke cherries, sweet cherries, sour cherries, corn and apples, Some farmers displayed honey that they had gathered from their beehives and some sold honey still in the honeycomb. Other farmers sold butter and cheese that they had made. Mid June's strawberry season saw people buying crates full of fresh handpicked strawberries to make jam preserves. Several farmers only sold fresh eggs; white, brown and duck eggs. Several farmers sold plants, flowers. large bunches of brightly coloured cut gladiolus, live rabbits and live poultry; chickens, ducks, geese, turkeys and pigeons. Fresh produce including live chickens, ducks and rabbits were purchased after a lot of bargaining over prices, appearance, size, freshness or whatever. In autumn and winter some farmers braving the cold, sold firewood and home preserves, honey and braided garlic. Usually they took turns interacting and negotiating with customers while the other person was getting warmed up. Dried tobacco leaves sorted into different grades were sold. The cured tobacco had a sweet hay, tea, rose oil, or fruity aromatic flavor. Besides being smoked, tobacco was snuffed (inhaled into the nasal cavity) for its swift 'hit' of nicotine and a lasting flavoured scent; most often however it was chewed. Men placed tobacco between the cheek and gum or upper lip and chewed until it was crushed to release flavor and nicotine. Unwanted juices were then spit out hopefully into a spittoon but more often on the ground.

The market closed on Saturday evenings at 6 pm with the departure of the outdoor farmers and was reopened on Monday morning. The indoor meat and fish market were closed on Saturday at 5 pm. Every summer Saturday night was awaited with great expectations, it was a very special night. The vacated outdoor farmer stalls were filled with unsold vegetables, carrot greens, cabbage trimmings, corn husks, potatoes, onions, fruit and perishables depending on the season, together with whatever garbage that the farmers disposed of. By 7 pm the mounds of produce became a gold mine. No sooner were the farmers gone when the "scavengers" moved in like vultures who had waited biding their time with great anticipation for the choicest spots. There was a flurry of activity as people went through the mounds to find edible fruit and vegetables. Armed with open cloth shopping bags, women and children crawled on the dumped produce, picking up whatever they could and filling up bag after bag. They found carrots, parsnips, turnips, cucumbers, tomatoes, potatoes, corn, onions, lettuce, strawberries, currants and the occasional cabbage. For Jean Guy and Lionel it was likely the start of their entrepreneurial careers. On Monday and Tuesday they peddled their meager pickings augmented perhaps by a smaller picking selection on those days, door to door selling the produce for pennies. Some housewives were thankful for their services; some even who felt ashamed ever to be found even close to any of the recognized scavengers bought from them. Did Jean Guy and Lionel know what they wanted to be when they grew up? That was a question that would be asked year after year of me and my friends as we were growing up. Around 9pm Saturday night, the municipal garbage trucks picked up all of the garbage. The market was then swept clean and the pavement was washed by a water truck with brushes late that night. It was so clean that on Sunday one would never know that it had been a market the day before. The market was considered outdated in the era of new food supermarkets and was closed in 1961 and demolished in 1966 to make way for a parking lot. In 1991, the parking lot and Lozeau Street were replaced by parc des Amériques.

Live chickens bought from the outdoor farmers or from the indoor poultry stores were cheaper than chickens that were plucked and cleaned. Many found it a lot more convenient not having to kill the chicken and plucking off all of the feathers before the chicken could be eviscerated prior to being cooked. Some people kept chickens in their backyard, raising them from little chicks. Some bought live chickens and killed them by slitting their throat over a bucket in the shed and then faced the smelly job of plucking off all of the feathers before further processing. Everyone enjoyed chicken soup and most people made their own; there was no other "prepared" chicken soup to be had, except that in a restaurant which offered it with noodles or with matzo balls. My mother often made a wonderfully delicious tasting chicken soup with very thin homemade noodles. While visiting my friends I was often invited to eat chicken soup made by their mothers. No two pots of chicken soup tasted exactly alike but they all were very nourishing; however, I preferred the soup made by my mother. It seems that people always ate chicken soup when they were sick; it was reputed to be the Jewish penicillin and a cure for whatever ails you, including the common cold and the flu. People saved chicken fat, which neighbours called schmaltz. It was used in frying and cooking when butter was in short supply. A close runner up to chicken soup was borscht a ruby-colored beet soup with sour cream which was served either warm or chilled; I preferred it served hot with beets cut julienne style in it and topped with cold sour cream.

While visiting with my friend Frank, Yaroslav, the cabinet maker, rushed in very disturbed and asked Frank's father, Witold the shoemaker, for some help. Yaroslav said, "My wife bought a live chicken. Would you kill it for me?" Witold very calmly answered, "Look it's not hard to do, I'll tell you how to do it and then you will always be able to do it." After some back and forth animated discussion, Yaroslav very agitated agreed. Witold said, "You will need a very sharp, heavy knife or a sharpened ax and a tree stump from the wood shed on which to place the chicken's neck on. You may even want to put two nails into the wood block just to make it easier to place the head between the nails so that the chicken's neck is straight for you to get a clean cut. Handle the chicken calmly, tie or hold the chicken's legs tightly together in your left hand and watch out that it doesn't scratch you. Support its weight by placing the chicken's chest on your thigh. The chicken will now be upside down with the head hanging down and with you holding the legs. Position the chicken's head in place on the block, then very quickly cut or chop. I prefer to cut with a sharp knife but you can chop the chicken's head off with an ax. That is all there is to it. Now go and do it."

Yaroslav kept pleading saying, "Show me, show me". When Witold firmly refused, Yaroslav left waving his arms, repeating, "And that is all there is to it."

Frank and I ran to his back yard where we could see through the cracks in the wooden fence into Yaroslav's back yard. We waited to see how he would kill the chicken. We watched as Yaroslav brought out the wood stump and his ax. After a short while he came out holding the squawking chicken. He was saying something to the chicken as he held its legs and positioned the chicken head down on the wooden stump. Frank and I thought that he was reassuring himself saying, "And that is all there is to it." He lifted his ax with his right hand and chopped the chicken's head right off. There was blood everywhere. He let go of the chicken's legs and off the chicken went flapping its wings, running around in circles. Yaroslav just stood there dumb stricken watching the chicken. Finally the chicken dropped, twitched and just lay there. Yaroslav looked scared as he approached the chicken. Frank and I were expecting him to run if the chicken had made a move. He stood over it for quite awhile before he picked it up and took it into the house. After that experience Frank and I thought that he probably left the cleaning up to his wife. We wondered if he even wanted to eat any of the chicken after his ordeal. People often saw men struggling with their chickens in the backyards. Regularly they witnessed the drama of a headless chicken running around the yard wildly flapping its wings and spurting blood everywhere. I guess that is where the expression "running like a chicken with its head cut off" originated to describe someone who is frenzied.

In the 1940s and 1950s the Rachel Street Market was a meeting place and the heart of the neighbourhood with a diverse population of hard working new Canadians from Central and Eastern Europe; countries such as Germany, Poland, Lithuania, Belarus, Ukraine, Estonia, Galicia, Hungary, Romania and Russia. Included was a large population of Ashkenazi Jews who had emigrated from these same countries. Jewish settlement had started in the 1800s and became more established after the heavy immigration of the early to mid-1900s on the lower Main, in the vicinity of St. Lawrence and Dorchester Street, in a section that now is part of Montreal's Chinatown. The community started the first Jewish educational institution, the Talmud Torah, located at the corner of Saint Urbain Street and De la Gauchetière Street. As the community prospered people moved up the Main towards Sherbrooke and Prince Arthur Streets and with the growth of the city, they moved from the downtown area of original settlement further north to the area outlined by Sherbrooke Street on the south, Mount Royal Avenue on the north, Esplanade Avenue and Bleury Street in the west and Saint-Denis Street in the east. These few blocks were the traditional heart of the Jewish district with St. Lawrence Boulevard known as "The Main". In 1907 the Main was a centre of Jewish publishing. A young Polish Jewish immigrant, Hirsch Wolofsky, started the Yiddish-language daily newspaper Keneder Adler (Canadian Eagle) published from an office on St. Lawrence near Ontario Street. Later the paper moved to its own building at 4075 St. Lawrence, near Duluth Street. The first Jewish city councillor in Canada, Abraham Blumenthal had been elected in 1912; the Jewish Peretz School had been founded in 1913; the Jewish Public Library, the Jewish People's School and the Canadian Jewish Chronicle, the Keneder Adler's English sister newspaper, had been founded in 1914. The Protestant School Board of Montreal had opened Baron Byng High School on St

Urbain Street near Rachel mainly for Jewish students in 1921. The school was closed in 1980.

The Main was the dividing line between the French to the east and the English to the west. Montreal had been the main destination for the 125,000 Jews who settled in Canada between 1905 and 1920, making the area a centre of Yiddish language and culture. The district was home to the second-largest Yiddish theatre in North America from 1896 to the 1940s, with shows at vaudeville houses along the Main as well as the Monument-National, now a National Historic Site. Between 1920 and 1950, a wave of immigration from Eastern Europe settled in the neighbourhood. During the period between 1947-1952, Canada admitted 11,064 Jewish refugees into the country, 40% of them settled within Jewish Montreal, giving Montreal the third-highest population of Holocaust survivors. Among them were orthodox observant Jews, and non-observant Jews alive with every shade of political opinion. They came from small towns and villages where, apart from those dedicated to a scholarly study of the Bible, they had worked as tailors, peddlers, traders or small store keepers.

Gradually the Jewish migration spread northwards as far as Van Horne Avenue, into an area between Henri-Julien Avenue in the east and Hutchison Street in the west and then even into Outremont. Many families of earlier migrations had thrived and moved on to more affluent neighbourhoods in the suburbs such as Snowdon, Hampstead, Cote St. Luc and even NDG (Notre-Dame-de-Grace) and Westmount. They became "Uptowners"; always well groomed and able to afford tailored suits. Those that remained in the area became known as "Downtowners", the majority of whom were Jewish along with those from different ethnic backgrounds; Polish, Ukrainian, Romanian, Hungarian, Irish, British, Slovakian, and French. The "Downtowners" aspired to become "Uptowners"; while the "Uptowners" felt embarrassed by the "Downtowners" shabby dress, poor grooming and way of life. The "downtowners" only knew a few words in English and even less in French; they spoke in their mother tongues, the languages from their various countries of origin and of course many of them spoke Yiddish. They did not find life easy upon settling in Montreal. in fact, it was very difficult. They generally brought little with them but their families, their traditions, a very few personal possessions and perhaps knowledge of some kin or fellow villager who had crossed the Atlantic in earlier days. Most were extremely poor and had brought very few assets and even fewer belongings with them to start their new life in Canada, With little or no money they had to hustle. There were no free lunches to be had. They worried about where their next nickel would come from. As recent immigrants, short of money, they were generally absorbed into the lower echelons of the work force, often in textiles or clothing, called the "shmata" business, which was concentrated in the heart of Jewish Montreal. "Shmata" is the Yiddish word for "rags". Yiddish was the common language in the Jewish district on Saint Laurent Boulevard, with the largest group of immigrants working in clothing factories. By the 1930s dozens of synagogues were established by the communities already in the area which helped the new Canadians to get settled.

So it was in the 1940s that the great majority of Montreal Jews lived in this area east of the mountain (Mount Royal), an area encompassed by Saint Laurent Boulevard, Clark Street, Saint Urbain Street, Esplanade Street and Park Avenue; in a world of immigrants, small shops and working-class housing. They moved into the vacated former houses that had been occupied by the now wealthier Jewish families who had moved on and the tell-tale relics of their former presence were evident everywhere. This was witnessed by the brass mezuzahs that were on every door of the homes inhabited by the downtowners, both Jewish and gentile. The brass mezuzahs were mounted at an angle on the upper part of the right-hand side of the door frame as one entered the premises. The top of it was slanted toward the inside of the entrance into which the door opened and the bottom of the metal case was pointing toward the outside. As an observant little boy, I noticed that when my Jewish neighbours entered their home, they glanced and touched the mezuzah and some kissed their fingers. Being curious I enquired about the practice and was told that I was a very observant sheyneh boychickal. After I persisted, I was told that it was a reminder that God is always with us inside or outside our homes and it was done to observe God's commandment called a mitzvah. The outside is simply a brass case, the mezuzah is actually a piece of parchment on which a Jewish prayer called the "Shema Yisrael" had been hand written in Hebrew by a highly trained and qualified scribe (called a "sofer stam"). The Hebrew verses are from the Hebrew Bible called the Torah (Deuteronomy 6:4-9 and 11:13-21) and the writing is done with a quill pen in black India ink. The parchment is then rolled up and placed inside the case. A Mezuzah on the doors of a home protects the inhabitants against all the surrounding dangers in life whether they are inside or outside.

The Roman Catholic Church was a major force in Quebec society. It exercised the greatest influence and had the most impact on Quebec. It played a major role in the exploration of the continent, a dominant role in the government of the colony of New France from its very beginning. The Church provided community services, taking care of education, health and social services and regulated the life of individuals. The Church had the official support of the province and enjoyed many privileges in Quebec. Church and State were united but the State was subordinated to the Church; one being a divine institution while the State was manmade. The Church operated with the full understanding that it alone determined the extent of its jurisdiction, authority and influence and that nobody could interfere with that. Only confessional schools (Roman catholic and Protestant) were permitted in Quebec; the Church kept all civil registries; a church wedding (religious marriage) was the only form of marriage that was acceptable; divorces could only be achieved through an act of the Federal Parliament and Church corporations were not taxed. To restore belief in the banking system and to discourage people from burying their money in the backyard, the Church supported and sponsored the establishment of a large number of cooperatives, especially the Caisses Populaires which were all organized on a parish basis with strong clerical support. The Church wielded a great deal of power and influence. There was no public education for girls in Quebec beyond elementary school. Catholic women started dozens of independent religious orders, funded in part by dowries provided by the parents of young nuns. The nuns of Quebec operated many of the institutions of the province, including most French-language schools and charitable organizations, hospitals with thousands of beds, orphanages, hundreds of boarding schools for girls. homes for unwed mothers and cared for the long-term sick and the homeless.

Several times a year during the 1940s and 1950s throughout Quebec, Roman Catholic faithful paraded through the streets honoring a saint or celebrating a religious feast day. These processions were organized by religious communities to encourage the faith of their followers. Two important annual processions were those organized for Corpus Christi and the Sacred Heart. The processions in the Saint Jean Baptiste parish involved all of the parish members and started after Mass at the church. The faithful assembled in groups behind a banner; children behind their school banner, etc. Each group followed another in an orderly manner and joined in the long procession that stretched for several city blocks. There were several groups of nuns wearing their traditional religious habits or tunics with coif (the garment's headpiece) and silver crosses hanging from a black cord around their necks and a rosary of wooden beads and metal links hanging from their belts. Also present was a group of well dressed Chevaliers de Colomb (Knights of Columbus) wearing their traditional black bow tie, plain white tuxedo shirt, black cummerbund, black footwear, black tuxedos, white gloves, coloured capes, baldric worn from right shoulder to left hip and black chapeaus (plumed hats). They paraded through the streets, reciting prayers and singing hymns. All of these parish members carried lit candles, a cross or banners or the statue of a saint and preceded the priest along the road strewn with flower petals. At the rear of the procession the priest wearing his liturgical vestments of white alb, a decorated coloured silk stole and fully embroidered chasuble with densely stitched fine gold thread walked under a canopy held by four attendants in their white church vestments (gowns). Priests or altar servers dressed in white vestments swung their golden thuribles suspended on golden chains and incensed the area. The priest carried a monstrance (a vessel consisting of a circular pane of glass set in a cross and surrounded with metal rays) in which the eucharistic host was carried in processions. Along the procession route, houses, window sills, balconies and outdoor staircases were decorated with coloured ribbons, flowers, papal flags, Quebec fleur de lit flags and pious images and one or several temporary altars were set up outdoors for the holy sacrament. These altars were constructed of lumber with stairs rising up to the second storey of a building. The stairs were lined with red carpet and pots of flowers all the way up to the decorated altar at the top. The procession stopped at the altar location and the priest and his attendants mounted the stairs to the altar while the hymn singing continued. At the altar the priest blessed the faithful and invited them to pray. Following the service and sermon the procession continued and ended where it began, back at the church where the priest blessed the faithful a final time and everyone dispersed.

With the Quiet Revolution of the 1960s these popular religious practices disappeared completely. However, they are not to be forgotten because they had a profound impact on Quebec culture and identity. Before the 1960s, the French Catholic Canadian province of Quebec was a more pious territory than France itself with the church monopolizing cultural and moral power. Today, most of the province's people still identify as Catholic and Quebec politicians who are not especially religious are very protective of the Catholic patrimony, seeing how enormous its influence was in the evolution of the province's culture. The Catholic heritage is everywhere, in street names, monuments and church buildings many of which today have been converted to secular use.

The early 1900s were a time of massive Jewish immigration from Eastern Europe to Montreal with many children being enrolled in elementary school. The social and religious climate of the day did not allow non-Christian people in Catholic schools. The Catholic Church did not want Jews attending Catholic schools fearing that Jews would have a negative influence on their students. Consequently Jews were drawn to the Protestant school because of its non-sectarian approach to religion. The principal source of school funding was the local property tax, supplemented by provincial governrnent grants and tuition fees. The newly arrived immigrants came with nothing, they were not property owners; they were tenants. Property taxes were paid by people who owned real estate and not by tenants. All of these circumstances took on a significance with the 1903 Pinsler court case. The British North America Act of 1867, Article 92 had made education an area of provincial responsibility. It mandated a confessional and religiously organized school system in Quebec guaranteeing that Catholics and Protestants had separate schools, administered by confessional school boards. Under pressure from the Catholic Church in 1875 Québec had abolished its Ministry of Public Instruction in 1868. The Catholic clergy deemed that it alone was able to provide appropriate teaching to young people and that the Province should not interfere in educational matters. Education was entrusted to the authority of a Department of Public Instruction (DPI) made up of a Catholic committee and a Protestant committee who operated separately and independently of each other.

In 1901 Jacob Pinsler, a poor Jewish student unable to afford high school, took part in a Protestant School Board scholarship competition and finished first in his graduating class at Dufferin Elementary School. Because of his very high marks on the examination, he was granted a Protestant Board of Commissioners' scholarship entitling him to attend Protestant high school tuition free. However, once it was discovered that he was Jewish, the scholarship was denied on the grounds that his father was not a property owner contributing taxes to the Protestant School Board. Jacob Pinsler's father's status as a tenant and not a ratepayer made the boy ineligible for the scholarship. The Pinsler case went to court in 1903. Quebec Superior Court ruled against the Pinslers. Jews were considered "guests" of the Protestant system and were therefore not legally entitled to awards or scholarships. The presiding judge held that "a resident of the Jewish religion who does not own real estate, cannot claim as a right to have his children admitted to the public schools (Pinsler, 1903). Public education was thus a right guaranteed to all Protestants, whatever their financial status; for Jews and other non-Protestants the right was limited to property owners. Responding to joint demands by Protestants and Jews for remedial action in light of the Pinsler decision, The Quebec National Assembly passed a law in 1903 titled "An Act to amend the law concerning education, with respect to persons professing the Jewish religion" (Statutes of the Province of Quebec, 1903). This Act designated Jewish children as Protestants for school purposes. Section 1 reads as follows: "persons professing the Jewish religion shall, for school purposes, be treated in the same manner as Protestants, and for the said purposes, shall be subject to the same obligations and shall enjoy the same rights and privileges as the latter." The law also gave Jewish pupils the right to exempt themselves from religious exercises in Protestant classrooms and ordered Jewish property owners to pay their taxes to Protestant schools.

By the late 1920's the Jewish inhabitants of Montreal had developed an identity and a sense of community and had formed institutions that served their own religious and social needs. The gentiles with differing languages and customs were not as united and their progress seemed more competitive rather than cooperative. The Jewish community of Montreal although incredibly diverse with people from different European backgrounds had established educational (Hebrew schools), leisure (YMHA), mutual aid associations, charitable and health institutions (Herzl dispensary, Montreal Jewish General Hospital) and sick benefit associations. Philanthropic work was organized by synagogue, and the people were committed to looking after each other. Some congregations in the neighbourhood did not have a permanent building for worshipping, nor were they well financed; they made do with second floor, dingy, ill-equipped synagogues. However they did not lack generosity and they all pitched in donating nickels and dimes or whatever they could to the many worthy causes. One of their first concerns was the chevra kadisha (burial society), an imperative for all Jewish communities. Many gentile ethnic groups adopted the burial society or sick benefit association model established by the Jews in their church sponsored organizations. They basically formed a fraternal organization to which people paid memberships in order to, at a minimum help cover the cost of burial. Having Yiddish as a common language was a tremendous advantage in building a united caring community. Yiddish, a Germanic Judeo language influenced by Hebrew and other Eastern European languages was the mother tongue, spoken at home, in the synagogue and on the street by these Eastern European Jews.

Many of the early Jewish immigrants started out at first dealing in second-hand and scrap goods such as clothing, furniture, metal and timber. The reason was simple. Scavenging (or modern day recycling) was the most efficient mode of business for an immigrant group with little access to capital. Moreover, although a difficult way to make a living, the collection and resale of castoff articles and materials in one form or another afforded a measure of independence unavailable to the common laborer. Self-reliance meant having the power to set one's own hours and to observe one's own Sabbath and holidays. Some received interest free loans from mutual aid societies and either rented or bought a horse and cart and started a scrap business, or worked as rag men that came around every day, singing out "Rags, Old Clothes" collecting all sorts of bric a brac, junk, bottles, metal, furniture and clothes. Most of the scrap-dealerships were Jewish-owned family businesses up until the 1990s. Some rag men even sold what had been discarded to people who would come to them, pick through the items and buy them for a few cents. A woman came out of her house with a nickel in her hand and picked an old, long, flowery red skirt. Two ladies were seen fighting over a high-necked, silky green dress. Women often haggled with the ragman over price and also with each other as to possession. After selling the bargains, the rag man was on his way again pulling on the reins of his horse and shouting: "Bottles, Rags, Clothes." The horse's furry face appeared majestic. Her brown sheen, silky fur, adorned with a long, silvery mane stretched across her back as she obeyed the rag man's every command. It is interesting to remember that most of the driving force in transportation of persons and goods of the first half of the twentieth century was realized thanks to the horse. Delivery people, milkmen, bakers, ice men, everyone used a horse. There were few if any gas stations, but lots of stables and hay sheds. The horse did not produce carbon emissions and it polluted by its sole production of unique and very specific gifts of manure which people used to fertilize their gardens.

Other immigrants began as peddlers starting with a small investment or securing merchandise on credit from a metropolitan wholesaler and selling dry goods, notions, clothing and jewelry from small carts or buggies in rural areas, or along the streets. For many Jewish immigrants peddling was a way to get a start. In the 1940s and early 1950s peddlers made their rounds, selling clothes, dresses, ice, rags, fruit and vegetables, sharpening knives, etc. We were visited regularly by Mr. Rosen, a peddler. We liked to think of him as a travelling salesman or vendor with a varied assortment of goods and services. The reason people dealt with peddlers was that they would extend credit and then come every week to collect, marking it down in the little books that they carried with them and updated the book that their customers had. Mr. Rosen's selling method of weekly collections ensured his return every week with new items to show and sell. He had connections and could get most items that people wanted. Many people bought the new small table model Northern Electric brown radio from Mr. Rosen to take advantage of it's portability or to replace the large RCA Victor radio that they had. Peddlers had a significant role in supplying people with fairly basic and diverse goods such as pots and pans, appliances, irons, toasters, tin ware, radios, clothing, a dress, leather belts, clocks, bread boxes, ice boxes, tables, chairs, tin, steel and iron goods. The peddlers brought people goods that were highly valued and appreciated. Instead of cash, some peddlers took livestock or produce as payment, while still others accepted any scrap metal, hides, or furs that people had for barter. Those seeking scrap metals, for example, sometimes offered new kitchen utensils in exchange for cast-off implements. Such metals would be hauled back to the peddler's yard, knocked apart with crow bars and sledge hammers, thrown into piles, and sold off to brokers who shipped it by rail or truck to the nearest steel mills. The knife and scissor sharpener visited us at least once a month. He made his way slowly up the street pushing his cart and clanging his bell to announce his presence. Housewives rushed out and had him sharpen their knives and scissors on the spot with his foot-powered grinding wheel. He repaired rivets and dents in pots and pans. There were many peddlers that went door to door including many charlatans who hawked their own quack remedies promising freedom from pain, a cure for whatever ails you. People walking along the Main were able to buy bagels topped with either poppy seed or sesame seed, a dozen tied with a string, from a cart marked Montreal Bagel Bakery in a laneway around 3835 St Lawrence Street. It was in operation throughout the 1940s until 1956. Hand rolled Montreal bagels continue to be very popular to this day. They are made following an ancient baking technique of boiling the doughy ring shaped bagels in honey-sweetened water, where after draining them, they are placed on wood paddles, sprinkled with sesame or poppy seeds, and baked in a hickory wood fired open flame oven. They are smaller, sweeter and have large holes. The Fairmount Bagel shop was opened on St Viateur Street in 1957. As more people began to shop at specialty and department stores who also began to extend credit, peddlers, except in rural areas, were put out of business.

People who were able to get their hands on some capital, established connections and either adopted peddling as a livelihood or frequently opened their own businesses. Many peddlers settled in one of the small communities they serviced and opened small stores. There were , tailors, dressmakers, shoe repairers, restaurants, herring stores on St Lawrence Street. Peddlers and storekeepers served as commercial intermediaries between the rural community and the growing populations in their towns. As purchasers from Montreal, Toronto, and Winnipeg wholesalers, they linked the towns to the metropolises. One man's junk was another's treasure. Bones were ground into meal for fertilizer; old clothing, if beyond repair, was processed into "shoddy" to make paper; and discarded furniture was broken down to make fuel, or refurbished as antiques. Clothes were repurposed. Children's clothes for example dresses for little girls were made from material gathered from adult dresses. Buttons were reused and wool was reclaimed to be knitted into something new. Many of the new Canadians continued in the occupations they knew, working out of their homes, setting up a small store or sewing machine in the front parlor. They cut and stitched garments. They bought produce at stalls at Bonsecours Market and sold it to their neighbors. They began to produce the foods familiar to them but new to this country such as smoked meat, marinated fish, spiced vegetables and bagels. A banquet hall, club and restaurant known as the Bucharest (3956 St Lawrence) served Romanian Jewish food and always had lively music. Culinary landmarks that still remain on Boulevard Saint Laurent such as Schwartz's (3895 St Lawrence) founded in 1927 by Reuben Schwartz and Moishes Steakhouse (3961 St Lawrence) was opened by Moishe Lighter in 1938 bear witness to the existence of this historic community. They opened shoe stores, grocery stores, fruit and vegetable stores, clothing stores and small clothing factory workrooms where they made coats, pants, vests, caps, etc., Stores such as Caplan's hardware store where they also sold fine china; or Moses Bidner's dry goods where they sold school uniforms, imported novelties and bed linens.

Those who were not able to have their own businesses generally worked in the textile and garment factories, bakeries or the many small shops along the "Main", Many took work where they could find it and laboured long hours for little pay because it was their only option. They worked countless hours to earn the wages necessary to support their families. Working conditions were poor and because of the abundance of these immigrants, disgruntled workers were quickly and easily replaced. Labour activist meetings, strikes and unions were used to slowly better the working conditions of all concerned. There were unions for type setters, shirt makers, bakers and even a Yiddish actors union. The garment industry was the street's main industry where the workers had formed and became part of the Ladies Garment Workers Union. Jews were part of the struggle for an eight hour day and were also among the elements who saw unionism as part of a greater movement for social reforms.

The "Main" (St Lawrence Boulevard), was the small business hub of the city and the hub of Yiddish Jewish Montreal particularly from just south of Sherbrooke Street to just north of Mount Royal Street where store signs were often in Yiddish. The large department stores namely Eaton's, Simpson's, Morgan's, Woodhouse, Ogilvy's and Dupuis Freres were all concentrated on St Catherine Street in downtown Montreal. The Main was messy, bedraggled and dirty but it smelled of things ambrosial, appetizing and enticing. The "Main" was filled with humanity; trading posts and emporiums; spicy scents from around the world mingling with oriental exotic perfumes and the strong gagging stink of perspiration and rotting cabbage. Most people's solution to body odor was to wash regularly and then to overwhelm any emerging stink with perfume. Those concerned about sweat percolating through clothing wore dress shields, cotton pads placed in armpit areas which protected fabric from the floods of perspiration on a hot day. It was a cosmopolitan place with people speaking in all manner of languages. It was easy to pick up all types of words in Polish, Ukrainian, Yiddish, Greek, Italian and of course English and French. Whatever an individual needed could easily be found in the shops on the street which in some locations resembled a bazaar, in other places it was like a flea market with people elbowing one another, loud haggling over prices, quality, freshness and size. The bickering or bargaining as some called it, was deemed necessary since the minimum wage in the mid 1940s was somewhere between $.25 and $.40 per hour for those who could find work and the average annual salary was somewhere around $1,040. For children, the "main" was a merry go round with lots of movement, people milling about and shops with wondrous things to see, smell, touch and eat.

The baking industry attracted immigrants who didn't have any English or French and took on a Yiddish old world environment sharing the workplace with the same people it shared with in the old world, namely; Russians, Ukrainians and Poles. The district was very well served with bread and cake by the many bakeries. Across the street from the Rachel Street market was Richstone Bakeries at 4200 St Lawrence that had opened in 1900. In addition there was Workmen's Bakery, Levine Bros. Bakery, Main Bakery, St Lawrence Bakery, Montreal Bagel Bakery, Kosher Quality Bakery, Original Knish Bakery and the Arena Bakery within a couple of city blocks of one another. Arena Bakery specialized in fancy birthday cakes. There was also an Italian Bakery on Mount Royal street closer to St Denis Street where people bought plain pizza and delicious white Italian bread. The Montreal Bagel Shop had its bakery on St. Viateur Street but its founder sold the bagels from a pushcart on the Main. These bakeries always excited the senses with their tantalizing smell of fresh bread. The bakeries were full of people who were happy to wait to be served, where they gathered to chat and looked forward to the next batch of bread coming out of the oven and took in the mouth-watering delicious aroma of fresh bread.

All of the bakeries carried Kimmel bread, a rye bread baked with whole caraway seeds, giving the bread a pungent, anise-like flavor and aroma. Kimmel is the Yiddish word meaning caraway bread. They also carried a wide variety of breads, buns, rolls, pastries and fancy decorated cakes, including:

Breads

- White and rye sandwich bread - a thick, protein-rich bread.
- Whole wheat grain bread.
- Pumpernickel bread - a very heavy, dense, slightly sweet dark brown almost black bread; pure rye made with coarsely ground flour.
- Sourdough bread - a bread made from fermented dough giving it a mildly sour taste.
- Challah - braided egg bread; often shaped into forms having symbolical meanings.
- Cornbread.
- Baguette also called French bread - a thin elongated loaf, made of water, flour, yeast, salt, instantly recognizable by slits cut on the top surface before baking to allow gas expansion.
- Mandelbrodt - a hard, baked almond bread;
- Babka - a raisin, cinnamon infused egg bread.
- Kalach - a ring-shaped bread.
- Matzo - unleavened bread.

Buns & Rolls
- Bread rolls, ranging from white rolls made with wheat flour, to dark rolls containing mostly rye flour, with many variants which included spices, such as coriander and cumin, nuts; or sesame seed, poppy seed or sunflower seeds.
- Small crusty rolls.
- Kaiser rolls –crusty round rolls, often topped with poppy seeds or sesame seeds, made by folding corners of a square inward so that their points met.
- English muffins - small, round, thin, bread usually dusted with cornmeal.
- Bialy or Onion rolls (cebularz in Poland) with a dimple on top, filled with a bit of butter and diced onion or garlic.
- Bublitchki - small hard bagel-shaped sweet breads, usually eaten with tea or coffee.

Pastries
- Hamantashen - triangular pastry or turnover filled with fruit preserves, prune paste, or fruit jams; or honey and black poppy seed paste.
- Kichels - large diamond shaped cookies made with egg and sugar; there was also the mohn kihel, a circular or rectangular wafer sprinkled with poppy seed.
- Knishes - a kind of turnover, filled with either mashed potato, ground meat, sauerkraut, onions, kasha (buckwheat groats) or cheese.
- Pirushkes, or turnovers, little cakes fried in honey or dipped in molasses after they were baked.
- Strudel a layered pastry with a sweet filling such as apple strudel, sweet cherry, apricot Strudel, Plum Strudel, poppy seed strudel, raisin strudel and nut filled strudel.
- Macaroons - almond/coconut cookies.

- Chocolate éclairs - a French oblong pastry filled with a cream or custard and topped with chocolate icing.
- Mille-feuille a French pastry made up of three layers of puff pastry alternating with two layers of pastry cream or custard. The top pastry layer is glazed with icing in alternating white (icing) and brown (chocolate) stripes, and combed.
- Pretzels - knot-shaped breads, either soft or hard, and either sweet or salty.
- Zwieback Crisp, sweetened bread - made with eggs and baked twice producing crisp, brittle slices resembling melba toast. Babies often were fed this soaked in milk.

Cakes
- Lekach or Honey cakes.
- Sponge cakes.
- Fancy decorated birthday cakes

I loved chocolate éclair pastries and lemon meringue pie. When my mother was in hospital giving birth to my brother in the 1940s, my father in order to keep me from being too choosy about what foods I would eat and to keep me quiet, provided me with what seemed a limitless supply of lemon meringue pies. I didn't want anything else to eat, but lemon pies. My over consumption of the abundant supply resulted in an over saturation with the associated nausea, throwing up and wobbliness. I believe that my father did it to teach me a lesson more than anything else and it worked! I felt the queasiness every time I saw these pies. I avoided lemon meringue pies, lemon curd filling and the fluffy meringue topping for many years after. Only lately have I had some and have not experienced any ill effects; but neither have I ever consumed any with the same gusto as I did that abundant supply.

North of Richstone Bakery and the newsstand was a little store where people bought smoked whitefish or chubs, a real delicacy sold whole by the pound. Both fish are found in the Great Lakes and average about 2 1/2lbs each. These fish are cleaned, salt brined, cooked, and smoked whole turning golden in color. The shop was well stocked with Eastern European delicacies like halva, cream cheese cut from a bulk package and Kraft cheese which the store owner sliced thinly into individual slices with what looked like a chrome coping saw. They had barrels of sauerkraut, a finely shredded fermented cabbage with its own sour flavor; delicious black olives, schmaltz herring and kosher dill pickles kept in separate large wooden brine filled barrels. Schmaltz herring is a whole herring with insides intact but with the head cut off, cured by being covered with coarse salt and left with a weight on top. Stores on the Main had barrels of it available for sale. Before being used, it had to be soaked in a few changes of water to remove the salt; each herring was then cut diagonally into two-inch pieces and arranged in a glass jar, alternating it with a layer of sliced onion. The marinade was made by boiling vinegar with peppercorns, cloves, sugar and bay leaves for about five minutes. When the marinade was cool it was poured over the herring and onions in the glass jar and sealed. After about two days it made for delicious eating with bread and butter. Today, supermarkets around the world offer a variety of marinated herrings ready for eating as herring remains one of the great Jewish favorites.

My friends and I frequented the candy store at the corner of Lozeau Street and St Dominique where we bought candied apples and toffee. My friend Solly lived next door to the candy store. His father was a tailor and his uncle played violin and gave music lessons. Their home was large and every room had textiles and bolts of material some cut to pattern and many other bolts of cloth waiting to be cut. There was a sewing machine in the corner with clothes all around and another sewing machine in the other corner. There were several wire pattern figures and a big press where suits were ironed. Solly's mother often asked me to stay for supper and Solly's uncle would often play beautiful music on his violin which sometimes made Solly's mother cry. Looking homeward was a daily routine for many families and home was somewhere in Europe where with the war it was impossible to go to. However it did not stop them dreaming about earlier times. My friends Solly, Israel and Label came from very devote orthodox Jewish families; always blessing sabbath candles and salting meat to get the blood out of it. Label had his zaida (grandfather) living on the first floor. During the early 1940s there was a lot of talk about Zionism at the time. The Zionist movement's, objective was the creation of a Jewish homeland in Palestine. My friends' parents were very happy to hear about the United Nations decision to partition Palestine between Arabs and Jews which finally gave the Jews a land to call their own. All of the families of my Jewish friends were ardent readers of the Forward which was the Montreal Hebrew newspaper along with the Eagle (the Keneder Odler). These along with the Montreal Standard Saturday newspaper were the most read. Occasionally Life magazine was looked at as well. As families had more money to go to Plattsburg or for a visit to New York, they would talk about it for years. Superstition was rampant affecting social behaviour as many believed in the evil eye and in throwing salt over their left shoulder to ward off the works of the evil one. Most people dreamt of a better life in Canada and all worked hard to put bread on the table for their families and to see that their children had a better future. Both Israel and Solly soon moved away to St Urbain Street and then possibly to Cote St Luc which is where the more affluent families moved to.

The phonograph and the song Anniversary Waltz by Al Jolson are indelibly stuck in my mind because of an event that happened when I was around ten years old. One evening my friend Rickey, myself and Isaac were in Isaac's house sitting and talking. His father had taken his mother out to celebrate their wedding anniversary. Isaac showed us the vinyl 78 rpm phonograph record that his father had brought home and he played it too. It was Al Jolson singing "Oh, how we danced on the night we were wed!", i.e. the Anniversary Song. It was a very beautiful song and lovely melody. The music was a waltz named, "Waves of the Danube" composed by Iosif Ivanovici (1845–1902) in 1880, and is one of the most famous Romanian tunes in the world. "The Anniversary Song" is a title given by Al Jolson when he and Saul Chaplin released an adaptation of the song on Decca label in 1946. It was very popular and many artists recorded it.

Anniversary Song
Oh, how we danced on the night we were wed!
We vowed our true love, though a word wasn't said.

> The world was in bloom. there were stars in the skies,
> Except for the few that were there in your eyes.

Isaac's home had an electrified record player which was a self contained turntable box that sat atop a large self standing radio. The turntable had wires into the radio so that sound was emitted through the radio speakers. The radio with record player was angled in a corner beside a telephone which was mounted on a wall. Across from the wall with the telephone was an icebox which was close to the dining room table. Rickey being very nosy checked out the icebox and found a brown paper bag of chocolate marshmallow biscuits. Isaac explained to Rickey that it was a gift that his father had brought home for his mother. This did not prevent Rickey from taking a handful and offering some to Isaac and me. It was okay with Isaac so long as some were left in the bag. We ate the biscuits and talked some more. When Isaac went to the bathroom Rickey raided the biscuit bag in the icebox once more. I refused to participate and told Rickey to put them back; but instead Rickey packed them into his mouth and ate them. Just as Isaac came back, the telephone rang and Isaac answered it. It was our friend Zoolie. As Isaac talked with Zoolie and me, Rickey emptied the bag of chocolate biscuits. Isaac was annoyed when Rickey waved the empty bag in front of our faces; but not wanting to be impolite he continued talking with Zoolie with his back turned to us. I told Rickey that he did wrong and to sit still until Isaac was off the telephone. Instead Rickey got up and kicked Isaac in the rear end as he continued to speak on the telephone. The reaction was terrible! As the kick landed, Isaac pushed forward into the radio; it sent the record player flying down the back of the radio into the corner. At the same time Isaac swore loudly into the telephone and hung up on Zoolie. Beside the swearing, we helped Isaac push the radio aside and retrieved the record player. The vinyl 78 rpm record was broken into four pieces. We were all feeling very bad. Isaac even more so, explaining that his father was sure to kill him; first for the chocolate biscuits and now for the Anniversary Song.

Rickey quickly fit the record pieces into place on the turntable and we replaced the record player on top of the radio; all as if nothing had happened. We all hoped that we could just for once turn back the clock. Feeling that his parents may come back at any time soon; the three of us sat outside on the doorstep to Isaac's house, trying to invent some believable reason to explain what had happened, but to no avail. When Rickey spotted Isaac's parents coming up the street both he and I decided to leave, Rickey turned right and I turned left and we both went home. At home I joined my mother at the front window where we both leaned on our elbows and watched the goings on in the street. About fifteen minutes later there arose quite a loud clatter with lots of yelling and shouting and then up the middle of the street came Isaac running as fast as his legs could carry him with his father chasing him close behind wielding a thick leather strap in his hand. They disappeared around the corner. Looking back on this episode it now seems humorous but at the time I felt very sorry for Isaac and very annoyed with Rickey. I often wondered what Isaac would say to his own wife when they hear the Anniversary Song. I wonder if he would sing it as:

> Oh how we danced on the night we were wed
> I needed a friend like Rickey like a hole in the head.

CHAPTER 2   The Wonderful People

In the 1940s people lived without any of our modern day conveniences, there was no television, no computer, no internet, no video games, no washing machine, no dish washer, no refrigerator, no air conditioner, no prepared or fast food. Fast food did not appear until the 1950s. Children were active and spent their time mostly outdoors. We played and watched baseball games both hardball and softball on Fletcher's Field. Our favourite hardball team was the "Wanderers". We watched soccer on Fletchers Field and McGill College football at Molson stadium. We played in the playground on Duluth and Park Avenue. We hitch hiked on Mount Royal. We played touch football (ragball) on Vallieres Square, our corner park. Our football was made from old socks sewn tight on top so as not to unravel. We played hide and seek in the backyards under flapping clothes that had been washed and hung out to dry on clotheslines. People spent more time in meaningful conversations, developing relationships, learning, in prayer, listening and helping one another. Language was never a barrier and everyone got along well with one another.

The 1940s and '50s were tough for parents, who worked ceaselessly and had little money to feed and look after their families and keep the home in good repair. Yet these were happy times. We had fun hanging around, making do with whatever we had and what we played with didn't cost any money. Everyone made do and enjoyed one another. My friends and I had our parents and each other and the street was our playground. Our neighbourhood was a closely knit community, where the word "neighbour" signified a very warm, unique, special friendship regardless of race, colour, belief or language. We played "hitting out" with a tennis ball on the street corner; a game that was based on baseball. We threw a tennis ball at the gray stones of the corner house and ran two bases and back to the wall to score a point. Anyone of the fielders catching or retrieving the ball could tag you out. There was one particular area of the gray stones angled just right that almost always yielded a home run. Getting along with your neighbors and maintaining good relationships was most important.

As a child I had many colouring books and enjoyed drawing my own illustrations and colouring with wax crayons. In the summer, when my friends were busy with music lessons, or attending parochial schools or were otherwise engaged and nowhere to be found; I sat on my doorstep and read comic books and story books that our landlord had given to me. He belonged to a book of the month club and I was given a veritable library to explore and enjoy. The well worn doorstep had a smooth knot which formed an uncomfortable bump that tortured my backside as I sat there reading. On occasion an annoying fly or mosquito came around buzzing in my ears, interrupting my concentration. I read mysteries, historical fiction, science fiction, memoires, mysteries and adventure stories. I was very interested in self help books and read "The Magic of Believing", "The Power of Positive Thinking" and "How to Make Friends and Influence People" I learned that the will to do springs from the knowledge that we *can* do. Thoughts of doubt and fear are the great enemies of knowledge because purpose, energy, power to do, and all strong thoughts cease when doubt and fear creep in. In order to grow in any field, you have to throw a lot of time at it! Many people get discouraged and give up way, way, way too early! For most people, it takes several years of practice to achieve a kind of basic mastery. It helped to explain the countless hours of practice that several of my friends endured in learning how to play the mandolin, the violin and the piano. You had to persevere. It's like music or sport in that way; you have to learn techniques, you have to show up for daily practice, you have to have high tolerance for your mistakes and the ability to learn from your mistakes; they are your guide. I discovered that mistakes were not to be dreaded or hidden but that they were learning in disguise. Trying and never giving up is not a mistake; failing at something meant try harder. I found tremendous meaning and inspiration in the phrase "when the going gets tough, the tough get going". Most importantly I rose to the challenge telling myself that I could learn and had to rely on doing so myself. I often would come back to that conclusion and promised action especially when I caught myself not following this very basic tenet.

Living close to St Lawrence Street meant being close to stores where it seemed that one could buy anything that was needed. There were hardware stores that carried tools, nails, screws, utensils, wrenches, screw drivers, water tap washers, paint, stove pipes, coal ash sifters, etc. Lumber yards that carried wood of every size and mouldings of every design. Dry good shops, china shops, groceries, butcher and fish stores, herring shops, bakeries, fruit markets, snack bars, ice cream parlours, hair salons, tobacco shops, drug stores; even stores that sold used postage stamps as stamp collecting was very popular then. We had a S. S. Kresge Company five and dime discount department store on the corner of St Lawrence and Mount Royal and a larger F. W. Woolworth Company five-and-dime store on St Denis Street north of Mount Royal Street. These stores sold just about anything in general merchandise undercutting the prices of other local merchants. Both stores had a popular luncheon counter serving sandwiches, milk shakes, pies and coffee among other items and wide display counters filled with merchandise that the shopping public could handle and select without the assistance of a sales clerk. They were different in that regard from other retailers who kept all merchandise behind a counter and customers had to have a sales clerk present them with whatever they asked for.

After supper during warm summer evenings when it was not raining, the favourite pastime of people in the neighbourhood was to sit on their doorstep and talk with their neighbours. Others sat on their kitchen chairs brought out on the sidewalk outside their front door and watched the activity on the street in the setting sun. Still others opened their windows, placed a pillow on the window sill to rest their elbows on and talked to their neighbours from their flats. Many stood smoking cigarettes and spoke with neighbours as they passed by. People often engaged in loud animated discussions. Our neighbourhood treasured our diversity, our different ethnicity, language, geographic area of origin, customs, beliefs, practices and skills both mental and physical. There was a trusted cooperation with people working together and watching out for each other. They took one another to the doctor and doctors made house calls. There were no nursing homes, so relatives took care of the old as needed. Many of our neighbours had zaideh and bubbe (Grandfather and Grandmother) living with them. The average life span in Canada in 1900 was fifty years, today it is eighty one. Certainly many people lived to be much older, but the great number of child deaths brought the average way down. There were many ailments such as small pox, diphtheria, cholera, typhus, tuberculosis and poliomyelitis that contributed to the high death rate. Children strong enough to survive beyond the age of five were expected to live a long life.

Today most doctors are specialists and serious illnesses are diagnosed in hospitals using modern techniques, the practice of medicine was very different in the 1940s. Some doctors had hospital work but the rest were in private practice made house calls on call 24 hours a day, seven days a week and treated whole families. Physicians examined patients in their bedrooms or in the kitchen where the table served as an operating surface and the tea kettle acted as a sterilizer. They diagnosed diseases as best as they could and relied heavily on what the patient told them, the color of the eyes and tongue or the presence of fever as these were all they had to go by. They performed minor surgery, delivered babies, and worked to heal infections and diseases of all kinds while the entire family were active spectators watching the doctor at work and occasionally lending a hand. When someone was sick or in an emergency, a doctor had to be summoned by a person delivering a message or by telephone call. The family physician came to the house with his black leather 'Gladstone' bag. Gladstone bags were carried by everyone. Tradesmen, businessmen, carpenters and laypeople of all kinds. They were used as weekend-bags and overnight bags by travelers going by train, carriage or ocean-liner, and even as equipment-bags by adventurers and archaeologists. Even though many people used these bags they were most commonly associated with physicians and to this day, they're still called 'doctor's bags'. Physicians who made house-calls were prepared for absolutely anything; from childbirth to mumps, boils to appendicitis, influenza to rampant diphtheria. Because of this, they carried a wide array of equipment in their bags. Not just measuring-tapes, a fragile glass thermometer filled with mercury and a stethoscope, but most things that doctors today wouldn't normally carry around such as surgical and amputation-kits, bottles of medicine, poisonous drugs like chloroform or ether in the event that they had to sedate a patient during an operation, swabs, measuring-cups, needles, syringes, tourniquets and other nasty and potentially deadly items.

Physicians on a house call were expected to do anything from listening to a heart-beat, taking temperatures, prescribing medicines, and checking pulses, to more serious stuff, like re-setting broken bones, stitching up wounds, stitching up a gash to the head, removing a fish-bone from a patient's throat, or even removing a patient's appendix. Family physicians were general practitioners, meaning that their training and education, covered a wide range of areas of medicine from minor operations and surgeries, to how to deliver babies, how to treat a broken arm or a case of influenza, how to take a person's temperature and how to prescribe medicines for head-cold and rashes. Such physicians did not specialise in one particular area but had to cover a wide range of skills, since they had no idea what they may be called out to attend to, at any hour of the day, or night.

After the end of the Second World War house-calls steadily decreased as a medical priority as did the number of general practitioners. In our increasingly litigious society, some physicians have stopped making house-calls over fears of being sued. Today there is a much higher number of specialists rather than general practitioners. Specialists concentrate on one part of the human body. Eye-doctors, hearing specialists, Ear-Nose-and-Throat doctors, cardiologists who look into heart-conditions, podiatrists, who handle feet, dermatologists who handle skin-issues and so-forth. This spreading-out of knowledge means that there are fewer and fewer doctors who can handle a wider range of diseases and illnesses which results in fewer doctors who can handle the unpredictable nature of house-calls. With modern emergency services and improved communications and transportation, there's less need for physicians to make house-calls.

During these get togethers many neighbours remembered the hardships that everyone suffered during the depression. They talked about the collapse of Wall Street in October 1929 that precipitated the financial crisis that devastated the European banking systems of Austria, Poland, Hungary, Czechoslovakia, Romania, Germany, Switzerland, France, the United Kingdom, Turkey, Mexico, Egypt, and the United States. The 1930s were extremely difficult times with most people out of work, scarce job openings and millions of people who had lost their homes. With so many men unemployed or on lower wages, it was a major challenge for housewives to cope with the shortages of money and resources. Homemakers used various strategies in budgeting, shopping, cooking, cleaning and childcare essential to the economic maintenance of the family. They purchased the cheapest cuts of meat, sometimes even horse meat, recycled the Sunday roast into sandwiches, served more soups, beans and noodles. They sewed, darned and patched clothing, traded outgrown items with their neighbors or the rag man. They kept the house colder and postponed buying new furniture and appliances until better days. Extended families helped each other with extra food, spare rooms, repair-work and cash loans. Many worked outside the home, or took boarders, did laundry for trade or cash, knitted sweaters and socks from repurposed wool, did sewing for neighbors in exchange for something they could offer.

The people remembered how during the depression, Montreal Mayor Camillien Houde commissioned public works projects in Montreal, including more than twenty pissoirs or vespasiennes which were public restrooms (lavatories) that locals called "Camilliennes." No mere pissoir, these public washrooms were designed to resemble "miniature palaces" to convey Montreal's status as a modern metropolis, They served as information stations, places where people could get their shoes shined or even use a telephone. At the time, Camillien Houde quipped that the project would provide the unemployed with "two kinds of relief." The Montreal vespasiennes were built underground in places such as Phillips Square, Place Jacques-Cartier, and Place d'Armes and were accessible by two wide sets of granite stairs. In Dominion Square, Cabot Square, Victoria Square and Viger Square, the toilets were housed in octagonal stone kiosks with large windows and copper roofs. These were fully operational in the 1940s and 1950s. By 1980, most vespasiennes had become run-down and dirty and were closed for "moral and cleanliness reasons." Many of these palaces to our basic functions have since been transformed and now serve other needs. The Camillienne in Cabot Square became the Café Roundhouse. The ice cream parlour in St. Louis Square was once the Camillienne located in Viger Square.

The local newsstand on St Lawrence and Rachel outside the Richstone Bakery had many newspapers on display. In French we had La Presse, Le Devoir and Le Journal de Montréal. English language newspapers included The Montreal Star, the Standard. the Gazette and the Herald. There were Polish, Ukrainian, Hungarian, Slovak and Italian newspapers, many published weekly in the U.S.A. and delivered by mail. We had several Yiddish newspapers. There was Der Keneder Adler (The Jewish Daily Eagle) a Yiddish daily newspaper which was published right in the neighbourhood. The Eagle newspaper had been founded in 1907 and provided news of the community, the city, the country (Canada), America (United States), the old country (Europe, their homeland) and the world. Canadian Jewish Chronicle was another newspaper published from the same location on the Main north of Duluth Street but it was published every two weeks and was in English. The people were well informed and were easily able to discuss and debate current events with their neighbours and countrymen.

The neighbours discussed what they had read in the newspapers and what some of them had experienced years before. Newspapers had reported thousands of bank failures in the United States and the fact that millions of investors had been ruined, Despite all the trauma inflicted on banking customers and staff by the depression they marvelled at the fact that Canadian banking survived without a single bank failure even though the credibility in Canadian banking sagged. Rumours of bank troubles had been widespread. Banks instinctively had tried to minimize their exposure to liabilities by adopting hard-nosed lending (tight money) policies. Wage earners and professionals drew out their money from the banks because at the time the government did not guarantee the savings and they were afraid of losing the little they had. With decreased consumer spending, companies were having trouble paying their bills. Companies laid off workers, banks and investors stopped lending money to borrowers. The banks were being pushed toward the brink of bankruptcy with a dangerous accumulation of bad debts and the stifling effects of tight money across the country. The Bank Act allowed banks to foreclose delinquent loans and they seized homes, business inventory, cattle, tractors, etc. Banks sent out loan collectors and inspectors intent on shaking out loan payments that the local bank manager knew were unshakable and the bond of trust between the local manager and townsfolk was broken.

Bank deposits decreased and money withdrawn was often buried in the garden or under the floorboards in the house. With no central bank regulating the Canadian nation's appetite for credit, the banks concentrated on preserving their own solvency as their first duty. New loans were vigorously scrutinized, old loans were vigilantly policed, and interest rates were raised above the usual seven per cent. Banks could charge whatever interest they liked on loans, but the Bank Act only allowed them to legally recover 7 per cent. Rumours were a banker's nemesis, and worked to dissolve the public's trust and withdrawals continued. The Depression had severely dented the credibility of Canadian banking and people were worried and wanted to safeguard the little money they had. People were scared to buy homes even many years later afraid that banks could repossess their homes in the event of a mortgage default.

I paid Chaim, the newsstand owner for the Montreal Herald newspaper as he continued talking to Benny. I heard him say, "Yesterday Izzie who as you know works for Abe Goldfinkle came by and told me something that could happen to anybody." "What was that?", asked Benny. Chaim continued, "Izzie had watched his boss Goldfinkle trying over and over again to open the safe in his office. He finally had to call Itzhak the locksmith and safe cracker. Itzhak had no problem opening the safe and told Goldfinkle to write down the combination in a book so that he would not forget it which Goldfinkle did without question. Earlier today Izzie came by and said that Goldfinkle again was having trouble opening the safe. So Izzie said to him, remember the book, you wrote the combination down in a book. Goldfinkle answered him saying, I know, I know but the book is in the safe.

Sitting on his doorstep Max delighted in telling and retelling his neighbours about his last doctor's visit. Max had complained to his doctor of aches and pains all over his body. After a thorough examination, the doctor gave him a clean bill of health, saying, "Max, you're in excellent shape for an 60 year old man. But I'm not a magician, I can't make you any younger". To which Max had replied, "Who asked you to make me younger? Just make sure I get older!" Of course Max's story led to other neighbours recalling their stories. Marvin told the gathering about when he had broken his leg riding a bicycle. He found himself in the Montreal General Hospital on Lagauchetiere street and St Dominique in a ward where all the patients in it were not only in bed, but also had one of their legs suspended in a sling above them. This particular day, Doctor Wallace, the resident doctor, together with some of his staff, was making the rounds in the ward. Dr. Wallace stopped at the first bed and pulled and twisted the patient's suspended leg. The patient screamed in agony. This was repeated along the row of beds, and each patient screamed and yelled during the examination. Dr. Wallace finally reached Marvin in the last bed. But when Marvin's suspended leg was pulled and twisted as was done to all the others, Marvin says that he remained silent and smiling throughout the procedure. When Dr. Wallace and his entourage left the ward, all the patients marvelled and congratulated Marvin on his bravery and fortitude, as they all seem to have had the same ailment. Marvin laughed heartily and said that he told them that he was not brave at all but neither was he a klutz and he explained by saying, "I saw what Dr. Wallace was doing to you, so I switched my legs and put my good leg in the sling."

Of course Benny Finklebaum had to get his two cents in and told everyone about his lying in bed in the hospital wearing an oxygen mask tightly over his mouth and nose. A young student nurse was giving him a partial sponge bath. "Nurse," mumbled Benny from behind the mask, "are my testicles black?" Embarrassed, the young nurse replied, "I don't know, Mr Finklebaum. I'm only here to wash your upper body and feet." Benny struggled to ask again, "Nurse, please check for me. Are my testicles black?" Concerned that Benny might elevate his blood pressure and heart rate from worrying about his testicles, the nurse overcame her embarrassment and pulled back the covers. She raised Benny's gown, moved his manhood to one side, looked very closely at his testicles and said, "There's nothing wrong with them, Mr Finklebaum. They look fine." Benny said that he looked at her for a few seconds, then slowly pulled off his oxygen mask, smiled at her, and said, very distinctly, "Thank you very much nurse. That was wonderful. You have very soft and silky hands. But now listen very, very carefully to what I'm saying: Are - my - test - results - back?" Everyone laughed even us younger kids who really didn't have a clue about such matters.

At this point Benny's wife Sharon sitting with the ladies chimed in with her story about Benny who sometime in the past spoke to their doctor because he was getting more and more worried about what he felt was his wife Sharon's aggressive behaviour towards him. Benny was surprised that she knew about his conversation with the good doctor. He asked, "How do you know? The doctor must have told you! What a double croser!" Sharon ignored him and continued. So Benny sees the doctor and tells him, "I've not come about me, doctor, It's mine Sharon I've come to talk about. I just don't know how to handle her anymore. Every time I'm with her, Sharon seems to quickly lose her temper for no reason at all - and it's beginning to scare me." "Don't worry Benny," said the doctor. "You'll be pleased to hear that curing such behaviour is now no longer difficult." "So what medicine are you going to prescribe for her?" asks Benny. "I don't need to prescribe medicine for her," replied the doctor. "Whenever you think Sharon is beginning to lose her temper, just drink some water. But don't swallow it - just swish it around in your mouth. And keep swishing it around until Sharon calms down or else leaves the room." "Thank you doctor," answered Benny. "I will try it as soon as I get back home." Ten days later, Benny saw the doctor again. "So how is Sharon's temper problem?" asked the doctor. "Your cure really works, doctor," replied Benny. "I've been swishing water around my mouth every time Sharon starts to get aggressive, and she's now almost normal. I can't thank you enough, doctor. But do tell me, how can a plain glass of water work so well?" "I must be honest with you Benny," replied the doctor, "the water itself does absolutely nothing. It's you keeping your mouth shut that is the solution". All of the ladies laughed and approved the doctor's solution. Benny just sat there nodding his head.

I enjoyed these summer evenings as I joined my friends and their families sitting outside their homes listening to the stories that the grownups recounted. Sometimes the conversations went on for hours. Some people thought that they were an authority on everything. Others simply listened. People talked about their differences, the news, their activities and their dreams. They traded knowledge, gossip, home remedies, dietary habits, recipes, and bargain locations. They expressed their opinions and beliefs; some more forcefully than others. They discussed family matters and talked about their cousins and uncles. I listened as my friend's mother talked to her neighbour about her aunt Sadie. The neighbour was surprised that Aunt Sadie never married. My friend's mother explained that, "she was two thirds married once. She was there, the rabbi was there but the man didn't show up." There may have been loud words but there was no swearing or physical violence of any kind. The people in our neighbourhood recognized that some groups of people were often portrayed as stereotypes, but collectively felt that no person was exactly like another person or a clone of another member of a group. If there were individual attitudes toward a particular ethnic group or stereotype prejudices from the old country they were not openly evident in our neighbourhood. I think that awareness and discussion gave everyone a clearer picture of cultural diversity. Appreciation and understanding of cultural diversity meant not just tolerating differences among groups, but supporting and nurturing them.

Neighbours were aware of and were comfortable about dealing with diverse issues. They discussed each other's culture and values and often laughed at remembering events that happened in the old country. They valued personal learning and encouraged each other to do well. People were not judged because of accent or grammar; they were all struggling with English and adapted their communication style to fit their situation. This nurturing environment exposed them to new issues, ideas, information and opportunities. They were tolerant and respectful of each other. Everyone was committed to whatever they were doing. The common goals were to put food on the table, raising a happy family while doing their best to do well in their newly adopted country. I believe that this opportunity fostered an environment of cross-cultural understanding. There was a lot of news on the world scene that kept the newspapers fed with stories, opinions and editorials. Our neighbours discussed, rehashed, argued and even verbally fought over events that they had no control over and many had proposals and a multitude of solutions for world leaders that never left the neighbourhood doorsteps. At times the discussions about politics, about religion, about health matters, job opportunities and socialist views were heated and on occasion were pretty rowdy. At times differences were resolved, often they were left in limbo and that's when the fun began. For example, my friend's father would say to his brother, "Admit what?" "There is no dishonour in learning from

one's own mistakes; but it's better to learn from the mistakes of others; so that is why you read books". "Why not? It helps".
His brother then countered with, "Nu, so tell me why do people who make mistakes write books?
My friend's father answered, "Moe, why don't you ask them?"
Then, as usual, followed a period of silence until a new subject came up and there was no lack of new subjects. Some discussions were interspersed with loud laughter, some with swear words especially if there was an argument. There they sat from after supper until ten o'clock or so; talking with each other, laughing, discussing and loudly arguing over the war, Hitler, Mussolini, Stalin and Churchill. These were tumultuous times before the widespread use of television, portable radios, refrigerators, air conditioners, washing machines and microwaves.

Most men smoked cigarettes either readymade or they rolled their own using Chanteclair or Vogue cigarette paper and cigarette tobacco such as Turret, Vogue or Ogden. Some men smoked real stinky cigars imitating Winston Churchill. People also enjoyed KiK cola or beer while sitting outdoors while others drank tea or water. Because of rationing neighbours brought their own tea bags which were often reused. Kool Aid was popular which along with water was kept cold in a glass jug in an ice box. Residents knew everybody on the street and shared their stories of the old country; of pogroms in Russia; of their first days in Canada; their home life; childhood games; youthful idealism; their children's school fees; first jobs, union building activities and stories of hard times and high spirits. They exchanged news with their neighbours and passersby and information on where to get a good deal or a bargain. They traded recipes, tools, ladders and what have you. Gossip was rampant in those days and it seemed like everyone knew everyone else's business. This was not necessarily a bad thing since they tried to help one another as best as they could. Doors were never locked at night and there was no fear of being vandalized. Talking with their neighbours they would get sleepy and begin to doze off. At which point they got up, wished one another "zie ga zink" (wishing good health) and proceeded to "gay shlafen" (go to sleep). The only interruption to this daily evening ritual was when it rained or when the city water trucks and sweepers came around cleaning the street, then everyone moved indoors.

During the 1940's it was common to see horse drawn chip wagons plodding the streets of Montreal stopping to serve fries or hot dogs every few feet. We received a nightly visit from our friendly neighbourhood horse drawn chip wagon and the smell of french fries and vinegar fragrance that permeated the air. Next we saw our neighbours scrambling for money and standing in line by the wagon waiting to be served a small brown paper bag full of fries that cost them five cents. People would salt them and add vinegar to their liking and take away their purchase allowing the next person in line to be served. The wagon had a small chimney vent on top; was brightly lit inside and was all enclosed with glass windows with the two side windows capable of being opened. These had a wide ledge to accommodate the salt and vinegar. You could also buy steamed hotdogs with mustard and shredded cabbage for a dime. Many people did not buy anything from the chip wagon mostly because they did not have the money and besides "Mom could make better fries in fresher oil" so they said. However no one could deny that the french fries from the chip wagon were delicious especially when accompanied by cold KiK cola.

My friends and I were devout readers of classic comics, Moby Dick, Superman, Archie and Little Orphan Annie all supplied by an elderly Jewish lady named, Molly. She sat in a dirty dress in a dark shop on Duluth Street, weary, short, grey and half blind but with a big smile. She sold Coke for 6 cents and small open bags of potato chips for 2 cents and different candy. We bought black licorice babies, wax lips, rock candy and comics. Whatever coins we had soon were spent. Some of the kids discovered alchemy; they could turn copper pennies into silver dimes. Rubbed with mercury from old thermometers, a magical enzyme, turned pennies into dimes. They would push the loot across the counter at Molly who unknowingly was taken advantage of. Some of the kids called it making a profit. I called it stealing. Molly had a good heart but once she didn't trust someone, she did not welcome them into her store and checked everything very carefully.

On our street language was never a barrier. One often heard people ask, "Farshtayn Yiddish?" The phrase meant do you understand Yiddish. If the person shook their head or said no then the person would try their best to converse in English. We had almost all nations represented on our street with an overwhelming majority of Jewish neighbours. At the time of the Second World War, the inhabitants of the whole district including the Jewish community of Montreal considered themselves fortunate to not be living in Europe under the dictatorship of Adolf Hitler. Some evenings sitting on their doorsteps neighbours reminisced with one another about the old country. At the time songs about gypsies and fortune tellers was very popular. Song lyrics were memorized by people after hearing them on the radio. Lyrics such as:
> One more village, one more town,
> One more girl to put your arms around
> And say goodbye when the moon is pale,
> And ride, ride, the gypsy trail.

There were great vocalists who sang memorable songs that people adored. Peggy Lee, was an American popular music singer, songwriter, composer, and actress who started as a vocalist on radio singing with Benny Goodman's big band. People loved her singing Golden Earrings.

> There's a story the gypsies know is true
> That when your love wears golden earrings
> She belongs to you
> An old love story that's known to very few
> But if you wear those golden earrings
> Love will come to you
>
> By the burning fire, they will glow with every coal
> You will hear desire whisper low inside your soul
> So be my gypsy
> Make love your guiding light

> And let that pair of golden earrings
> Cast their spell tonight

Sitting outdoors with their neighbours ladies related their visits to fortune tellers in Montreal and in the old country. They also related their fear of gypsy men in the old country who camped on the outskirts of their village with their caravans. The gypsies that Lou's wife Esther remembered were a nomadic people who constantly were on the move. She remembered them playing lovely violin music and having beautiful horses. Her friend Golda remembered that they were always begging for food and money and that they had a reputation for stealing and for kidnapping children. Golda as a young girl, was intrigued by the mystery and the glamour of the strangers to whom so many ladies went to have their fortunes told. Much to Golda's surprise, Esther described her visit to a gypsy fortune teller very close to our Montreal neighbourhood. She described her as being a very friendly good looking elderly lady with dark eyes who wore a colorful shawl and a matching head kerchief. She told fortunes by reading cards, although she had also closely examined Esther's palms.

The fortune teller had spoken to Esther's deceased father who had passed on several years before she came to Canada. Esther found that the gypsy described him in great detail and that she was spot on. Esther thought that the gypsy was fantastic and recommended her to Golda. Golda although intrigued said that she was not brave enough to go. Lou who had listened patiently to the discourse said that he thought that fortune tellers were nothing but trouble. He said that men coming to his barber shop had complained that their wives were told that they (the men) were having an affair with some mysterious woman thereby causing lots of domestic trouble. He asked Esther if the gypsy was married. Esther didn't know but asked Lou why was that important? Lou said, "One of my customers had asked his wife to ask her fortune teller the following question, Do you believe that departed people can communicate with you? Do you know what the fortune teller replied? She said. Yes, my husband sends me alimony every week." Lou couldn't stop laughing. Esther and Golda on the other hand did not appreciate Lou making fun of the matter. After all they said that fortune telling was a practice that dated back centuries, permeating all cultures , spanning continents and cognizant of no religious barriers had to have some truth attached to it. After all, people of different nations consulted fortune tellers to gain hidden knowledge into business decisions, financial investment, decisions of career, matters of the heart. love, family friendships and health. Lou said, "If it's so popular, maybe I should install one of those electronic coin operated gypsy style fortune teller machine in the barber shop. You know the kind that they have in Belmont Park with a full size enclosed figure in an elaborate oak cabinet. Where the gypsy's head moves from side to side, her hand moves across the cards, and her left hand raises up and then slowly dispenses a fortune card through the ornate card slot." He continued laughing. Esther and Golda looked disapprovingly at Lou and warned him not to tempt fate as people looked to the supernatural for answers and who was he to say that there were no gifted people with a genuine ability to ask the universe for answers. That was how it was in our neighbourhood. people spoke with each other and with their neighbours about all sorts of things ranging from personal stuff to food, recipes and gardening.

Stories not only concerned everyday life but on occasion reflected on religion. One evening after supper Saul, my friend Zoolie's father speaking to his neighbour John said that he had heard a conversation where a rabbi, a priest, and a minister were discussing what they did with donations to their respective religious organizations. The minister said that he drew a square on the floor, threw the money up in the air, and whatever landed in the square, he gives to God, and whatever lands outside the square, he keeps. The priest said that he uses a similar method. Except that he draws a circle, and whatever lands in the circle, he gives to God, and whatever lands outside the circle, he keeps. They both ask the rabbi, interested in how he divided the money. The rabbi said that he had a slightly different method of dividing the money. He did not draw any circles or squares but he also threw all the money up in the air and he said, "Whatever God wants, he keeps and what falls down I keep." John turned to Saul and said that he had heard a better one still. He said that "Ariel had gone into a Church, took out his tallis, yarmulke, and proceeded to pray. The priest entered to start services and said: "Will all non-Christians please leave." Ariel continued davening (reciting Jewish liturgical prayers). Again the priest said, "Will all non-Christians please leave." And again, Ariel prayed, even harder. Finally, the distraught clergyman moved to Ariel and said. "Will ALL JEWS please leave." At this, Ariel removed his yarmulke, packed up his tallis, then went to the altar, picked up a statue of Jesus and said, "Come bubbela they don't want us here anymore." Both Saul and John laughed long and hard.

At one warm evening get-together with neighbours Meyer told everyone who wanted to listen about the experience his friend Itzhak had on an airplane trip from New York, Itzhak said that as he sat in the airplane taking off from New York he saw the rabbi sitting next to him cross himself, not once but several times. It bothered him so he asked the rabbi if he had abandoned the Jewish faith and had converted to being a Christian explaining that he had seen the rabbi crossing himself. The rabbi looked at Itzhak somewhat perplexed and said, "What? I was simply checking spectacles, testicals, wallet and watch. They all had a good laugh. Meyer always appeared to be deep in thought, He read a lot of newspapers and magazines, some of which he brought home from the barber shop. He said that he always made sure to return them so that others could read them too.

My neighbours talked with passersby, watched the goings on the street and watched the orthodox Jews walking up the street after their prayer meetings at the synagogues. People relaxed, talked with one another and watched the drunks staggering and meandering home after their habitual visit to the local taverns (establishments serving beer exclusively to men) of which there were many along the Main, Rachel and Mount Royal streets. Taverns did not admit women. This was a hold-over from earlier times when beer drinking was regarded essentially as a man's pastime and a tavern was not a place for a lady. At the time a women's beverage room or a mixed beverage room as in Ontario simply did not exist in Quebec. Of course, women could frequent a bar proper and most of these were in full-scale restaurants or hotels, but they were not allowed in taverns. Taverns attracted middle and working class men of all backgrounds, and male students. Typically taverns had a clean plain vinyl tiled or hardwood floor. The space was populated with solid round tables with ironwork supports surrounded by solid banker's-type wooden chairs, a counter that had beer pumps and a washroom. They had glistening 10 ounce (used to be 12 oz.) glasses stacked on the counter next to the beer pumps at the ready to serve cold draught beer and several waiters scurrying around. Behind the counter were large oak paneled refrigerators stocked with bottles of beer. Occasionally a drunk stopped by asking for directions and the conversation went something like this. The inebriated fellow would ask, "Which is the other side of the street?" One of the neighbours would reply, "Over there." pointing to the other side of the street. The drunk would then say something like, "That's funny, I was just over there and a guy said it was over here." One late evening with the street lights on we saw a drunk searching for something on the ground under the light. A neighbour asked him, "What's the matter?" He replied, "I just lost a dollar down the street." So the neighbour said, "Why are you looking for it here?" The drunk replied, "Because the light is so much better here."

In taverns on the west side of Montreal one usually heard English spoken. In the downtown taverns it was either mixed or French-speaking except in pockets around Guy and Ste. Catherine and parts of Verdun where English endured. East of Bleury Street the taverns tended to be French-speaking. The food was similar in all taverns: pizzas, hamburgers, french fries (I never saw poutine when growing up in Montreal), ham steak, "farmer" sausages (McGarry's or La Belle Fermiere) with brown gravy and onions, pork chops, veal escalope, tourtiere and a variety of omelets; cheese, plain, ham and cheese, with mushrooms, Spanish-style, etc. An omelet with french fries was a popular order as were grilled cheese sandwiches. They also served pickled eggs with soda crackers or extra old cheddar cheese and crackers which went well with cold beer. The beer was a draft from Molson, Labatt or O'Keefe.

Tavern patrons sometimes called for a "tablette" (shelf beer); which meant the drinker wanted it unchilled. The odd dark beer called Champlain Cream Porter was served. It tasted a bit like black licorice. In the spring, some breweries released a "bock" which was stronger than regular beer and tawny-coloured. Brador from Molson was popular for its extra strength. Apparently at one time it was an "ale" and was considered better before it became a "malt liquor". Sometimes, people would order beer and say, "la table", which meant, cover the small round table in draft beers. Students did this after exams. Normally one heard "two drafts please" or "a big Molson" meaning Molson Export in the so-called quart bottles (22 oz.) that were popular. Patrons had a choice of bottled beers from the big three brewers but draft beer in each tavern only came from one of the brewers. The typical tavern beers were Molson Export, Labatt 50, Labatt Blue, O'Keefe Ale, Laurentide Ale or Dow Ale.

There were no imports available until licensed American beers, Miller and Bud came in the later 70's. Imported beers were available at English-style pubs and some restaurants but not in a tavern. Carlsberg - a locally licensed version - came in the mid-1970's. Some of the taverns specialized in a certain kind of food. Kraussman Tavern on Philip's Square made great pig's knuckles cooked in beer. Once a year they had several weeks of a special such as frogs legs. Their tourtiere and fish and chips were outstanding throughout the year. Magnan Tavern in Pointe St Charles specialized in huge rib steaks and roast beef dishes. By the early 1970's male-only establishments were outmoded and taverns changed themselves into a different style of bar called a "brasserie" or "bistro" which offered better décor, food, drink and admitted women.

Beer was promoted as the symbol of hospitality everywhere, a greeting to the welcome guest, a boon to the weary wayfarer; a restorer of strength to the tired worker. It seemed like nothing else on earth bestowed so many favours at so trifling a cost. The ads positioned the best beer as being Dawes " Black Horse " Ale. The brand was owned by Dow Breweries. The ale was fermented in huge vats of selected wood, in a room where even the air was temperature controlled at all times, No other beer could be brewed anywhere approaching the purity and the uniformly high standard of full bodied and robust Black Horse Ale which contained only the finest ingredients; the pick of barley from Canada's finest grain fields; vitamin B yeast developed in the Black Horse brewery from one perfect cell and brewed by brewers of many years experience aided by the best equipment money could buy and brewed under conditions governed by exact science, regulated by every mechanical device for timing, temperature and pasteurization known at that time. A blend of selected hops from several world-famous areas and malt to produce thousands of gallons of ale were boiled together at one time in the immense brew kettles of Dawes Brewery gave balanced flavour to Dawes "Black Horse" Ale. This sort of promotion and the following it had, made " Black Horse " Ale the most popular ale in Canada. Taverns and beer stores sported little statues of a Black Horse and signs advertising Black Horse beer were everywhere.

Dow Breweries was formed in 1952 in Quebec City and used the Boswell Brewery (1843-1952) facilities. In August of 1965, a patient was admitted to a hospital in Quebec City with symptoms suggestive of alcoholic cardiomyopathy. Over the next 8 months 50 more cases with similar findings appeared in the same area with 20 of these being fatal. It was noted that all patients were heavy drinkers who mostly drank Dow brand beer consuming an average of 24 pints of alcohol per day. Epidemiological studies found that Dow had been adding cobalt sulfate to the beer for foam stability since July of 1965 and that the concentration added in the Quebec city brewery was 10 times that of the same beer brewed in Montreal where there were no reported cases. The government began an inquiry and the company panicked. Although Dow denied any responsibility, the Dow Brewery in Quebec City temporarily shut down and the remaining beer (some 500 000 litres) was dumped into the Saint Lawrence River. At the time of the incident, Dow Ale was the number one selling beer in Quebec. Consumers were not reassured and as a result of the "tainted beer scandal" sales of the brand soon dropped dramatically never to recover. Dow was acquired by Carling O'Keefe and stopped its activities on March 31, 1966. Molson Brewery purchased Carling O'Keefe and the Dow brand disappeared from the Canadian market in the spring of 1997. Brands brewed by Dow included Dow Ale, Kingsbeer Lager and Black Horse Ale.

The evening get togethers were sometimes interrupted by horse contributions of smelly piles of manure. On these occasions people quickly moved indoors leaving the immediate area quiet and stinky. Usually someone with a shovel quickly scooped up the manure into a pail for later use as fertilizer in the back garden. The chairs and cushions that had disappeared indoors re-emerged again if it was not too late. If the contribution occurred after the water truck had made its rounds it supplied food for the birds who crowded over it in the morning. Usually though the water trucks succeeded in keeping the street clean. Ten o'clock seemed to be the invisible mandated go to bed time; cushions, chairs and people all went indoors and the street became completely silent. That is when the large water tanked truck with mounted spray nozzles in the truck's front and on its sides took on water at the fire hydrant by the fire station and then came up the street spraying water through the pressurized nozzles all controlled by the driver using a system of in-cab controls.

During these evening conversations people exchanged views on many topics and repeated what they had heard and read. Moishe informed everyone and anyone who would listen about what he had heard at the social club he belonged to. He had met his friend Arnold at the social club and asked him how Abe's funeral went the other day. "It went OK, Moishe," replied Arnold, "but at the end of the Rabbi's eulogy, I had to try and stop myself from laughing aloud." "Why was that?" asked Moishe. "Well," said Arnold, "throughout his marriage to Miriam, she was always telling me what a mean guy he was. He never had a steady job and the money he brought home to her wasn't enough for food and clothing, let alone holidays. Yet he drank heavily and often stayed out all night gambling. Altogether, a good husband he was not. But at the funeral, the Rabbi spoke of how wonderful the deceased was - so considerate, so beloved, so thoughtful to others. Then, when the Rabbi had finished, I heard Miriam say to one of her children, "Do me a favour, David, go see whether it's your father in the coffin."

We had a large Steinberg's grocery store, (number 18) on St Denis Street near Mount Royal Avenue just a few yards north of the F. W. Woolworth store. Steinberg's was the largest grocery supermarket chain in the province of Quebec. Store outlets could be spotted in nearly every district of the island of Montreal. The store displayed bread, dairy, meat, fish, fruit, vegetables, bottled, boxed and canned groceries on its well stocked shelves giving the shopper a wide choice at the best prices and most families in the neighbourhood shopped there every week. Given a list of needed items and money by my mother, I did the shopping and used a red wagon that I had received for my birthday to bring the groceries home rather than having to carry them from the distant store. It was at Steinberg's that most people learned about Kool-Aid and used the different flavours to make a lemonade like drink in the summer to quench their thirst. In 1951 while attending high school I worked at the store on weekends as a wrapper standing behind a cashier and wrapping groceries in bags or boxes for customers at twenty five cents an hour. During the summer holidays I worked as the assistant dairy and bread manager packing the shelves with bread, cake and pies and the refrigerators with butter, cream, milk and cheese. The pay was thirty five cents an hour. The following year my pay was increased to fifty cents an hour. Steinberg's was so entrenched in Quebec culture that English speaking people referred to going grocery shopping by saying "I'm doing my Steinberg's" and French speaking people said, "Je fais mon Steinberg". Most of the weekly heavy grocery shopping was done at Steinbergs while local small grocery stores were used for convenience and purchase of last minute items.

Our neighbourhood grocery store was the FX Lafleur Grocery Store located on the corner of St Dominique and Marie Anne streets. It was a typical Quebec

French dépanneur that sold groceries, dairy, milk, meat, cheese but in addition it was licensed to sell beer and offered free delivery. The Lafleur family lived above the store on the second and third floors. What made it unusual was that only certain licensed dépanneurs that were non-state owned stores were allowed to sell beer, a situation which lasted until the 1990s.

Mr. Lafleur's eldest son, Andre, and I were good friends and we frequently helped with deliveries which we made using a wagon; although the store did employ a full time delivery fellow who made deliveries by bicycle. There were many types of beer being brewed and Lafleur's stocked them all. Dow Breweries produced Dow Ale, Kingsbeer Lager and Black Horse Ale. Labatt 50 was a blonde ale launched in 1950. It was the first light-tasting ale introduced in Canada and was Canada's best-selling beer until 1979 when, with the increasing popularity of lagers, it was surpassed by Labatt Blue. Molson produced Molson Canadian and Molson Export. There was Champlain Cream Porter a dark-coloured beer brewed with dark malts; and Champlain Stout also a dark beer made using roasted malt or barley, hops, water, and yeast. Stouts were traditionally the generic term for the stoutest porters, produced by a brewery. Historically, there were no differences between stout and porter, though there has been a tendency for breweries to differentiate the strengths of their dark beers with the words "extra", "double" and "stout". The term stout was initially used to indicate a stronger porter than other porters issued by an individual brewery.

In the 1940s there were several breweries in Quebec. There was Molson Brewery, which still exists today; Boswell Brewery (1843 - 1952); Champlain

Brewery (1911-1952); Labatt Brewing Company (1847 - 1995); Frontenac Breweries (1911 - 1952) became Carling Brewery in 1952; The Carling Brewery (1840-1930) which in 1930 was sold to Canadian Breweries Limited, founded by E.P. Taylor but the label carried on as Carling's Black Label, Carling Premier and Carling's Red Cap ale; O'Keefe Brewery (1862-1934) which was one of the first to use trucks for beer delivery and the first to build a mechanically refrigerated warehouse, In 1934 it was sold to Canadian Breweries Limited but the label carried on; Dawes Brewery (1811 - 1915) which became National Breweries, and then became the much more famous "Dow Breweries"; Dow Breweries (1952 - 1997) stopped its activities on March 31, 1966 and was purchased by Molsons Brewery and disappeared from the Canadian market in the spring of 1997.

Another small grocery store in the neighbourhood was Averback's on the corner of Colonial and Marie Anne streets. Mr. Averback was a very friendly and helpful Jewish grocer who always had fresh kimmel bread, kaiser rolls, Kraft and cottage cheese, milk, butter, even schmaltz herring on occasion, and halva along with canned goods and soft drinks in glass bottles which cost ten cents a bottle. Across the street on the southwest corner was another general store called Kaufmans. We sometimes bought candy there. Another small grocery store located on St Dominique St between Rachel and Duluth was Klyms owned by Mr. Klym, a Ukrainian, who lived with his family on the second floor above the store. It served as a local meeting place where almost every evening Polish, Slovak and Ukrainian men gathered and discussed world news, politics and current events. On any evening the store was transformed into a friendly social congress where same language immigrants ceased being laborers, who on the job could hardly make themselves understood to those around them, and once again regained their true identities.

The men crowded around the front entrance heatedly debating the political realities of the day while smoking cigarettes and filling the place with smoke. The store was their social club. Accompanying my father I sat in a corner at the back of the store in the corner unnoticed and listened to discussions about the war and its players: Stalin, Hitler, Mussolini, Churchill, Roosevelt, Eisenhower, Tojo and Truman. During this time I petted and played with Mr. Klym's cat, a gray and white tabby that enjoyed my company while I had a cream soda to drink or candy to munch on. I admired the large glass drink bottles of Jumbo with an elephant on them, bottles from KiK Cola, Denis cream soda, Denis Nectar, Corona Cream Soda, Pepsi, Peers, Denis Cola, Snow White Cream Soda, Coca-Cola, 7up, Nesbitt's Orange, Allans, Orange Crush, Royal Stewart, Gurds Dry Ginger Ale, Biere D'epinett (Spruce Beer), Hires Root Beer, Cott, and Canada Dry Ginger Ale. I watched as the tobacco smoke clung heavily to the ceiling. I think that Mr. Klym sold a lot of tobacco and Zig-zag, Vogue or Chantecler cigarette paper as everyone in those days rolled their own cigarettes. Every time someone came in to buy something the men would make space so that the person could reach the counter where Mr. Klym did his best to serve their needs. Opening the door exhausted the tobacco smoke and freshened the air in the place. At times the store was so crowded that customers found it difficult to enter and approach the counter where Mr. Klym was. I frequently returned home with a bag of cookies or David chocolate biscuits in a brown paper bag or Viau biscuits shaped like maple leaves. When I did not accompany my father I would lie awake in bed and wait for him to come home with a small brown paper bag filled with my favourite chocolate biscuits.

Although my neighbours brought nothing material with them to this country, they brought their dreams and hopes for a better life and they knew and were more than willing to do the work that it would take to make their dreams a reality. They possessed a committed purpose to their lives and approached it with optimism in a brighter future. They proceeded to establish a foothold in their newly adopted country and continued to weave the fabric of who they were and they made a difference. We all lived harmoniously together and looked for opportunities. Hard working people engaged in various commercial activities inhabited our street and the surrounding area bounded by Sherbrooke street to the south, Laurier street to the north, Park avenue in the west and St Denis street to the east. There were shop keepers, barbers, billiard and pool room keepers; locksmiths, electricians, plumbers, blacksmiths, tailors, tinsmiths, upholsterers, chip wagon owners, tobacconists, butchers, waiters, cafeteria workers, cooks, housekeepers, bookbinders, bookkeepers, insurance agents. scrap dealers, bill collectors, bakers, cabinet makers, dentists, doctors, furriers, lawyers, notaries, painters, milliners, lumbermen, machinists, musicians, labourers, iron workers, pressers, window cleaners, printers, publishers, peddlers, taxi drivers, opticians, peddlers, salesmen, storekeepers, clerks, delivery men, some who worked for the city, or the railways, on the docks; in shipyards and some selling newspapers on street corners and some with their own newsstands and those who worked at the many stores. There were bakeries, meat. fish and fruit markets, ice cream parlors, book stores, candy stores, furniture stores, delicatessen stores, restaurants, hardware stores, dry goods stores, boots and shoe stores, drug stores, clothing stores, grocery stores and shops that sold appliances, jewellery, radios, picture frames and factories.

People all had stories about their workplaces; they spoke about their home life, their work and their experiences. Beryl driving a Diamond Taxi recalled how this one day he had just picked up his first passenger of the evening. After about five minutes of driving, the passenger suddenly tapped Beryl on his shoulder to ask him a question. Beryl screamed, lost control of his taxi, nearly hit a streetcar, went up onto the pavement and stopped only inches from a shop window. For a second, everything went very quiet in the taxi, then Beryl said, "Look sir, don't ever do that again. You scared the living daylights out of me." His passenger apologized and said, "I didn't realise that a little tap could scare you so much." Beryl replied, "Sorry, it's not really your fault. Today is only my second day as a cab driver – I've been working at Papermans Funeral Home driving hearses for the past two years."

With the usual assembly of neighbours in the evening Moishe asked Sidney what was new with him since Sidney looked pretty miserable blowing and wiping his nose with his handkerchief. Sidney with a somewhat heavy nasal voice said, "You remember the heavy cold rain and terrible wind we had the evening before yesterday? The streets were almost deserted, puddles of water everywhere and the 'Workmen's Bakery' was just about to shut when I walked in. I am very sure that I looked absolutely drenched and half frozen. I was shivering and felt very cold. My umbrella had blown inside out and I was thoroughly miserable. As I unbuttoned my coat, I said to the lady behind the counter, "Two bagels, please." She looked at me very surprised. "Only two? Don't you want anything else?" "No. I only want two," I replied. "One for Esther and one for me." "Is Esther your wife?" the lady asked. "Don't ask silly questions," I said, "Of course she is. Do you think my mother would send me out on a night like this? So today I'm suffering with the sniffles" Meyer who sat and patiently listened to Sidney's tale of woe said, "Sidney take some Aspirin and a hot water bottle to bed with you and you'll be fine in the morning. That's what my doctor had told me to do. At least you don't have the problem that Shlomo told me about". Both Moishe and Sidney were curious to find out. Meyer continued, "As you know Shlomo and Rifka had just got married and had been on their honeymoon visiting her family near St Denis street. On the first night, as he was making love to Rifka for the first time, Shlomo looked down at her and asked, "Am I the first man to make love to you, Rifka?" Rifka looked up at him and replied, "No Shlomo. I'm sure I would have recognised you." All three of the men shook their heads, no one laughed.

This sort of nightly exchange was not limited to the men. The ladies had their stories too. Leah, Max the peddler's wife was talking to her neighbour. "Oy, my daughter-in-law is just so lazy! She sleeps until after ten o'clock every single morning! My poor son, Solly, wakes up at the crack of dawn and has to make his own breakfast. The house she won't clean; she made my Solly get her a maid so she wouldn't have to lift a finger. Then, when he comes home after a long, hard day at work, Solly has to make dinner because she can't be bothered even with that!" The neighbour sighs and asks, "Nu...and how is your daughter?" "Oh, now my daughter Rebecca has an absolute gem of a husband. He insists my Rebecca pamper herself by sleeping late in the morning; he hired help so she shouldn't have to work so hard, and he even comes home from work and tells her to relax while he takes care of dinner!" Sidney was somewhat of a gossip and in his hushed voice informed everyone who was listening about Solomon who at the age of seventy-five, suddenly began to chase much younger women. Solomon kept to himself mostly and did not participate in the evening get togethers much. Sidney said that he was going to bring up Solomon's behavior to his wife Ruth. Leah said, "Why don't you just forget about it? Besides do you think that she really cares?" She shrugged and continued, "Who cares? Let him chase girls! After all dogs chase after cars; but when they catch them, can they drive?"

Among the hard working people there were also those who were after easy money, gamblers. card sharks and poker players. Benny, a well known freeloader was a horse player always hanging around the newsstand at the corner of the Main and Rachel streets and always with the latest "Racing News" paper rolled up in his hand. He kept Chaim, the newsstand owner, company every noon hour, mostly gossiping and trying to solve the problems of the world. One day while I was getting the Montreal Herald newspaper I overheard Benny telling Chaim that his friend George, another horse player, had chased after and retrieved a Hassidic rabbi's fur hat that had been blown off by the strong wind. Returning it to the rabbi, the rabbi said, "Thank you, are you Jewish?" "No," replied George. "Well," said the rabbi, "I can't bless you, but I see a day of great wealth for you." When George spoke with Benny he wondered what could the rabbi have possibly meant and finally said, "I know, I can make the last four races at the horse track." So he looked at the racing programme and saw a horse named Top Hat in the next race. "An omen," he thought, and he bet $100 and what do you know - he won. The next race had a horse named Stetson, so again he bet it all and he won again. The next race featured a horse named Beret, and he naturally won again. On the next race he bet everything again and he lost big time. "How come? What horse did you bet on?"' enquired Benny. George said "Chateau, French for hat." "Oy Vey" Benny said, "Chapeau is French for hat, not Chateau. Chaim asked, "So what horse was the winner?" Benny said that is what I asked him, I said, "By the way, who won the race?' George answered, "I don't know, Some Japanese horse called Yarmulka!". Benny and Chaim both exclaimed. "How do you like that?"

Most houses didn't have a phone. Every neighbourhood had several telephone booths (pay phones) situated in convenient places enabling those without access to a telephone at home or while travelling to communicate with others whether for business or personal use. It enabled people to talk to someone without physically going to see them. Public telephones could be found in hotel lobbies, drug stores, hospitals, taverns, market places, most public places and on city streets. The Mount Royal Hotel had a long line of luxurious sit-down pay phones on the mezzanine. Labows Drug Store had several public telephone booths. Each telephone booth had a door to provide privacy; windows for anyone to see that the booth was occupied, an interior light, a printed telephone book or directory and the pay phone itself which accepted coins. In the 1940s and 1950s a local call cost five cents which had to be prepaid by inserting coins into the pay telephone enabling you to talk for as long as you wanted. During the 1960s and 1970s, the same call cost ten cents. In the late 1970s and early 1980s, this price gradually changed to twenty cents, and again rose to twenty five cents between 1985 and 1990. Long distance calls were placed by an operator who asked the caller to deposit the amount of the call for a given number of minutes ahead of the call. Coins had to be deposited in full in the telephone for the allotted time before the call was placed. Long distance prices were high - some calls could cost an hour's wage for a single minute. People tried to outsmart the phone company by making collect calls to phone booths, which invariably went unpaid. Bell Canada fixed the pay phones so that they would not be able to receive incoming calls. In the 1970s, pay phones and booths began to disappear chiefly because of mayor Jean Drapeau's attempt to rid the city streets of them along with newspaper boxes and mailboxes. There are very few public telephone booths remaining at present and they are rapidly disappearing as cell phones gain in popularity.

Only a few homes on our street had a telephone, In the 1940s the telephone company made two types of telephone service available; private and party line. Party line meant sharing the line with other subscribers somewhere else on the street. A majority of telephone subscribers were serviced by party lines which provided no privacy in communication and were used as a source for much gossip. Telephones had a rotary dial or finger wheel, with numerical digits and letters arranged in a circular layout with holes so that a finger could be inserted. The dials had letters and numbers displayed under the finger holes in the following pattern: 1, 2 ABC, 3 DEF, 4 GHI, 5 JKL, 6 MNO, 7 PRS, 8 TUV, 9 WXY, and 0 (sometimes Z) Operator. The letters were associated with the dial numbers to represent telephone exchange names. The finger wheel was rotated with one finger from the position of each digit to a fixed stop position, a mechanical barrier to prevent further rotation. When released at the finger stop, the wheel returned to its home position by spring action. This dialing action was decoded by the telephone exchange and the number was connected. The exchange names were assigned by area and were good identifiers as to place of residence, The named telephone exchange prefixes in Montreal were:

AMherst	ATlantic	AVenue	BElair	BYwater
CAlumet	CHerrier	CLairval	CRescent	DExter
DOllard	DUpont	ELwood	EXdale	FAlkirk
FItzroy	FRontenac	GIffard	GLenview	GRavelle
HArbour	HEmlock	HOchelaga	HUnter	LAfontaine
LAncaster	MArquette	MElrose	PLateau	POntiac
RAymond	REgent	RIverside	TAlon	TRenmore
TUrcotte	UNiversity	VEndome	VIctor	WAlnut
WIlbank	WEllington			

Between 1961 and 1966 all exchange names were phased out in favor of "all-number calling" (ANC). Although the push-button phone using a keypad for dialing was showcased at the Seattle World's Fair in 1963, it took a further twenty years for the push button phone to displace the rotary dial phone. By the 1980s, party lines were replaced with individual service lines to accommodate computer modems and answering machines.

Mayer and his wife Dinah would often join the evening get together on the doorsteps outside their home. They had a party line telephone, one of four on the whole block. This one evening Mayer wasn't home, he was still at work. Dinah was sitting nursing her ankle but she sprang to the telephone when it rang and everyone sitting outdoors could hear her say, "Hello Mamma, I'm so happy to hear from you." .... "I'm having a bad day; the baby won't eat, kept me up all night, diapers and laundry is piling up." Breaking into bitter tears, she continued, "I haven't had a chance to go shopping, and besides, I've just sprained my ankle and I have to hobble around. On top of that, the house is a mess."............."Oh Mamma, you're so kind, I really appreciate it" ...."Jakob?" said Dinah. "Who's Jakob?" ...."No, this is Harbour 1892". There was a short pause, then Dinah said, "Does this mean you're not coming over?" ....Dinah hung up the telephone and came back, saying, "wrong number".

Her two neighbours Golda and Dora asked, "What happened to your Mamma?" Dinah said that the call was from a women who sounded just like her Momma who after hearing all of Dinah's troubles told her. "Sit down, relax and close your eyes. I'll be over in half an hour. I'll do your shopping, clean up the house and cook your dinner for you. I'll feed the baby and do the washing. Now stop crying. I'll do everything. In fact, I'll even call your husband Jakob at the office and tell him he ought to come home and help out for once. When she said my husband Jakob I didn't know who she was talking about and then when she told me the number she thought that she had called we knew it was the wrong number." After a longer pause, Golda asked "so is she still coming over?" Dinah laughing said. "I did ask her that, didn't I?" She could have verified that by talking with the other folks who shared the party line and who had listened in. Our neighbourhood had few secrets.

The radio evolved from the huge parlour furniture pieces to table top models and portable boom boxes; eventually to pocket size transistor units. Radios were the main source for news, weather forecasts and entertainment. The song, "Goodnight, Irene" was a real favourite played over and over again on the radio and jukeboxes everywhere. The lyrics tell of the singer's troubled past with his love, Irene, and express his sadness and frustration. "Goodnight Irene," was one side of a two-sided hit vinyl record. It was number 1 while number 2 "Tzena, Tzena, Tzena" was on the flip side. "Tzena, Tzena, Tzena" was originally written in Hebrew by Issachar Miron (a.k.a. Stefan Michrovsky), a Polish emigrant while serving in the Jewish Brigade of the British forces, he composed the melody for lyrics written by Chagiz. The song became popular in Palestine and was played on the Israeli radio as well.

Tzena, Tzena, Tzena
Tzena, Tzena, Tzena, Tzena
Can't you hear the music playing In the city square
Tzena, Tzena, Tzena, Tzena
Come where all our friends will find us With the dancers there

Another favourite was a novelty song titled, "The Thing". The lyrics took the form of a first-person narration, describing the discovery of a box on a beach. Whatever is in the box is never revealed, nor is it called "The Thing" in the lyrics. When the lyrics call for The Thing to be named, the vocals simply pause for three percussive knocks. Initially, the narrator is overjoyed by his discovery and tries to sell it. Instead, he is thrown out by a proprietor with a threat to call the police. Undaunted, the narrator decides to give it to his wife, who also kicks him out and requests that he never return with it. After going through life unable to rid himself of the Thing, the narrator dies and arrives in Heaven where Saint Peter tells him to take it "down below" to Hell. In the final verse, the narrator warns the listener not to open boxes on the beach as he did.

From the 1940s to 1960 The Barry Sisters, Clara and Minnie Bagelman, first known as the Bagelman Sisters, were popular Yiddish jazz singers. They performed on the New York Radio Show "Yiddish Melodies in Swing" which played jazz, swing and klezmer songs in the Yiddish language. One of their biggest hits was Tumbalalaika, by no means a jazz song, but a Russian-Jewish folk and love song in the Yiddish language. Tuml is the Yiddish word for noise and a balalaika is a stringed musical instrument of Russian origin. The Barry Sisters recorded a Yiddish and English combination version. The song went like this:

A young lad stands, and he thinks
Thinks and thinks a whole night

Whom to take and not to shame
Whom to take and not to shame

Tumbala, Tumbala, Tumbalalaika
Tumbala, Tumbala, Tumbalalaika
Tumbalalaika, strum balalaika
Tumbalalaika, may we be happy
Girl, girl, I want to ask of you
What can grow, grow without rain?
What can burn and never end?
What can yearn, cry without tears?

Foolish lad, why do you have to ask?
A stone can grow, grow without rain
Love can burn and never end
A heart can yearn, cry without tears
What is higher than a house?
What is swifter than a mouse?
What is deeper than a well?
What is bitter, more bitter than gall?
A chimney is higher than a house
A cat is swifter than a mouse
The Torah is deeper than a well
Death is bitter, more bitter than gall

People could be heard humming and then singing the melodic refrain "Tumbala, Tumbala, Tumbalalaika" over and over again as they were doing their chores.

CHAPTER 3 - Dark Clouds of War

My friend Yurie's father, Pavel explained the soviet farm system at one of the evening get togethers, The Soviet Union had established collective farming called kolkhozy in 1917 under then leader Lenin. The people in a kolkhoz were called kolkhozniks and were supposed to receive a share of the farm's product and profit according to the number of days worked. However, in practice, the kolkhozy paid no cash for labor at all, instead they paid 500 grams of grain or less per day worked. All of the grain and other crops produced had to be sold to the State at the very low fixed prices set by the Soviet government, which paid less than one third of the cost of production and those prices hardly changed at all between 1929 and 1953. Each able-bodied adult kolkhoznik could hold about 1 acre (0.40 ha) of private land with some animals and had to work a minimum of 130 days a year on the kolkhoz and on other government work (such as road building). Boys aged between 12 and 16, had to work for 50 days each year. If the required minimum of work was not performed the private plot of land could be confiscated and at a trial of a People's Court the individual could be sentenced to several months of hard labour in a corrective labor camp. In urban areas the movement of population was controlled by a system of internal passports and residence permits which were legally necessary for all domestic travel. In the countryside kolkhozniks did not have internal passports and therefore were prevented from leaving a kolkhoz or from moving from rural areas to urban areas. According to the law children born on a collective farm had to work there as adults unless they specifically received permission to leave. People living on a kolkhoz were tied to their kolkhoz. The Stalinist bureaucracy took over and administered this so called soviet farm system, filling the role formerly held in Russia by tsarist-era serf-owners.

Itzik's father Jacob added that throughout history antisemitism was based on Christian theology blaming Jews for killing Jesus. in Europe, Jews were subjected to expulsions and pogroms i.e., attacks against Jews and physical destruction of Jewish property, as well as looting of Jewish homes and businesses. The economic strains of the Great Depression led some in the German medical establishment to advocate the euthanasia of the "incurable" mentally and physically disabled as a cost-saving measure to free up funds for the curable. In reference to the disabled and mentally ill the Nazis used the phrase Lebensunwertes Leben (life unworthy of life). Even before the Nazi rise to power in 1933, there was a tendency to save the racially "valuable", while ridding society of the racially "undesirable". Some even believed that Marxism was a Jewish doctrine; that Jews had created communism as part of a conspiracy to destroy Germany. The Nazis did not see humans as racial equals with equal hereditary value. Nazi ideology believed that the Roma, originally an Aryan population, had been "spoiled" by non-Romani blood. The Germans saw the Roma as hereditary criminals and "asocials"; (they were given black triangles to

wear). The Nazis considered the Slavs as subhuman and Hitler's 1942 General Plan East planned on exterminating, expelling, or enslaving all or most Slavs from their lands over a period of 20–30 years to make living space for Germans. It was estimated that over ten million Slavs were murdered by the Germans. The ideology of Nazism was based upon a concept that the ancient Aryan race was a superior race, and that the German people were the most racially pure people of Aryan stock in existence today. Nazism embraced the view that Jews as a race were locked in mortal combat with the Aryan race for world domination. This ideology was adopted and became commonplace throughout Germany. With the birth of the Third Reich in 1933, Nazi policies divided the population into two groups; those who belonged and those who did not (enemies). The enemies were divided into three groups:
1. Racial enemies, such as the Jews and Roma.
2. National Comrades, such as political opponents of Nazism, such as Marxists, liberals, Christians, and the reactionaries.
3. Moral opponents, such as gay men, the "work-shy", and habitual criminals.

The latter two groups were to be sent to concentration camps for "re-education", with the aim of eventual absorption into the belonging category. Tens of thousands of German gay men were convicted between 1933 and 1944 and sent to camps for "rehabilitation"; they were identified by pink triangles. Hundreds were castrated, sometimes "voluntarily" to avoid criminal sentences. Many victims kept their stories to themselves because homosexuality remained criminalized in postwar Germany. The Gestapo raided gay bars, tracked individuals using the address books of those they arrested, used the subscription lists of gay magazines to find others, and encouraged people to report suspected homosexual behavior and to scrutinize the behavior of their neighbors. Lesbians were left relatively unaffected; the Nazis saw them as "asocials", rather than sexual deviants. Blacks and persons of color including prisoners of war were subjected to incarceration, sterilization, murder, and other abuse. Jehovah Witnesses were given the option of renouncing their faith and submitting to the state's authority by pledging allegiance to the Nazi party or by serving in the military; if they refused they were sent to concentration camps where they wore purple triangles. Racial enemies namely Jews and Roma could never belong; they were to be removed from society. However only the Jewish people were singled out for annihilation. Itzik's father and the other neighbours struggled trying to understand the stupidity of the Nazi thinking. Often attention was diverted to some other event when it became too painful to persue what they had been talking about any further.

Often discussions were held concerning some social event that was published in the newspaper like a wedding, or bar mitzvah which all Jewish boys receive when they attain their thirteenth year. The newspaper articles emphasized those given by the more affluent Jews that were particularly noteworthy. My working class neighbours were stunned by the magnificence and utter lavishness of everything, the description of the dresses, the table settings, the meal, the music, etc. They talked about the food that was served since no Jewish celebration is complete without food. They pictured the proud fathers standing talking with the guests having a great smile but hiding an aching wallet. At times they spoke about the celebrations and proceedings, traditions, rituals and prayers at a bris

(circumcision - the removal of the foreskin from an eight-day-old baby boy's penis). They talked about the mohel (a rabbi specially trained in circumcision). an act that was usually performed in the district by Rabbi Colton. The subject of circumcision generated lots of discussion and many stories. My friend Label's father, Lazarus related his story of looking for a watchmaker when his watch was not working. He had passed a little shop with clocks and watches in the window on Mount Royal street, so he took the watch in for repair. "Can I help you?" asked the man behind the counter.
"I want this watch repaired," said Lazarus.
"I'm sorry. I don't repair watches."
"Well, how much for a new one then?" asked Lazarus.
"I don't sell watches."
"You don't sell watches?"
"No, I don't sell watches."
"Clocks, you sell clocks then? How much for a clock?"
"I don't sell clocks." Lazarus said that he was getting exasperated. "You don't sell watches, you don't sell clocks?"
"No, I'm a mohel," replied the man.
"Then why do you have all those clocks and watches in the window?"
The mohel asked, "If you were a mohel, tell me, what would you put in your window?"
Everyone sitting around laughed loudly at that story.

My friend David's father, Izzy related his story about the birth of his eldest son Itzhak. To celebrate his birth Izzy had bought a round of drinks for everyone at his social club as he announced that his wife Hanna had just given birth to a baby boy weighing 20 pounds. Everyone in the social club congratulated him and many told him that they found it hard to believe that his baby weighed in so heavy. But Izzy assured them, "It's true, it's really true." When Izzy came back to the club three weeks later, those present asked him, "Nu Izzy how much does your baby weigh now?" Izzy proudly replied, "Twelve pounds." His colleagues could not understand this, so they asked Izzy, "Vus machs da? Is he ill? What happened? He weighed 20 pounds at birth, why has he lost so much weight?" Izzy said that he took a big swig from his beer, wiped his lips with the back of his hand and proudly replied, "Had him circumcised." The neighbours all laughed, but underlying this discussion was a growing problem that came up several times and were very serious and ponderous conversations with relatively much hard thinking by all of these good neighbours and the community at large. The subject involved a bris, a ceremony that includes prayers and the surgical procedure called circumcision to remove the foreskin from an eight-day-old baby boy's penis according to the commandment in Leviticus 12:2, In the 1940s the mohel had to be a rabbi specially trained in circumcision. The popularity of circumcision among non-Jews presented problems for religious Jews because the penis remained a key sign of Jewish difference. The great scholar Elliot Wolfson called Jewish circumcision 'the cut that binds,' it's a severance that connects Jewish boys to their fathers and grandfathers, to Jews across time and borders." The intrusion of science on the ritual of circumcision was posing a problem for my Jewish neighbours. Expert opinion endorsed circumcision and its health advantages from a variety of medical subfields which included urologists, surgeons, gynecologists and even psychiatrists.

Circumcision changed from being mainly a Jewish religious custom to a surgical procedure available to everyone. Babies delivered in a hospital were being circumcised by an attending physician. Even Jewish parents who had insurance were having their sons circumcised in hospitals, paid for by insurance companies, instead of at home or at synagogue by a rabbi who was a mohel. This posed a threat to Judaism because it seemed to strip the Covenant of Circumcision of its mysteriously potent spiritual power. The neighbours discussed the influence of the New York Board of Rabbis, founded in 1914 who trained mohels in the newest surgical techniques, methods of asepsis and hygiene, newly developed clamps and devices; they certified mohels and provided malpractice insurance and acted as a guild for Jews entering the profession. They felt that it was the board's job to keep circumcision Jewish in the face of the changing norms. Meanwhile the Board had worked hard to represent mohels at hospitals, requiring that mohels be certified for hospital-regulated circumcision encouraging hospitals to provide space to perform the rite.

My friend Sidney's father, Moe, was smoking a cigar to the harsh disapproval of his wife Ruth. She kept saying and probably everyone sitting there agreed that it smelled like dreck (shit). Moe said that it was a gift he received at the social club and that it was an expensive Montecristo Cuban cigar. Not to change the subject, our neighbour Moishe wondered since circumcisions were being performed by physicians whether many mohels were under threat and would have to retire. Saul chimed in wondering what kind of mal practice insurance did mohels carry. Moe who always had an opinion on everything said that he did not see why they should not carry such insurance if for no other reason than to safeguard themselves. Discussion then shifted to what the premium for such an insurance could possibly be. Moe was sure that the premium would depend on the deductible. He felt that a two inch deductible was probably the standard and anything shorter than that would be much more pricey.

The conversation about conditions in Germany resumed several evenings later and Itzik's father, Jacob continued. After Adolf Hitler's rise to power in 1933, the Nazis intensified their restriction of legal, economic, and social rights for Jews. They led a campaign of violence against opponents and suppressed all potential opposition. The Law for the Restoration of the Professional Civil Service was passed excluding Jews and other "non-Aryans" from the civil service. Jews were disbarred from practising law, from being editors or proprietors of newspapers. Jewish doctors were dismissed or urged to resign. On April 6, 1933, the weekly official journal of the German Medical Association, "Deutsches Ärzteblatt" distributed to all physicians in Germany, reported "Germans are to be treated by Germans only." Works by Jewish composers, authors, and artists were excluded from publications, performances, and exhibitions. Companies fired Jewish workers. The Nazis closed and boycotted Jewish businesses and targeted them for forcible sale to Germans. Jews were not allowed to own farms. Jewish faculty and students were dismissed from universities and quotas were imposed restricting Jewish students from attending schools and universities. On July 14, 1933, the Nazis passed the Sterilization Law, titled the Law for the Prevention of

Hereditarily Diseased Offspring, also known as Aktion T4 which allowed compulsory sterilization. Estimates for the number of involuntary sterilizations during the whole of the Third Reich range from 300,000 to 400,000.

Nazi racial policy was forcing Jews to emigrate. On September 15, 1935, the Reichstag passed the Reich Citizenship Law and the Law for the Protection of German Blood and German Honor which stated that only those of "German or kindred blood" could be citizens. Anyone with three or more Jewish grandparents was classified as a Jew. Marriages between Jews and those of German or related blood were forbidden and any sexual relationships between them were criminalized. Moishe added that conditions turned violent on November 9 and 10, 1938 when the Nazis instigated a pogrom against Jews throughout the Third Reich. It was carried out by SA paramilitary forces (the "Brownshirts") and German civilians while German authorities looked on without intervening. The pogrom was called Kristallnacht ("Night of Broken Glass") from the shards of broken glass that littered the streets after the windows of Jewish-owned stores, buildings, and synagogues were smashed. Jewish homes, hospitals, and schools were ransacked, as the attackers demolished buildings. The rioters destroyed 267 synagogues throughout Germany, Austria, and the Sudetenland and over 7,000 Jewish businesses were either destroyed or damaged. A decree on November 12, 1938 barred Jews from most of the remaining occupations they had been allowed to hold. Kristallnacht marked the end of any sort of public Jewish activity and culture, and Jews stepped up their efforts to leave the country.

Ghettos were set up to segregate and confine Jews into tightly packed areas of a city and were closed off from the outside world at different times and for different reasons. Bureaucrats identified who was a Jew, confiscated property, and scheduled trains that deported Jews into the ghettos. A ghetto could be closed to force the Jews inside to give up money and valuables as happened at the Łódź ghetto in 1940. Food supplies were restricted, public hygiene was difficult, and the inhabitants were often subjected to forced labour. In the labour camps and ghettos at least half a million Jews died of starvation, disease especially typhoid, and poor living conditions. The murder, looting, destruction of property, and terror on an unprecedented scale sent shock waves around the world.

Starting in 1933, the Nazis built a network of concentration camps in Germany for people deemed "undesirable". The initial purpose of the camps was to serve as a deterrent by terrorizing Germans who did not conform. After 1939 more than 42,000 camps, ghettos, and detention sites were set up. The reason given for setting up concentration camps was that in the long run it was not possible to keep individual undesirables in the state prisons without overburdening these prisons. The first concentration camp was opened in Dachau, Germany with room for 5,000 people. German communists, socialists and trade unionists and whomever the Nazis felt endangered state security were among the first undesirables sent to the camp at Dachau. About 30,000 Jewish men were arrested and incarcerated in concentration camps. In 1939 Hitler signed a "euthanasia decree" authorizing his personal physician, to carry out a program of involuntary euthanasia also known as Aktion T4. Between 1939 and 1941, the number of mentally and physically handicapped adults and children in institutions murdered was about 150,000.

On May 22, 1939, Italy and Germany signed the Pact of Steel joining both countries in a military alliance designed in the event of war against France and Britain. On August 23, 1939 Germany signed a nonaggression pact with the Soviet Union where they agreed to divide Poland between them. In this way Germany neutralized the possibility that the USSR would come to Poland's aid. On August 25 Britain signed a new treaty with Poland, promising military support should it be attacked. On September 1, 1939 Germany invaded Poland and on September 3, Britain followed by Australia, New Zealand, India and France declared war on Germany, starting World War II. Germany unleashed its blitzkrieg, or "lightning war," with air support provided by the Luftwaffe, armored panzer tank divisions smashed through Polish horsed cavalry. By September 8, German forces had reached the outskirts of Warsaw, having advanced 140 miles in the first week of the invasion. The Polish armed forces hoped to hold out long enough so that an offensive could be mounted against Germany in the west. All hope was lost when on September 17, 1939 the Soviet Union invaded the eastern regions of Poland and annexed territories totaling 201,015 square kilometres (77,612 sq mi) with a population of 13,299,000 inhabitants. On September 18, Poland's government and military leaders fled the country.

The pretext for the Soviet invasion of Eastern Poland (including Western Ukraine and Belarus) was the "need to protect" the Ukrainian and Belarusian majority populations in the wake of the Nazi invasion of Poland. On September 28, Germany and the USSR concluded an agreement outlining their zones of occupation. Soviet authorities immediately started a campaign of sovietization of the newly acquired areas. They nationalized and redistributed private and state-owned Polish property and attempted to erase Polish history and culture, They regarded service for the pre-war Polish state as a "counter-revolutionary activity" and as a "crime against revolution" and justification for arresting and taking between 230,000 to 450,000 Poles prisoner, some of whom were executed. On March 5, 1940 they executed 25,700 Polish POWs, labeled as nationalists and counterrevolutionaries in occupied western Ukraine and Belarus. This became known as the Katyn massacre. Sovietization policies in Polish lands included confiscation of property and mass deportations of the hundreds of thousands of local citizens to Siberia. During 1939–1941 1.45 million people (63.1% Poles and 7.4% Jews) inhabiting the region were deported to Siberia of whom 350,000 people died. Local populations in some occupied Soviet territories actively participated in the killings of Jews and others. Besides participating in killings and pogroms, they helped identify Jews for persecution and rounded up Jews for German actions. In western Ukraine many locals were deeply involved in the atrocities many even serving as concentration and death-camp guards for the Nazis as well as for the NKVD.

Despite their declaration of war against Germany, Britain and France did little militarily to aid Poland. With the exception of a few dramatic British-German clashes at sea, no major military action was taken during the subsequent seven months. In November 1939, with Poland under German occupation, Nazi plans called for the complete removal of the Polish population from all Polish territories in 15 to 20 years and have the country settled by German colonists. German expansion had begun in 1938 with the annexation of Austria and then continued with the occupation of the Sudetenland (Czechoslovakia except for the eastern part) and then all of Czechoslovakia in 1939. Both had been accomplished without igniting hostilities with the major world powers and Hitler had hoped that his invasion of Poland would likewise be tolerated. The policy of the Germans in Poland included reducing food rations, depriving the people of medical services and the deliberate lowering of public hygiene, It was estimated that almost two million non-Jewish Polish citizens perished at German hands during the course of the war, about four-fifths of whom were ethnic Poles with the rest ethnic Ukrainians and Belarusians. It had been reported that about 5.6 million of the victims of World War II were Polish citizens, both Jewish and non-Jewish, and over the course of the war Poland lost 16 percent of its pre-war population. Over 90 percent of the death toll came through various deliberate actions by Germany and the Soviet Union.

Hostilities escalated dramatically in 1940 with Germany's April invasion of Norway and May invasion of the Low Countries and France. On June 10, 1940, as the French government fled to Bordeaux during the German invasion, declaring Paris an open city, Benito Mussolini, the dictator of Italy with the title Il Duce ("The Leader") felt the conflict would soon end and declared war on Britain and France. Mussolini had ruled Italy as its fascist leader since 1922 and as dictator from 1925.

The Soviet Union under its leader, Joseph Stalin, developed a new category of concentration camps; called gulag camps which were forced labor camps. They were used for the imprisonment of millions of people who were not criminals, but political opponents and various so-called undesirables under the totalitarian, both communist and fascist regimes. Some kolkhozy became gulag camps. Some of them were dubbed "re-education facilities" for political coercion, but most others served as the backbone of industry and agriculture for the benefit of the state especially in times of war. Officially gulag camps were called "Corrective labor camps". They existed throughout the Soviet Union and were a significant part of Stalin's campaign to turn the Soviet Union into a modern industrial power and to collectivize agriculture in the early 1930s reaching their peak in the 1940s to the 1950s. The largest camps lay in the most extreme geographical and climatic regions of the country from the Arctic north to the Siberian east and the Central Asian south. The Gulag (Glavnoye Upravleniye Lagerej) was the government agency in charge of the Soviet forced labor camp system where prisoners were engaged in a variety of unskilled, manual, and economically inefficient activities. The combination of endemic violence, extreme climate, hard labor, meager food rations and unsanitary conditions led to extremely high death rates in the camps. Following Stalin's death in 1953 the Gulag was radically reduced in size, however forced labor camps and political prisoners continued to exist in the Soviet Union for many years after.

In June 1941, Hitler attacked the USSR, breaking his nonaggression agreement with the Soviet Union, and Germany seized all of Poland. During the German occupation, nearly three million Polish Jews were killed in the Nazi death camps. The Nazis also severely persecuted the Slavic majority, deporting and executing Poles in an attempt to destroy the intelligentsia and Polish culture. A large Polish resistance movement effectively fought against the occupation with the assistance of the Polish government-in-exile. Many exiled Poles also fought for the Allied cause. The Soviets completed the liberation of Poland in 1945 and established a communist government in the nation.

Melvyn's wife Anita said that she had something to contribute to the evening's discussion after her husband excused himself and went indoors to go to the bathroom. She spoke about the time that Melvyn had ordered a new pair of reading glasses and they had gone to his optician to collect them. After he picked them up and on their way home, they stopped off at their local snack bar for a bite to eat. As they looked at the menu, Melvyn said, "Anita, I can only see everything double with these new glasses, so please order for me - I'm going to the toilet." When Melvyn came back, the front of his trousers were soaking wet. "Oy vay, I said, What happened?" "Well I'll tell you," said Melvyn, "As I was standing in front of the urinal, I looked down and I saw two, so I put one back." Moe laughed so hard at Anita's story that he almost swallowed the cigar he had been smoking and stubbed it out on the sidewalk. Everyone thought that Anita's story was hilarious and were still laughing when Melvyn returned. He did feel his trousers though when he noticed that everyone was looking at them.

In the neighbourhood news whether acquired from the newspapers or on radio was shared by word of mouth and many expressed their own opinions. Canadian Broadcasting Corporation (CBC) began "farm broadcasts" in 1939 and provided full coverage of the six-week visit of King George VI and Queen Elizabeth. Regular broadcasting began of the Montréal Canadians' hockey games from the Montréal Forum the same year. With the declaration of World War II, CBC/Radio-Canada sent a team of announcers and technicians to accompany the Canadian Armed Forces' First Division to England, and so began special wartime broadcasts. In 1940, the Canadian Press provided the CBC with free news for their CBC News Service that had news bureaus in Halifax, Montreal, Winnipeg, Vancouver and Toronto. They went on the air four times daily and broadcasted to Canadian soldiers overseas, using the BBC facilities in London, England. As well as listening to CBC for war time news, everyone who had access to a shortwave radio tuned in nightly to BBC news.

We were living during a period of war and everyone with access to a radio listened daily to CBC Radio and very attentively at the supper hour to short wave radio for the chimes of Big Ben in London, England and the announcement that it was the BBC news with the latest from the front. On September 1, 1939 German forces had invaded Poland attacking across all frontiers and bombing Warsaw, the capital and other Polish cities and two days later Britain and France declared war on Germany. On May 10, 1940 British Prime Minister Chamberlain was replaced by Winston Churchill as German forces invaded the Low Countries by air and land. The last Allied soldier left Dunkirk on June 4, 1940 and British Prime Minister Churchill vowed his forces "shall never surrender". German troops marched into Paris on June 14, 1940 forcing French and allied troops to retreat. On July 10, 1940 the Battle of Britain was launched by the Luftwaffe German Air Force after a series of attacks on shipping convoys off the south-east coast of England. German bombers unleashed a wave of heavy bombing raids on London on September 7, 1940, killing hundreds of civilians rather than going after purely military targets. Hitler attempted to crush the British people after the Luftwaffe's failure to gain air superiority frustrated Hitler's plan to invade Britain. On September 15, 1940 British RAF Fighter Command claimed victory over the Luftwaffe after a day of heavy bombing raids ended with the destruction of 176 enemy aircraft and at least another nine aircraft hit by anti-aircraft guns. On November 15, 1940 Coventry was bombed into smithereens during a massive German raid which lasted more than ten hours. We all prayed each in our own way that our boys, our neighbours sons and daughters, and all of the munitions workers would safely return home.

From 1932 to 1953 Canadians were required to have a licence to listen to radio. Every radio sold had a warning sticker attached cautioning people that if they did not have a licence, they could be prosecuted. The warning stated, "Any person installing or operating this Receiving Set without having first obtained a license from the Minister of Transport of Canada is liable, on summary conviction, to a fine not exceeding twenty-five dollars; and the said Receiving Set may be forfeited to His Majesty by order of the Minister, for such disposition as the Minister may direct." All this came about in March 1932 when the government passed the Radio Broadcasting Act creating the Canadian Radio Broadcasting Commission (CRBC) which later became the Canadian Broadcasting Corporation (CBC). Originally the Act imposed a licence-fee of $1.00 and created an army of inspectors to enforce licensing of radio receivers. In 1937 the fee was raised to $2.50. In the 1950s each licence cost $2.50 per year if the set was A.C. powered and $2.00 if it ran on batteries. Dealers and vendors got a commission of 25 cents or 15 cents per licence. All dealers who sold broadcast receivers were required by law to send the names and addresses of all purchasers to the Broadcast Receiving Licence Office in Ottawa. Licences could be bought from any radio dealer or post office. Inspectors checked each house on every street and trying to find an unlicensed radio. In 1953 the receiving set licenses were discontinued. We had an RCA Victor floor model console multi-band radio which was about four feet high with a shiny dark mahogany-style finish and with multiple vacuum tubes inside. We added a table model Northern Electric radio later in the 1940s.

Radio's "golden age" lasted ten years from January 1944 until about 1954. During this time we listened to shows like The Happy Gang, Wayne and Schuster, Make Believe Ballroom, Superman, Lux Theatre and a lot more. On September 1, 1941 Dorval International Airport was opened in Montreal and in 1943 synthetic rubber was invented, along with the Slinky toy and Silly Putty. Friends of my parents came to visit unannounced and they were always welcomed. We also visited them. Together with them at lunch or supper, I listened while they recounted stories, exchanged gossip and talked about politics. I sat in a corner of the room, unnoticed and listened to discussions about the war and its players: Stalin, Churchill, Eisenhower, Hitler, Mussolini, Roosevelt, Tojo and Truman.

People listened to the radio not only for the news and weather forecasts but also to some very interesting programs. Radio featured popular entertainment formats such as adventure, comedy, drama, horror, mystery, musical variety, romance, thrillers, classical and big band music concerts, farm reports, panel discussions, quiz shows, sidewalk interviews, talent shows along with news and commentary. Classical music programs on the air included the Bell Telephone Hour, the Metropolitan Opera broadcasts, the New York Philharmonic and one of the most notable of all classical music radio programs featured the celebrated Italian conductor Arturo Toscanini, considered the greatest living maestro, conducting the NBC Symphony Orchestra, which had been created especially for him. Also featured were popular songwriters such as George Gershwin. Country music was very popular. NBC carried the Grand Ole Opry from Nashville, Tennessee from 1944 to 1956.

Top comedy talents such as Fred Allen, Jack Benny, Victor Borge, George Burns, Jimmy Durante, Phil Harris, Bob Hope, Groucho Marx and Red Skelton generated much laughter as did shows such as Abbott and Costello, Amos 'n' Andy, Burns and Allen, Fibber McGee and Molly and Our Miss Brooks. Some shows were adapted from comic strips, such as Blondie, Dick Tracy, Li'l Abner, Little Orphan Annie, Popeye the Sailor and Terry and the Pirates. I liked listening to Robert L. Ripley's Believe It or Not. The line-up of late afternoon adventure serials included The Adventures of Superman, Batman, The Green Hornet and The Make Belief Ballroom. Badges, rings, decoding devices and other radio premiums offered on these adventure shows, required listeners to mail in a box top from a breakfast cereal or other proof of purchase. Outstanding radio dramas were presented on such programs as CBS Radio Workshop. Orson Welles's Mercury Theatre on the Air and Campbell Playhouse. They included such titles as A Tale of Two Cities and the celebrated-but-infamous adaptation of H. G. Wells's, The War of the Worlds, formatted to sound like a breaking news program. Theatre Guild on the Air presented adaptations of classical and Broadway plays. Their Shakespeare adaptations included a one-hour Macbeth and a ninety-minute Hamlet. Lux Radio Theater and The Screen Guild Theater presented adaptations of Hollywood movies, performed before a live audience, usually with cast members from the original films. Suspense, Escape and Inner Sanctum Mysteries were a popular series of thrillers. I also listened to Edgar Bergen and Charlie McCarthy, Hollywood Theatre, I Love Lucy, Jack Benny, Kraft Music Hall, Life with Luigi, Sergeant Preston of the Northwest Mounted Police among others.

Memorable parodies were presented by satirist, Spike Jones. The entire neighbourhood enjoyed his music and antics. Lindley Armstrong "Spike" Jones (December 14, 1911 – May 1, 1965) was a musician and bandleader specializing in performing satirical arrangements of popular songs. Ballads and classical works receiving the Jones treatment would be punctuated with gunshots, whistles, cowbells, and outlandish vocals. The very name of Spike Jones became synonymous with crazy music. Among the series of recordings in the 1940s were humorous takes on the classics such as the adaptation of Liszt's Liebesträume, played at a breakneck pace on unusual instruments. My favourite was his rendition of Rossini's William Tell Overture rendered on kitchen implements using a horse race as a backdrop, with one of the horses in the race named "Beetle Bomb" but when the people of the street referred to it, that horse was called "Feedelbaum" .

> **William Tell Overture - Spike Jones**
> Now the horses are approaching the starting gate
> And there they go!!
> And it's Stooge Hand going to the front
> Cabbage is second on the rail
> Beautiful Linda is third by a length And ... Beetlebomb
>
> Around the turn heading for home
> It's Stooge Hand and Dog Biscuit
> And Girdle in the stretch Flying Sylvester is third
> And Mother-In-Law nagging in the rear Oh oh oh

The most popular show on Canadian radio during the 1940s-1960s was Don Messer and His Islanders which came from Charlottetown, Prince Edward Island. In the 1960s until the show ended in 1969, Don Messer's Jubilee, a half-hour television show produced out of Halifax, was the second-most watched television show in Canada. The most watched television show was Hockey Night in Canada. During the supper hour we listened to Tony The Troubadour which aired regularly on CBM, the Montreal CBC Radio station, at 6:00 p.m. from Toronto. Tony the Troubadour was a singer and guitar player who had been with the Navy Show during the war touring Canada, Great Britain and Europe, entertaining troops. Every week at ten p.m. I listened to The Prairie Schooner program aired from Winnipeg also on CBC radio. They played many reels and jigs, square dance music, The Quarter Deck; Silver Heels; The Campbell's Are Coming; The Farmer's Krakowiak; Nya Fiskar Vals; Wake Up, Susan; Lithuanian Hop; Kitty O'Neil; The Wonder. Vocalist; San Antonio Rose; The Texas Cowboy and My Adobe Hacienda among many others. A song titled, "Open the Door, Richard" an early rhythm and blues (R&B) novelty record was a runaway pop sensation. There were "Richard" hats, shirts, and jeans, and ads for products ranging from ale to perfume that incorporated references to the song. "Too Young" recorded by Nat King Cole was a million-selling record and stayed at number one for five weeks and on the Best Seller chart for twenty nine weeks. "On Top of Old Smoky" was a traditional folk song and well-known ballad that became a favourite song. Old Smoky was a high mountain somewhere in the Ozarks or the central Appalachians. The song was parodied and the parody became a hit in 1963, it was called "On Top of Spaghetti" by Tom Glazer with the Do-Re-Mi Children's Chorus. The song dealt with the loss of a meatball when somebody sneezed and discussed what happened to the meatball after it fell off of a pile of spaghetti and rolled away. Another very popular novelty song was "It's In The Book" which started off with, "I have a message for you, a very sad message! My subject for this evening will be Little Bo Peep" and led to a hymn being sung including a verse such as:

> Then let us sing right out for grandma's, for grandma's lye soap
> Used for, for everything, everything on the place

For pots and kettles, the dirty dishes
And for your hands and for your face

Inner Sanctum Mysteries were sponsored by Bromo Seltzer, Bromo Seltzer, Bromo Seltzer, the commercial sounding like a train. Bromo Seltzer was used to settle stomachs and for fast headache relief. We listened to many commercials and some for products that now no longer exist. There was Salhapatica to fight colds; Rinso soap for clothes and for dishes. Their commercial announced that Rinso had an ingredient Solium and that no other soap could make your wash so bright as Rinso White. We listened to the jingle about Ajax cleanser:
Use Ajax, the foaming cleanser,.
Cleans pots and pans just like a whiz,
Floats the dirt right down the drain.

Then there was the Pepsodent toothpaste commercial:
You'll wonder where the yellow went,
When you brush your teeth with Pepsodent.

And the Halo Shampoo commercial:
Halo Everybody Halo,
There is something that you should know,
Halo is the shampoo that glorifies your hair,

And the more familiar Pepsi commercial:
Pepsi Cola hits the spot
Twelve full ounces, that's a lot,
Twice as much for a nickel too,
Pepsi Cola is the drink for you.

Gene Autry, The Singing Cowboy, was very popular on the radio during the 1930 to the 1950 period having gained fame in the movies with his signature song was "Back in the Saddle Again." Gene Autry is best known today for his Christmas holiday songs, "Here Comes Santa Claus" (which he wrote), "Frosty the Snowman," and his biggest hit, "Rudolph the Red-Nosed Reindeer." He is the only celebrity to have five stars on the Hollywood Walk of Fame. Very popular during this time and into the 1970s was Roy Rogers, a cowboy singer and actor, nicknamed "King of the Cowboys". Rogers was a competitor for Gene Autry as the nation's favorite singing cowboy. He and his wife Dale Evans nicknamed "Queen of the West", his golden palomino horse, Trigger, and his German Shepherd dog, Bullet, along with George "Gabby" Hayes as a crotchety sidekick were featured in more than 100 movies and The Roy Rogers Show which ran on radio for nine years before moving to television from 1951 through 1957. Rogers and Evans's famous song, "Happy Trails", was written by Dale Evans Rogers, as their theme song for the 1940s and 1950s radio program and their 1950s television show. They sang it as a duet to sign off their show.

Happy Trails
Happy trails to you, until we meet again.
Happy trails to you, keep smilin' until then.
Who cares about the clouds when we're together?
Just sing a song and bring the sunny weather.

Happy trails to you, 'till we meet again.

Some of the older boys on the street addressed the question of what do you want to be when you grow up by enlisting and became soldiers. There were about 700,000 Canadians under the age of 21 who served in uniform. Sometimes boys as young as 13 lied about their age and If they looked old enough they were accepted and joined the army. Others were not accepted for one reason or another. Many who were rejected served in the Merchant Navy, where they transported troops and materials overseas. Their willingness to fight and sacrifice everything for peace and freedom was an inspiration for others to follow. The younger boys were left to continue dreaming but this time instead of being firemen they could dream of being soldiers. Canada joined the war effort on September 10, 1939. The Armoury of The Canadian Grenadier Guards at Rachel and Esplanade streets was and is home to a reserve infantry regiment in the 34th Canadian Brigade Group, 2nd Canadian Division of the Canadian Army. The regiment is the second most senior and oldest infantry regiment in the Primary Reserve of the Canadian Army. Its primary role is the provision of combat-ready troops in support of Canadian regular infantry.

My mother and I often joined a much larger group of residents who crowded on Esplanade street to watch the assembly and drills of The Canadian Grenadier Guards on Fletcher's Field. Weeks later we watched them march on Park Avenue on their way to the train station and off to war overseas. We were all filled with mixed feelings and emotions, some with tears in their eyes, and everyone overflowing with pride but also with fear and hope that they would all be safe and come back soon. The Canadian Grenadier Guards participation in the Second World War saw numerous heroic actions by men as the Regiment saw considerable action in North West Europe; in Normandy, France; in Belgium; the Netherlands and across the Rhine. We read and heard about warships, merchant ships, troop trains, air raid practices; collected materials for the war effort; bought war saving stamps at school; listened to the news broadcasts about the Blitz in England and watched newsreels of battles and raids, This was all a part of children's lives and these events undoubtedly shaped our view of human activity and the world around us. No one could live through the war years and experiences without being affected in some manner.

Canada became one of the largest trainers of pilots for the Allies. With industries pushing to increase production and with so many men overseas having joined the war, there was a dire need for employees in the workplace. Women took up positions to aid in the war effort and unemployment faded away. Without women to step-in, the economy would have collapsed. By autumn 1944 the number of women working full-time in Canada's paid labor force was twice what it had been in 1939, and that figure of between 1,000,000 and 1,200,000 did not include part-time workers or women working on farms. Women took on this intensive labor and while doing so they still found time to look after their children, looked after their homes, did the washing and ironing, made jam, clothes and volunteered in whatever way they could to aid the men overseas.

A large number of Montreal's industrial workers lived near the Lachine Canal neighbourhoods of St. Henri, Ste. Cunégonde and Point St. Charles. Many day labourers and other unskilled workers settled with their families in the districts adjacent to the sawmills, flour mills, refineries, shipyards and Grand Trunk railway shops. The Ogilvie and Robin Hood flour mills, the Canada Sugar Co. refinery, Stelco, Canadian Car and Foundry, and Dominion Bridge metalworking plants were all located along the Lachine Canal. A shortage of reasonably priced rental accommodation developed during the 1940 to 1945 period, when more people moved to the city to work in war material factories. Many workers at these factories lived in our neighbourhood and travelled back and forth daily on foot or by streetcar.

After the fall of France in May 1940, it became a priority to enlarge the Allies' merchant shipping fleet, to replace ships lost, and to make sure that there were naval escort vessels to guard convoys against German submarines. Britain was highly vulnerable, and North American arms and supplies became a lifeline. Canada in 1940 had just started to build patrol vessels for the protection of its own coasts, but Britain soon placed orders for 26 ten-thousand-tonne cargo ships and soon after orders for naval escorts and minesweepers. This was just the beginning, as Britain made clear it needed Canada to build as many naval and merchant ships as it possibly could. War production was ramped up quickly, managed by the Department of Munitions and Supply. Shipyards and repair facilities expanded dramatically as over a thousand warships and cargo vessels were built, along with thousands of auxiliary craft and small boats. The practically non-existent Canadian interwar shipbuilding industry - three shipyards employing fewer than 4,000 men - expanded to 90 plants on the East and West Coasts, the Great Lakes and even inland. More than 126,000 men and women were employed. In all, the shipyards built 4,047 naval vessels, most of them landing craft but included over 300 anti-submarine warships, among them 4 tribal class destroyers, and 410 cargo ships.

Canadian shipyards produced different types of warships; there were grim, grey corvettes, minesweepers, cruisers, patrol boats, cargo ships and many conversions of vessels to Royal Canadian Navy requirements. The pride of Canada's shipyards were the corvettes which with their cruising range could remain at sea for long periods of time and which were fast enough to mount deadly attacks on enemy submarines. Their service as convoy-escorts were invaluable and they played a big part in the Battle of the North Atlantic. Their guns were heavy enough to engage a submarine which dared to come to the surface and their high-angle armament was able to tackle enemy airplanes. For submarines lurking beneath the waves corvettes were equipped with deadly depth-charges. Minesweepers as well were equipped to encounter the enemy as well as to sweep death from the seas. Submarine chasers and motor torpedo boats, although small were also important units in a fleet.

My father worked at the United Shipyards and Canadian Vickers; two shipyards in the Montreal area who were in operation between 1942 and 1945. United Shipyards was a joint venture of Dominion Bridge Co. and Fraser-Brace Engineering Co., two major construction companies. The shipyard was located where the Bickerdike Basin is today in the harbour region of the city. Canadian Vickers shipyard was located on fifty acres of land at the foot of Viau street in the old Maisonneuve district of Montreal, Among the many emergency shipyards in Canada the Montreal based ones made a significant contribution towards building Canada's navy into a, strong offensive and defensive force .Being interested and very inquisitive, I was rewarded with several visits to the shipyards with my father. I enjoyed watching the construction activity. My father riveted the steel hulls of warships that were being built. I was fascinated watching the riveters who worked as a team. There was the riveter , the rivet heater and another riveter on the ship's interior. The riveter was equipped with an air-powered riveting hammer. The rivet heater was responsible for bringing each rivet point (the end opposite the head) to a glowing red heat. He had a little cast iron pot filled with burning coals. As each rivet was judged ready, he picked it up with tongs and tossed the hot red glowing rivet expertly into a bucket in the hands of the riveter who caught the rivet with remarkable dexterity. The hot rivet was picked up with tongs and placed into the hole of the steel plate. Then the riveter on the hull exterior and the riveter on the inside of the vessel went to work with their air-powered tools making sure that the rivet was driven in as far as the head would allow and until it added to the tightness of the fit. The riveter on the interior probably had a much harder time than the one on the exterior because he had to work in the imprisoning confines of the echoing steel frame interior which was deafening and had to be very uncomfortable. There were several teams that worked on each boat. Making a riveted hull water-tight, or oil-tight, required skillful, conscientious workmanship.

In later years vessels were welded instead of being riveted which led to some unpleasant surprises, each of which demonstrated the advantage of riveting. The most important discovery was that all-welded hulls showed an embarrassing likelihood of breaking in two. Even the slightest flaw in welding, or sharp discontinuity in structure, could trigger a brittle fracture that creeped around the hull and sank the ship. Cracks in riveted hulls generally stopped when they reached a seam because the stress concentration was dispersed as affected rivets yielded slightly and distributed the load over their neighbors. This occurrence in welded ships was recognized by the classification societies which asked that each of the built Liberty Ships be fitted with a crack arrestor strap: a riveted flat bar placed over a long slot burned in the shell a few feet below the main deck, port and starboard. In the design stage of all-welded ships the authorities required moderately expensive changes in the steel specification, making the hulls tougher and less notch sensitive. Greater care was taken in the design phase in order to avoid stress-raising discontinuities in hull structures. The soundness of rivets could usually be ascertained by sharply rapping on each rivet head with a little hammer, but poor welding was harder to detect without recourse to expensive X-ray procedures. In general, as riveting proceeded, the hull became more and more like the naval architect intended. In welding, however special measures were required to keep the keel from arching up at the bow and stern.

I particularly enjoyed watching the picturesque and impressive ceremony associated with the christening and launching of the completed vessels. The size and weight of a vessel during launching imposes stresses on the ship not met during normal operation, and is a considerable engineering challenge. Slipways are arranged perpendicular to the shore line and the ship is built with its stern facing the water. The vessel is built upon temporary cribbing that is arranged to give access to the hull's outer bottom, and to allow the launch ways to be erected under the complete hull. When it is time for launching the surface of these slipways are greased. On launching, the vessel slides backwards down the slipway until it floats in the water by itself. Each launch was treated as a great event in the ship's career. There always was a person who either sponsored or represented the sponsor standing on a platform built round the ship's bow as she rested on the slipway. The ceremonial ship launching was a long time naval tradition when transferring a vessel to the water. There were speeches and music played by military bands; members of the clergy said prayers. Attention slowly turned to a sacrificial bottle of champagne suspended from the bow of the ship linked to the sponsor with a white silken ribbon. The sponsor then named the ship and wished the ship and those who sailed in her, good luck and then released the ribbon sending the bottle to be smashed against the ship's side. At the same time the ship was released and slid stern first, slowly down the inclined dry-dock slipway into the water. There followed considerable applause, shouting and cheers from the people watching accompanied by lively military music the ship entered the water with steadiness and majesty filling every heart with joy, pride and an appreciation of the skill and the teamwork that went into each warship.

A sizeable industrial base had also evolved in the east end of Montreal. There was the Imperial Oil Company's refinery, the British-American and McColl-Frontenac (later Texaco) refineries, Dominion Oilcloth and Linoleum, MacDonald's Tobacco, Dominion Rubber, Vickers Shipyards, Canadian Car & Foundry and Molson's Brewery. Many people worked for the Canadian National Railway and the Canadian Pacific Railway or their busy railway stations; Windsor Station, Bonaventure Station, Viger Station and Central Station. Some people worked at Montreal's port facilities which was the most important grain port in the world. The port was very actively used for passenger and freight ocean liners. The Lachine canal with five locks passing through the southwestern part of the Island of Montreal from the Port of Montreal to Lake Saint-Louis made Montreal more convenient for trade. The canal was heavily used and expanded the city's industrial region from the east end and downtown to new working-class neighbourhoods such as Griffintown, St Henri, and Pointe St Charles. Railway transportation was very important for Montreal providing a link from the interior of Canada and the United States to the Atlantic particularly during the winter months. Industries were able to import coal, the source of power, from Nova Scotia, Ohio, Pennsylvania, and from Great Britain. The canal could not be expanded to handle larger great lakes vessels and was replaced in 1959 by the St. Lawrence Seaway that permitted ocean-going vessels to travel from the Atlantic Ocean as far inland as the western end of Lake Superior of the Great Lakes.

On June 22, 1941 German forces launched Operation Barbarossa and invaded the Soviet Union from the south, west, and from the north. They surrounded Leningrad (St Petersburg) and occupied Belarus and Ukraine, The retreating Soviet troops destroyed crops and burnt entire villages under Stalin's "scorched earth" policy to prevent supplies falling into German hands. The failure of

Operation Barbarossa was Hitler's first major defeat on land. On August 14, 1941 the British Prime Minister, Winston Churchill and the American President, Franklin D Roosevelt met in secret and forged the US-Britain alliance.

On December 7, 1941 hundreds of Japanese fighter planes launched a devastating surprise attack on Pearl Harbor, a U.S. naval base near Honolulu, on the island of Oahu, in Hawaii. In two hours, six battleships had been sunk, another 112 vessels were sunk or damaged, and 164 aircraft were destroyed. More than 2,400 Americans died in the attack, including civilians, and another 1,000 people were wounded. Japan declared war on Britain and the United States. On December 8, 1941, the United States Congress declared war on the Empire of Japan, ending its policy of isolationism. On December 11, 1941 Germany and Italy declared war on the United States. Under the Tripartite Agreement signed on September 27, 1940, Germany and Italy were obliged to defend its ally Japan. America immediately responded by declaring war on them.

During 1943–1944 ethnic cleansing operations or the Massacres of Poles took place in Ukraine resulting in an estimated 100,000 deaths and an exodus of ethnic Poles from the area. In 1939 the number of Poles in Ukraine was around 5.274 million, but after ethnic cleansing in 1939-1945 by the Nazi Germany, Soviet Union and Ukrainian nationalist forces there were only about 1.8 million inhabitants left. Citizens of Poland were executed by the Soviet NKVD as "enemies of the people," nearly 9,000 were murdered in the newly-acquired western Ukraine. The Soviet NKVD was the interior ministry of the Soviet Union called the People's Commissariat for Internal Affairs (Народный комиссариат внутренних дел, Narodnyy Komissariat Vnutrennikh Del). They carried out ordinary public order activities, as well as secret police activities and had a monopoly over law enforcement. The NKVD was known for carrying out the Great Purge or Great Terror under Joseph Stalin. It was a campaign of political repression in the Soviet Union which occurred from 1936 to 1938 It involved a large-scale repression of peasants, purge of Communist Party and government officials, and the Red Army leadership; widespread police surveillance, suspicion of "saboteurs", "counter-revolutionaries", imprisonment, and arbitrary executions. The NKVD undertook mass extrajudicial executions of untold numbers of citizens, and conceived, populated and administered the Gulag system of forced labour camps. They oversaw the protection of Soviet borders and espionage including political assassinations. Their agents were responsible for the mass deportations of entire nationalities to collective farms (kolkhoz) to work as slave labour or to uninhabited regions of the country; namely Siberia. Polish territories to the south namely : Drohobych Oblast, Lviv Oblast, Rivne Oblast, Stanislav (later known as Ivano-Frankivsk) Oblast, Tarnopil Oblast and Volyn Oblast were transferred to the Ukrainian SSR (The Ukrainian Soviet Socialist Republic). These divisions called oblasts (i.e., provinces) were created during the Second World War when both Nazi Germany and the Soviet Union invaded Poland. At the end of World War II, the Soviet Union annexed most of the territories it had invaded in 1939.

The Polish government-in-exile in London had been receiving a continual flow of information from 1940 on from the Polish leadership in Warsaw about the mass murders and the extermination camps. They in turn were informing the world of ghetto inmates being deported and being transported in freight trains to extermination camps. Operation Reinhard was the codename given to the secretive German Nazi plan during World War II to exterminate the majority of Polish Jews in the General Government district of German-occupied Poland. From the end of 1941, the Germans built Operation Reinhard extermination camps in occupied Poland: Auschwitz II-Birkenau (established October 1941); in the town of Oświęcim some 50 kilometres (31 mi) west of Cracow; Majdanek (October 1941); on the outskirts of the city of Lublin; Chełmno (December 1941); north of the city of Łódź; and three camps set up in 1942; namely, Belzec about 114 km (71 mi) south-east of Lublin; Sobibor close to the Bug River, which forms the border with Belarus and Ukraine; Treblinka II north-east of Warsaw, 4 kilometres (2.5 mi) south of the Treblinka train station; and Maly Trostenets on the outskirts of Minsk, the largest city of Belarus. These were used by the Nazis following their policy which they called the "Final Solution to the Jewish Question", All of these extermination camps were equipped with gas chambers using Zyklon B, a cyanide-based pesticide invented in Germany in the early 1920s. It consisted of hydrogen cyanide (prussic acid), as well as a cautionary eye irritant and one of several adsorbents such as diatomaceous earth. In June 1943, all ghettos were transformed into Nazi concentration camps, while some concentration camps had been transformed into extermination camps with the addition of gas chambers and crematoria. Victims were deported from the ghettos in sealed freight trains to extermination camps where, if they survived the journey, they were killed in gas chambers. Jews were murdered in mass shootings by paramilitary units between 1941 and 1945. The killings were systematically conducted in more than 20 occupied countries. The killing continued until the end of World War II in Europe in April–May 1945.

Victims arrived at the extermination camps by train. At some camps all arrivals were sent directly to the gas chambers after being told to hand over their valuables to camp workers and to undress and take a shower in the delousing chambers. They were then herded naked into the showers or delousing chambers which were in fact gas chambers. At Treblinka, to calm the victims, the arrival platform was made to look like a train station, complete with fake clock. At Auschwitz camp officials selected and sent some of the new arrivals to slave labour instead. At Auschwitz, after the gas chambers were filled, the doors were shut and pellets of Zyklon-B were dropped into the chambers through vents, releasing toxic prussic acid, or hydrogen cyanide. Those inside died within 20 minutes; the speed of death depended on how close the person was standing to a gas vent. At Chełmno victims were placed in a mobile gas van and asphyxiated, while being driven to prepared burial pits in the nearby forests. A mobile gas van was a vehicle reequipped with gas cylinders while others used the exhaust fumes rather than bottled gas and an air-tight compartment to accommodate the victims to be killed. The victims were gassed either with Zyklon-B or by carbon monoxide, resulting in death by poisoning and suffocation. Once dead, the bodies were removed, gold fillings from their teeth were extracted, and women's hair was cut by prisoner workgroups. At Auschwitz, the bodies were buried in deep pits and covered with lime. However between September and November 1942, they were dug up and burned to hide the evidence. Similarly in late 1942 Sobibór and Bełżec exhumed and burned bodies, as did Treblinka in March 1943. The bodies were burned in open fireplaces and the remaining bones were crushed into powder to hide the evidence. In early 1943, new gas chambers and crematoria were built to accommodate the numbers.

After 1942, it was commonplace for German companies to utilize labour camp prisoners forcing them to work as slaves. It is estimated that in the occupied countries the Nazis established about 30,000 slave labor camps and sub camps, almost 1,000 concentration camps, and another 1,000 prisoner-of-war camps. Villages throughout the Soviet Union were destroyed by German troops who also took foodstuffs away causing famines. They rounded up Soviet civilians for forced labour in Germany. On January 6, 1942, Moscow sent out diplomatic notes about German atrocities. They reported bodies surfacing from poorly covered graves in pits and quarries, as well as mass graves found in areas that the Red Army had liberated. In Belarus, Germany deported some 380,000 people for forced labor to help the German war effort and killed hundreds of thousands of civilians. In mid-1942 labor camps began to tattoo prisoners with an identification number on arrival. Prisoners had to wear colored triangles on their uniforms, with the color of the triangle denoting the reason for their incarceration. Red signified a political prisoner, Jehovah Witnesses had purple triangles, criminals wore black or green. Badges were pink for gay men and yellow for Jews. Jews had a second yellow triangle that was worn with their original triangle, with the two forming a six-pointed star. The work shifts were long and often involved exposure to dangerous materials. Prisoner transportation between camps was often carried out in freight cars with the prisoners packed very tightly. Long delays would take place, with the prisoners confined in the cars on sidings for days. Camp inmates were worked to death, or to physical exhaustion, at which point they would be gassed or shot fulfilling the Nazi extermination through labour policy. The guards became increasingly more brutal, beating, starving and killing prisoners. The Germans estimated the average prisoner's lifespan in a concentration camp at three months, due to lack of food and clothing, constant epidemics, and frequent punishments for the most minor transgressions. In late July or early August 1942, Polish leaders learned about the mass killings taking place inside Auschwitz. On December 17, 1942, eleven Allies issued the Joint Declaration by Members of the United Nations condemning the "bestial policy of cold-blooded extermination". Most of the Jewish ghettos of General Government were liquidated in 1942–1943, and their populations shipped to the camps for extermination.

Thousands of camp inmates were subjected to SS's medical experiments and most of them died as a result. Experiments took place at Auschwitz, Buchenwald, Dachau, Natzweiler, Neuengamme, Ravensbrück, Sachsenhausen, and elsewhere. The most notorious physician was Josef Mengele, an SS officer who was the Auschwitz camp doctor in 1943. Mengele's experiments included placing subjects in pressure chambers, testing drugs and new vaccines on them, freezing them, attempting to change their eye color by injecting chemicals into children's eyes, sterilization of men and women and amputations and other surgeries. Twenty-three senior physicians and other medical personnel were charged at Nuremberg, after the war, with crimes against humanity. As it was becoming more evident that Germany was losing the war, efforts were made to conceal evidence of what had happened. The gas chambers were dismantled, the crematoria dynamited, and the mass graves dug up and the corpses cremated. Local commanders continued to kill Jews and to shuttle them from camp to camp by forced "death marches". Already sick after months or years of violence and starvation, some were marched to train stations and transported for days at a time without food or shelter in open freight cars, then forced to march again at the other end to the new camp. Others were marched the entire distance to the new camp. Those who lagged behind or fell were shot. Around 250,000 Jews died during these marches.

In April 1945 Western Allied forces began to take large numbers of German prisoners (about 1,500,000) on the Western Front. In addition at least 120,000 German troops were captured in the last campaign of the war in Italy. In the three to four months up to the end of April, over 800,000 German soldiers surrendered on the Eastern Front. The advance of Allied forces into Germany uncovered numerous Nazi concentration camps and forced labor facilities. The camps were liberated by allied troops in 1944-1945 and allied forces began to discover the scale of the Holocaust. The Soviets liberated Majdanek on July 25, 1944; and Auschwitz on January 27, 1945 where they found 7,600 prisoners. On April 11, 1945 the Americans liberated Buchenwald. On April 15, 1945, the British 11th Armoured Division liberated some 60,000 prisoners at Bergen-Belsen and found 13,000 unburied corpses. Due to the prisoners' poor physical condition, another 10,000 people died from typhus or malnutrition over the following weeks after liberation. Treblinka, Sobibór, and Bełżec were never liberated, they were destroyed by the Germans in 1943. On April 29, 1945, the American 42nd Infantry Division liberated Dachau forcing the remaining SS guards to gather up and bury the corpses of dead inmates in mass graves. Captured SS guards were subsequently tried at Allied war crimes tribunals where many were sentenced to death. Ravensbrück was liberated by the Soviets on April 30, 1945; Mauthausen by the Americans on May 5, 1945; The Red Cross took control of Theresienstadt located in Czechoslovakia on May 4, 1945, days before the Soviets arrived. The Holocaust was a genocide during World War II in which Nazi Germany, aided by its collaborators, systematically murdered two-thirds (about 6 million) of the Jewish population of Europe. Jews, political opponents, ethnic Poles, Soviet prisoners of war, the Roma, and "incurably sick", homosexuals and Jehovah Witnesses were targeted for extermination.

By the autumn of 1943, Mussolini was reduced to being the leader of a German puppet state and was faced with the Allied advance from the south and an increasingly violent internal conflict with the partisans. On April 25, 1945, with the Allies breaking through the last German defences in northern Italy and a general uprising of the partisans taking hold in the cities, Mussolini and his mistress, Claretta Petacci fled Milan and tried to escape to the Swiss border. They were captured on April 27 by local partisans near the village of Dongo on Lake Como and were shot the following afternoon, executed by Italian partisans in the small village of Giulino di Mezzegra in northern Italy. On April 29, German forces in Italy surrendered unconditionally to British forces. They had signed a surrender document at Caserta after prolonged unauthorised secret negotiations with the Western Allies, which were viewed with great suspicion by the Soviet Union as trying to reach a separate peace. In the document, the Germans agreed to a ceasefire and surrender of all the forces under the command of Generaloberst Heinrich von Vietinghoff at 2 pm on May 2. Accordingly, after some bitter wrangling between SS Obergruppenführer Karl Wolff and Albert Kesselring in the early hours of May 2, nearly 1,000,000 German troops in Italy and Austria surrendered unconditionally to British Field Marshal Sir Harold Alexander at 2pm on May 2.

In Germany at the end of April 1945 the Battle of Nuremberg and the Battle of Hamburg had ended with American and British occupation. The Soviets had surrounded Berlin, while the Americans had cut off any escape route and with the Battle of Berlin raging above him German dictator Adolf Hitler realized that all was lost. On April 30, 1945 Adolf Hitler committed suicide in his Führerbunker along with Eva Braun, his long-term partner whom he had married less than 40 hours before their joint suicide. In his will, Hitler dismissed Reichsmarschall Hermann Göring, his second-in-command and Interior minister Heinrich Himmler after each of them separately tried to seize control of the crumbling Third Reich. Hitler appointed his successors as follows; Großadmiral Karl Dönitz as the new Reichspräsident ("President of Germany") and Joseph Goebbels as the new Reichskanzler (Chancellor of Germany). However, Goebbels committed suicide the following day, leaving Dönitz as the sole leader of Germany.

Benito Mussolini had been executed by Italian partisans on April 28, 1945. Adolf Hitler, Heinrich Himmler, Wilhelm Burgdorf, Hans Krebs and Joseph Goebbels had all committed suicide in the spring of 1945 to avoid capture. Reinhard Heydrich had been assassinated by Czech partisans in 1942. Josef Terboven killed himself with dynamite in Norway in 1945. Adolf Eichmann fled to Argentina to avoid Allied capture, but was captured by Israel's intelligence service the Mossad and hanged in 1962. Hermann Göring was sentenced to death but committed suicide the night before his execution as a perceived act of defiance against his captors. The Battle of Berlin ended on May 2, 1945 with German forces in Berlin unconditionally surrendering the city to General Vasily Chuikov of the Soviet army. On the same day the two armies of Army Group Vistula north of Berlin consisting of the German 21st Army and the Third Panzer Army surrendered to the Western Allies. Also on May 2 Hitler's deputy Martin Bormann attempting to flee Berlin to avoid capture by the Soviets, committed suicide. On May 4, 1945, German forces in North West Germany, Denmark, and the Netherlands unconditionally surrendered to the British Field Marshal Bernard Montgomery. The surrender included all naval ships between the cities of Hamburg, Hanover and Bremen. The number of German land, sea and air forces involved in this surrender amounted to 1,000,000 men. Also on May 4, 1945, German forces in Bavaria surrendered to the American 6th Army Group General Jacob L. Devers. On May 5, 1945, Großadmiral Dönitz ordered all U-boats to cease offensive operations and return to their bases. German forces in the Netherlands, surrendered to Canadian General Charles Foulkes. On May 6, 1945, Reichsmarshall and Hitler's second-in-command, Hermann Göring, surrendered to General Carl Spaatz, the commander of the United States Air Forces in Europe. Also on May 6, German forces in Breslau (Polish Wrocław) the largest city in western Poland that was surrounded and besieged for months, surrendered to the Soviets.

The Supreme Allied Commander, General Dwight D. Eisenhower, threatened to break off all negotiations unless the Germans agreed to a complete unconditional surrender to all the Allies on all fronts. Eisenhower explicitly told Jodl that he would order western lines closed to German soldiers, thus forcing them to surrender to the Soviets. Dönitz, accepting the inevitable, sent a signal to Jodl authorizing the complete and total surrender of all German forces. Thirty minutes after the fall of Fortress Breslau, German General Alfred Jodl arrived in Reims and, following Donitz's instructions, offered to unconditionally surrender all German armed forces fighting the Western Allies. News of Germany's unconditional surrender broke in the West on May 8, and celebrations erupted throughout Europe and parts of the British Empire. In the US, Americans awoke to the news and declared May 8, 1945 as V-E Day – Victory in Europe Day. World War 2 in Europe ended on May 8, 1945. . As the Soviet Union was to the east of Germany it was May 9 Moscow Time when the German military surrender became effective, which is why Russia and many other European countries east of Germany commemorate Victory Day on May 9. World War II between 1939 and 1945 was one of the most devastating wars in the history of mankind. Over 100 million people from more than 30 countries were involved in this global war. Even though the War had come to an end in Europe on May 8, 1945, Japan kept fighting.

On August 6, 1945, U.S.A. President Truman informed the American public that a United States B-29 bomber named Enola Gay had dropped an atomic bomb on the Japanese city of Hiroshima, Japan. Hiroshima was an important military center and had a civilian population of almost 300,000. The yield of the explosion was later estimated at 15 kilotons (the equivalent of 15,000 tons of TNT). By the end of 1945, because of the lingering effects of radioactive fallout and other after effects, the Hiroshima death toll was probably over 100,000. The five-year death total may have reached or even exceeded 200,000, as cancer and other long-term effects took hold. President Truman warned that if Japan still refused to surrender unconditionally the United States would attack additional targets. Schools advised students to duck under desks and bomb shelters were being promoted to protect people from radioactive fallout. On August 9, 1945 a second nuclear plutonium bomb was dropped on the Japanese city of Nagasaki. The yield of the explosion was estimated at 21 kilotons, 40 percent greater than that of the Hiroshima bomb. The day after the attack on Nagasaki, the emperor of Japan overruled the military leaders of Japan and forced them to surrender (almost) unconditionally. By January 1946, the number of deaths in Nagasaki probably approached 70,000, with perhaps ultimately twice that number dead total within five years. The war ended with the atomic bombings of Hiroshima and Nagasaki, and other large aerial bomb attacks by the United States Army Air Forces, accompanied by the Soviet declaration of war and the Soviet invasion of Manchuria on August 9, 1945, resulting in the Japanese announcement of intent to surrender on August 15, 1945. The formal surrender of Japan ceremony and signing of the official surrender documents took place on the deck of the battleship USS Missouri in Tokyo Bay on September 2, 1945. Japan's Shinto

Emperor was forced to relinquish much of his authority and his divine status through the Shinto Directive in order to pave the way for extensive cultural and political reforms. World War 2 was officially over on September 2, 1945.

In 1945 - 1946 International Military Tribunals (IMT) were set up in Nuremberg, Germany and war crime trials were held. Prominent members of the political, military, and economic leadership of Nazi Germany were prosecuted. The first of these trials tried 22 political and military leaders of the Third Reich. The prosecution entered indictments against 24 major war criminals and seven organizations—the leadership of the Nazi party, the Reich Cabinet, the Schutzstaffel (SS), Sicherheitsdienst (SD), the Gestapo, the Sturmabteilung (SA) and the "General Staff and High Command". The indictments were for: participation in a common plan or conspiracy for the accomplishment of a crime against peace; planning, initiating and waging wars of aggression and other crimes against peace; war crimes; and crimes against humanity. The tribunal passed judgements ranging from acquittal to death by hanging. Eleven defendants were executed, including Joachim von Ribbentrop, Wilhelm Keitel, Alfred Rosenberg, and Alfred Jodl. Further trials at Nuremberg took place between 1946 and 1949, which tried a further 185 defendants.

In 1961 Nazi leader Adolf Eichmann known as the architect of the Final Solution, was put on trial in Israel for his role in the holocaust after being found and captured in Argentina. At the end of World War II, Adolf Eichmann, like many top Nazi leaders, attempted to flee defeated Germany. After hiding in various locations within Europe and the Middle East, Eichmann eventually managed to escape to Argentina, where he lived for a number of years with his family under an assumed name. In the years after World War II, Eichmann, whose name had come up numerous times during the Nuremberg Trials, had become one of the most wanted Nazi war criminals. Unfortunately, for many years, no one knew where in the world Eichmann was hiding. Then, in 1957, the Mossad (the Israeli secret service) received a tip: Eichmann may be living in Buenos Aires, Argentina. After several years of unsuccessful searches, Mossad received another tip: Eichmann was most likely living under the name of Ricardo Klement. This time, a team of secret Mossad agents was sent to Argentina to find Eichmann. On March 21, 1960, the agents had not only found Klement, they were certain he was the Eichmann they had been hunting for years. On May 11, 1960, the Mossad agents captured Eichmann while he was walking from a bus stop to his home. They took Eichmann to a secret location and smuggled him out of Argentina nine days later. On May 23, 1960, Israeli Prime Minister David Ben-Gurion made the surprise announcement to the Knesset (Israel's parliament) that Adolf Eichmann was under arrest in Israel and was soon to be put on trial.

Adolf Eichmann's trial began on April 11, 1961 in Jerusalem, Israel. Eichmann was charged with 15 counts of crimes against the Jewish people, war crimes, crimes against humanity, and membership in a hostile organization. Specifically, the charges accused Eichmann of being responsible for the enslavement, starvation, persecution, transportation and murder of millions of Jews as well as the deportation of hundreds of thousands of Poles and Gypsies. The trial was to be a showcase of the horrors of the Holocaust. Press from around the world followed the details, which helped educate the world about what really happened under the Third Reich. As Eichmann sat behind a specially made bullet-proof glass cage, 112 witnesses told their story, in specific detail, of the horrors they experienced. This, plus 1,600 documents recording the implementation of the Final Solution were submitted against Eichmann. Eichmann's main line of defense was that he was just following orders and that he just played a small role in the killing process. Three judges heard the evidence. The world waited for their decision. The court found Eichmann guilty on all 15 counts and on December 15, 1961 sentenced Eichmann to death. Eichmann appealed the verdict to Israel's supreme court but on May 29, 1962 his appeal was rejected. The neighbourhood had followed closely the news of how Adolf Eichmann had been found, captured and the progress of his trial. Near midnight between May 31 and June 1, 1962, Eichmann was executed by hanging. His body was then cremated and his ashes scattered at sea.

People found solace in music; it helped them relax and eased the pain, confusion and anxiety of these tumultuous years. In the 1940s the vinyl record business aided by the development of the jukebox industry saw restaurants and snack bars install coin operated jukeboxes. They played music from a vinyl record once a nickel was inserted and a music selection was made. Jukeboxes originally were called nickelodeons and they reached their peak in the mid 1950s. Three companies Seeburg, Rock-Ola, and Wurlitzer manufactured jukeboxes at this time. The most popular design was the Wurlitzer introduced in 1946. Wurlitzer models were works of art, housed in art deco styled cabinets and bubble tubes they used rotating lights. In 1948, Seeburg introduced its Select-O-Matic 100, the first jukebox to include 100 selections enabling the unit to handle a variety of popular music such as folk, jazz, regional country and blues music. By 1956, jukeboxes with 200 selections were being manufactured. Billboard, the oldest weekly American trade magazine devoted to the music industry, began publishing music charts covering Pop, Rhythm & Blues, and Country & Western. It maintained an internationally recognized music chart that tracked the most popular songs and albums in various categories on a weekly basis. Cashbox magazine was another weekly publication devoted to the music and coin-operated machine industries. It was published from July 1942 to November 16, 1996. The music chart was referred to as the Hit Parade.

Before elections there was always considerable discussion among my neighbours about politics and candidates and opinions ran the gamut from anarchism to Zionism to communism. Campaign rallies along the Main frequently blocked streetcar traffic. Large crowds listened to speeches and participated either in support or dissention. The Communist Party of Canada was banned in 1940, under the wartime Defence of Canada Regulations. It refounded itself as the Labor-Progressive Party (LPP) in 1943 after the release of Communist Party leaders from internment. The LPP was the legal political organization of the Communist Party of Canada between 1943 and 1959. Our predominately Jewish neighbourhood had a distinctly left- wing slant. Only one LPP Member of Parliament (MP) was ever elected under that banner and he was Fred Rose. Our district was the center of the schmatta (garment) industry with factories being owned by wealthy Jews (Uptowners) who lived in Westmount and Outremont. It was represented in the Canadian House of Commons from 1925 to 1968 as the

federal electoral district of Cartier. The riding covered much of Montreal's old Jewish district. It was one of the smallest ridings in the country in area and was the only riding in Canada to have elected a Communist, Fred Rose, to the House of Commons. Every single MP to represent this riding was of the Jewish faith. They were:
- 1943–1945 & 1945–1947 Fred Rose, Labor–Progressive
- 1947–1949 & 1949–1950 Maurice Hartt, Liberal
- 1950–1963 Leon David Crestohl, Liberal
- 1963–1965 & 1965–1968 Milton L. Klein, Liberal

The electoral district was abolished in 1966 when it was redistributed into Laurier, Outremont and Saint-Jacques ridings.

In September 1945. Canada was shocked by the revelations of defected Soviet embassy clerk in Ottawa, Igor Gouzenko (January 13, 1919 – June 28, 1982) who revealed the extent of the Soviet spy ring in Canada. Gouzenko exposed Joseph Stalin's efforts to steal nuclear secrets, and the technique of planting sleeper agents. Gouzenko and his family were given another identity by the Canadian government out of fear of Soviet reprisals. In July 1946 a royal commission called by Prime Minister Mackenzie King investigated the Soviet spy ring in Canada and found that secret information had been leaked. One of those involved was Fred Rose, who had been elected in a 1943 by-election in our district, was re-elected in the 1945 federal election and was a sitting member of parliament.

Gouzenko's revelations led to the downfall of Fred Rose. In 1947, Fred Rose was charged and convicted for spying for the Soviet Union, and was expelled from the House of Commons. Fred Rose (né Rosenberg) had immigrated to Montreal from Poland as a child in 1916, and represented the Cartier riding until he was expelled in 1947. The LPP had strong pockets of support in working-class neighbourhoods of Montreal such as ours. Rose was released from prison in 1951 after four and a half years with his health broken. After being unable to find work in Canada, he went to Poland in 1953. His Canadian citizenship was revoked in 1957 making it impossible for him to return to Canada. Gouzenko remained in the public eye, writing two books, This Was My Choice, a non-fiction account of his defection, and the novel The Fall of a Titan, which won a Governor General's Award in 1954. Gouzenko also appeared on television always with a hood over his head to promote his books and to air grievances with the RCMP,. Gouzenko and his wife Svetlana lived the rest of their lives and raised eight children together under an assumed name. He died of a heart attack in Mississauga, Ontario in 1982.

In 1945 after World War II the UN was founded as a platform for dialogue to stop wars between countries and to replace the League of Nations.The first meeting of the United Nations (UN) was held in London on January 10, 1946. The UN was an international organization whose stated aims were facilitating cooperation in international law, international security, economic development, social progress, human rights, and achievement of world peace. The UN contains multiple subsidiary organizations to carry out its missions. In grade six we formed an informal debating group in session once a week after having received promotional information from the United Nations which was used to teach us procedure and skills in debate. We made a class visit to the parliament buildings in Ottawa, met the Prime Minister and sat through an hour watching parliamentary debate. 1945 was also the year that Maxwell House instant coffee was introduced to the public.

Space history was made in 1946 when a US Army Signal Corps project named Diana based at the Camp Evans, part of Fort Monmouth laboratory near Wall Township, New Jersey, succeeded in bouncing radar waves off the Moon, measuring the exact distance between the Earth and the Moon. This successful echo detection occurred on January 10, 1946 at 11:58am local time and was the first attempt to "touch" another celestial body. Project Diana marked the birth of the US space program, as well as that of radar astronomy; proving that communication was possible between Earth and outer space. The project demonstrated that artificially-created signals could penetrate the ionosphere, opening the possibility of radio communications beyond the earth for space probes and human explorers.

After the war, in 1947, Canada liberalized its immigration policy, no doubt influenced by the public revelation of the enormity of the Holocaust and the assassination of six million Jews under Hitler's reign. In 1947, the Workmen's Circle and the Jewish Labour Committee initiated the Tailors Project through the federal government's "bulk-labour" program that allowed labour-intensive industries such as the needle trades to bring European displaced persons to Canada, in order to fill those jobs. They succeeded in bringing into Canada roughly 40,000 holocaust survivors hoping to rebuild their shattered lives.

CHAPTER 4 HOME FRONT ACTIVITIES

Although the danger of an air raid on Canada seemed slight, air raid drills and blackouts were a common feature of life during the Second World War. Large horn-shaped air raid sirens were installed to alert the population to an imminent air attack, We had regular random air raid drills and we listened to the ear piercing, wailing sirens and ran for cover. At night, blackouts were enforced during the air raids. The purpose of the blackouts was principally to serve as camouflage. It was explained that although enemy planes could pinpoint targets using instruments, blackouts ensured that enemy planes had no way to be sure of their positions as there would be few visible landmarks even on a moonlit night. Defence of Canada regulations made it an offence for any lights to be left on in any building so as to be showing to the outside during any test air raid warning blackout. It applied to all businesses and residences. Emergency security lights had to be effectively shaded so that no light was visible to the outside. Police and air raid wardens (chief warden, zone warden, division warden, district warden, section warden), had the right to enter premises which were contravening the order and therefore being non compliant and the offenders were subject to prosecution.

The Department of National War Services had a fats and bones collection campaign encouraging housewives to collect fats and bones as these were essential for munitions production. Bones provided essential materials for industrial glues. Advertisements reminded people that fat was ammunition. One pound of fat supplied enough glycerine to fire 150 bullets from a Bren gun and that two pounds could fire 10 anti-aircraft shells or a burst of 20 cannon shells from a Spitfire. Canadian women responded to the urgent appeals to make-do, recycle and salvage in order to come up with needed supplies. They saved fats and grease; gathered recycled goods, handed out information on the best methods one could use to get the most out of recycled goods and organized many events to decrease waste. Volunteer organizations led by women also prepared packages for the military overseas and for prisoners of war in Axis countries.

The government of Canada introduced a universal price freeze in December 1941 and rationing on January 24, 1942 to limit imported food and to free up supplies in short supply for the military and our allies. Certain staple goods were rationed to ensure that there was an adequate supply to meet military and civilian needs. Prices were fixed along with the amount a person was allowed to buy. It was argued that price and rent controls would help to ensure that Canadians could continue to afford necessities like food, fuel, and shelter while rationing promised all Canadians a fair share of scarce necessities. In addition to price control and rationing, the Wartime Prices and Trade Board (WPTB), the federal agency responsible for overseeing and regulating Canada's wartime economy, imposed controls on the production and distribution of food. These ranged from prohibitions on sliced bread and iced cake in bakeries to the establishment of meatless Tuesdays and meatless Fridays in restaurants between 1945 and 1947. Other restrictions included reductions in the production of non-essential goods like chocolate bars and soft drinks, limitations on the number of tin can sizes that could be used from 116 to only 9 standard sizes, as well as the removal of foods like carrots, beets, apples, pork and beans, and spaghetti from the list of foods that could be sold in cans. These controls came on the heels of months of periodic food shortages and a precipitous spike in food prices. Each household coast to coast filled out applications and ration coupon books were mailed out to each family member on August 31, 1942. More than 11 million ration books were distributed. There were six series of ration books issued. Each book contained between 7 and 10 panes of sequentially numbered coupons for sugar, tea, coffee and with spare coupons for other foods that had not yet even been restricted and a postcard that needed to be sent in to get the next book. Strict rules about ration coupons were enforced. The coupons had to be detached in the presence of the grocer or butcher when the purchase was made. The penalties for breaking the rules ranged from small fines to imprisonment.

In July 1941 sugar was rationed because it was used in the manufacturing of shells and bombs. Each person was allowed 12 ounces (340 grams) per week and later only 8 ounces. Alcohol was also on the ration list. By mid 1941, silk was no longer being imported. Women were asked to donate their used stockings to the war effort since all available silk, nylon and rayon was needed to make parachutes, tents and other materials. Once word got out that there might be a shortage of silk stockings; stockings became a precious commodity and women flooded the stores, buying up all they could creating price inflation and shortages. To get the nylon look without hosiery, women started to stain their legs with household items. Max Factor quickly reacted introducing a stocking cream that gave the illusion of stockings. Tea and coffee were added to the ration list in August 1941 because they were imported and many merchant ships had been taken over by the military and many were lost. Butter was added to the list of rationed items in December 1941 with each person being allotted just 1/4 of a pound per week. Meat rationing of two pounds of meat per person per week was added in March 1942. Gasoline was rationed in April 1942. Tires were also rationed and civilians could not purchase them unless they could prove that driving was essential. Canning factories had their supplies of tin cans cut and items that came in cans were added to the ration list because tin was required for the war effort.

In 1943 more items, namely, maple syrup products, table syrups, molasses, apple or honey butter, and canned fruits were added to the ration list. On August 23, 1943 jams, jellies, marmalades, and honey were put in the rationed category. By October evaporated milk was only justified for priority use. On January 17, 1944, canned salmon made the ration list. Meat ration coupons were suspended in March, 1944. On July 1, 1944, canned blueberries, blueberry pie filling, and canned crab apples were added. At some point cheese was also included. Ration Book No. 4 came into use April 13, 1944. Ration Book No.5 was distributed between October 14 and 21, 1944 and was meant to cover a period of fifty weeks, the longest of any issue. Books 3 and 4 expired December 31,

1944. Late in 1944, sugar rationing became even more stringent with each person being allowed 8 ounces of sugar per week.

Rationing continued after the war ended. Meat, which had been taken off the list in February 1944, was back on in September 1945. The need for an increased supply for devastated Europe was urgent. During this second round of meat rationing the new meat ration was changed to one-and-a-third pounds of meat per person per week. Initially meat had been limited to two pounds per person per week. The problem for many people was that they would not need the two pounds of meat per week that each coupon allowed them to buy, and as a result had to forfeit a whole coupon for a lesser amount of meat or had to waste the excess. To solve this problem the Canadian Government issued stiff round navy blue cardboard meat tokens. Eight tokens were the equivalent of one meat ration coupon. If the amount of meat purchased did not take up the whole coupon, the customer could receive ration change in the form of tokens. If the customer wanted half the ration, the butcher handed him four tokens that could be used later. Because meat was scarce, a new product found its way on almost every table. It was named, Spam short for "seasoned ham". Even though the war officially came to an end in 1945, rationing continued in Canada until 1947. The last ration book was issued in September 1946. On June 10, 1947, dairy was taken off of the ration list and Canadians once again enjoyed larger quantities of cheese, milk and ice cream. Rationing in Canada ended in 1947. Residents of Great Britain however had to wait until 1954, a full nine years after the war, before they could put away their little books. For most civilians rationing was more of a nuisance than a hardship.

By the end of the war, it was estimated that Canadian exports to Great Britain accounted for 57 per cent of all wheat and flour; 39 per cent of bacon, 15 per cent of eggs, 24 per cent of cheese, and 11 per cent of evaporated milk consumed in Britain. Most people were happy to oblige with the new regulations, knowing full well that the foods they gave up and/or ate less of went towards feeding Britain, our own fighting forces overseas, prisoners of war, and starving refugees from many war-torn countries. Middle-income and upper-income families felt the greatest change due to rationing. Lower-income families were already used to making do. City dwellers were worse off than people who lived on or near farms which supplied them with fresh eggs and cream. People who were good at hunting and fishing had it a little easier since they could bring home lots of fresh game and fish, which were not rationed.

In the early spring (end of April, early May) our elderly Italian neighbours asked my mother who frequently visited Mount Royal park with me to forage some dandelion greens for them. At the time, pesticides were not used as extensively as they are today. Our neighbours used the greens to make a salad and they also used the greens in cooking. They called the dandelions "cicoria" but it is not "chicory". Dandelion in Italian is "dente di leone" meaning teeth of the lion; however apparently they all refer to it as "cicoria". We picked only the very young dandelions that had not yet flowered which are only available in the early spring. We cut off the roots and separated the leaves, one by one before giving our pickings to them. They prepared a salad which had garlic and olive oil added to the greens and even offered us some..It is a delicacy. They told us that later in the season the dandelions; even those that have flowered, are still edible, but they have to be cooked because the leaves are tougher and more bitter.

Many Canadians stretched their war rations by planting Victory Gardens, canning and preserving, fishing, hunting for game, mending and restyling their existing clothes. Despite the official discouragement of victory gardening by inexperienced gardeners in the early years of the war, new gardens appeared in backyards, laneways, front lawns and vacant lots almost everywhere. The Department of Agriculture felt that inexperienced gardeners would waste valuable commodities which were in short supply. One pamphlet suggested that these victory gardeners would create the demand for equipment such as garden tools, fertilizers and sprays, which were made from materials needed by Canada's war industries and that Canada's vegetable seed supply could best be employed by experienced gardeners with equipment on hand. The victory gardeners, on the other hand felt that what they were doing was an important contribution to the war effort, freeing up agricultural production and shipping space that could be used to send more food to Canada's allies. In the face of considerable protest by the country's avid victory gardeners The Department of Agriculture reversed its position in 1943. Reports estimated that in 1944 there were more than 209,200 victory gardens in operation nationwide producing a total of about 57,000 tons of vegetables.

My mother and I also picked the flowers from linden trees, also known as basswood and Tilia, on Mount Royal park. Linden trees are very attractive providing abundant shade with fragrant and nectar-producing flowers. Beekeepers, love these trees because bees feeding on the nectar of the flowers produce a pale but richly flavoured honey. We dried the yellow, mildly sweet and sticky flowers and used them to make a delicious tasting potent tea. Linden tea is reputed to help those who suffer from tension headaches and other inflammatory conditions, including arthritis and gout. In Europe linden flowers had been used as tea for treatment of disorders of the respiratory tract, colds, cough, fever and flu, infections, inflammation, high blood pressure, headache (particularly migraine), and as a diuretic (increases urine production), antispasmodic (reduces smooth muscle spasm along the digestive tract), and as a sedative. We also picked chamomile flowers, dried them and used them to make a potent tea. Chamomile tea had a reputation for being able to treat stress. anxiety and insomnia as a gentle sleep aid, sore stomach, irritable bowel syndrome, and as a mild laxative, Linden tea and chamomile tea were used as substitutes for rationed imported tea.

During the summer we picked ripe cherry red chokecherries on Mount Royal (our beloved mountain). Chokecherries grew in clusters on relatively small trees growing to 16 ft tall that were found along the roadside, ravines and on the hillsides. We ate the bitter, somewhat sour, astringent berries and spit out the chokecherry stones. We tried to avoid swallowing the stones because swallowing too many made you sick to your stomach. The chokecherry fruit with stones removed could be used to make jam, jelly, or syrup, pies and desserts but their bitter nature required sugar or honey to sweeten the preserves. Although home canning was promoted by the government, each single adult or family unit was required by federal law to apply for canning permission. Once applications were filled out, they were sent to local Rationing Boards for approval. The Department of Agriculture published helpful pamphlets and brochures that were available for pick up at the Post Office or Ration Administration offices, to which Canadians responded overwhelmingly. These canning guides provided directions on the type and amount of food allowed to be preserved in cans.

In September and October people went mushroom picking on Mount Royal and in the woods of Montreal east and in the Laurentians. Mushrooms typically started to grow around the second week of September and could be found until the middle to end of October. Weather conditions of course had a huge impact on their abundance. Mushrooms literally sprout and grow overnight on the ground near the base of trees, growing on all sides of a tree, around tree stumps and are also found several feet away from these. We usually brought home one to two pillow cases full. Once home my parents checked every one of the picked mushrooms ensuring that they were all familiar to them and that none were dangerous for human consumption. The mushrooms were washed and were preserved in jars of vegetable oil to be enjoyed all winter long. We had my mother's homemade, delicious mushroom soup, mushrooms sliced and pan fried and mushrooms added to gravies. Fall mushroom hunting in the forest was great fun.

In Protestant schools across the island of Montreal pupils formed school clubs such as the Junior Red Cross, adolescent girls knitted garments for soldiers and refugees, and students raised funds for specific projects. Organizations such as the Boy Scouts advanced citizenship, reinforced the social order and promoted patriotism, sacrifice and dedication, At assemblies, music classes, and concerts school authorities prominently displayed the Union Jack, pledged allegiance to the monarch, and sang "God Save the King", children memorized and sang Canadian and British patriotic songs such as "The Maple Leaf Forever", "Rule Britannia", "The British Grenadiers", "The Red, White and Blue", and "Men of Harlech", students marched and drilled sustaining a high level of patriotic sentiment.

The Montreal Protestant School Board noted that as a result of the urgent appeals of government and industry for workers to which many women had responded, there was a serious decline in parental control over school-age children. Juvenile crime was on the rise. According to the Dominion Bureau of Statistics, the number of juvenile delinquents rose from under 10,000 in 1940 to almost 14,000 in 1942. In Montreal the number of children appearing before the juvenile court judge increased by 20 per cent between 1940 and 1942 (from 2,979 to 3,680). The delinquents continued to commit the same offences that they always had; namely, petty theft, truancy, and loitering in the case of boys, and immoral conduct in the case of girls.

The Montreal Police expanded its Juvenile Morality Squad and focused on the surveillance of youth in public places through "tours of inspection" of restaurants, pool halls, bowling halls, etc. The morality squad was renamed the Juvenile

Prevention Bureau and included new bureaucratic measures of surveillance and police keeping records on "bad" youth. They instigated a curfew which was seen as a child protector since children were without surveillance in the evenings because mothers were working in war factories. In September 1942 the municipal government passed By-law 1715. The curfew stipulated that all children under 14 years of age, unless attending night courses, were forbidden to "circulate in the streets, lanes and public places" between 9 p.m. and 5 a.m. Exceptions were made for children in the company of a parent. The immediate impact of the curfew was that it created hoards of delinquent children whose only offence was that they were not at home in the evening. It was reported that records of the Montreal Juvenile Delinquents' Court show that most children aged 11, 12, and 13 who were brought to juvenile court for being on the streets at night pleaded guilty and were fined between 50 cents and $1. Failure to pay the fine within one week resulted in incarceration in a detention home. While this might appear to be a harsh measure, the youth were spared reform school and permitted to return home.

In 1940 unemployment insurance was introduced in Canada; Nazi, fascist, and communist groups were declared illegal and its leaders and members were jailed. Japanese Canadians were registered by the government and had to carry a registration card. A few years later, Japanese Canadians were interned and moved further inland. Their fishing boats were impounded by the government and Japanese-language schools and newspapers were shut down. Camillien Houde, the mayor of Montreal, was arrested for sedition due to his anti-conscription rhetoric.

There were several elementary schools in the area including Devonshire school, founded in 1921 located north of Pine avenue between Clark and Sewel streets; Aberdeen school founded in 1896 on St Denis Street near St Louis Square, Bancroft school founded in 1915 on St Urbain Street north of Mount Royal Avenue and Mount Royal School on Rachel street between Clark and St Urbain. The school started in 1886 as the St Jean Baptiste school until 1889 when it changed its name to the St Urbain Street school and then in 1894 it became the Mount Royal School which my friends and I attended. We had a fifteen minute recess in the morning and in the afternoon. At noon we went home for lunch and returned within the hour to the school. Before school and at recess when the weather was favourable we played in the schoolyard and when the bell rang we assembled in preassigned spaces. During inclement weather we assembled in the basement of the four storey school building and when the bell rang we lined up where our class teacher stood; usually beside the lockers where we hung up our coats and left our boots in winter. We mounted the stairs to our respective classrooms in a silent, very orderly manner.

The gymnasium and nurses room was located in the basement along with public washrooms. Grades one and two were on the first floor where the principal's office and administration office was located. The second floor had an assembly hall and grade three classrooms. The third floor had the grade four and five classrooms while the fourth floor housed the grade six and seven classrooms. The classrooms were bright with very large windows; with a black slate blackboard at the front and another one at one side. School children in all of the grades sat at wooden desks with ink wells and hinged desktops under which they kept books and pencils. The desks had folding seats that squeaked loudly when we stood up. The back of the seat was the front of the desk behind. The classrooms always smelled of sharpened pencils in the morning probably from the dust type cleaner that was sprinkled on the hardwood floors before being swept every night. In grade one and two there was a multi-purpose table that was used for such things as plasticine modeling or holding a sand box. I learned about Humpty Dumpty who sat on a wall and about Old Mother Hubbard who went to the cupboard, to give the poor dog a bone: When she came there, the cupboard was bare, and so the poor dog had none. Here's where I was introduced to Dick, Jane and Spot and I learned all about Jack and Jill and the alphabet.

>Jack and Jill went up the hill
>To fetch a pail of water;
>Jack fell down and broke his crown,
>And Jill came tumbling after.

In grade one and two (1942 - 1944) the pencils were very thick green pencils with large soft grey slate or graphite centers which we sharpened using a hand cranked pencil sharpener at the front of the class. Students helped teachers by doing simple chores such as dusting the erasers, washing the blackboards and bringing out new chalk. In later grades we learned numbers and how to count, how to tell time and how to add and subtract. We learned about HB pencils and then all about pen and ink. Teachers not only taught reading, writing and arithmetic as useful basic tools but also moral lessons and explained how learning these would help us to build skills that we would need and use later on in life. Teachers helped parents who also wanted students to learn obedience to superiors, to be polite to each other; to learn basics of cleanliness and neatness in personal dress and to have a good standard of deportment, called posture. I made good progress, which was interrupted by a bout of measles and chicken-pox. The students had a lot of respect for and held teachers in a high regard. Teacher's word was law, never to be questioned. You did as you were told or suffered the consequences, which might be to stand in the corner facing the wall, or to stand outside the room until told to return. If by chance you committed a major offence you were dispatched to the principal's office and possibly even expelled or given the strap. Teachers shouted a fair bit and had us repeat tables and spelling over and over again until we got it right.

Each school day began with us standing beside our classroom desks saluting the British Union Jack flag that was mounted on the wall above the front blackboard and pledging allegiance to Canada, "to the flag and the country for which it stands" and sang "Oh Canada" our national anthem and "God Save the King" and for good measure "The Maple Leaf Forever". We sang "God Save the King" until 1953 when King George VI passed away. In 1954, Queen Elizabeth II took his place and we sang "God Save the Queen". Daily we also recited the Lord's Prayer and sang a hymn. Every class was composed of Christians and Jews and we often all sang "Onward Christian Soldiers". At assemblies, music classes, and school concerts students marched, drilled and sang Canadian and

British patriotic songs. After all, these were war years; world war II had started on September 1, 1939 and was not officially over until May 8, 1945.

We were continually encouraged by our teachers, neighbors and friends to support the war effort. With most able-bodied men overseas, many children worked hard on farms to harvest crops ensuring a steady domestic food supply because there were not enough farm workers available. Many schools cooperated by not taking attendance or by not introducing any new material in classes until after the crops were in. Even the government lowered the minimum age to 14 for obtaining a driver's license so that children could legally operate farm trucks and other vehicles. Many high school students, both boys and girls, joined cadet corps, militia groups and learned how to march, perform arms drills and fire weapons. Boys in particular were encouraged to join the cadet league open to both Jews and Gentiles at the YMHA. We helped to collect tons of scrap, a lot of it donated during metal salvage drives and were active in fund-raising activities where the money raised was used to buy a truck, or an ambulance for the Royal Canadian Air Force. Teachers encouraged us to write letters to Canadian servicemen overseas, telling them about what was happening back home. We made art projects which were sent overseas to the fighting men for Christmas. Teachers also encouraged us to have "pen pals". I corresponded with some girls in a school in the British Channel Islands.

We bought War Savings Stamps in school and at the post office for 25 cents each and pasted them into special booklets for subsequent post-war redemption. After saving $4 worth of stamps the completed form was sent to the federal government and we received a War Savings Certificate worth $5. The government used the money to fund the war effort. This Victory War Savings program led to Canada Savings Bonds being introduced in October1946. These very popular investments were extremely safe and secure being guaranteed by the government. They were easy to purchase and were redeemable at any time without penalty. It was reported that about $5.5 billion had been raised in the Victory War Stamp appeals. In January 1947 the Canadian Citizenship Act came into effect. Two new Canadian nuclear reactors went online at the Chalk River research facility. Oil was discovered near Leduc, Alberta and the Dead Sea scrolls were discovered. 1,100 children, survivors of the Holocaust were brought to Canada, as part of the Canadian Jewish Congress's negotiated "war orphans" program; 525 of them were settled in Montreal.

In the early 1940s many children saw themselves as junior soldiers in training. We prepared for war by memorizing aircraft silhouettes and building airplane and ship models; learning Morse code and learning how to convey information at a distance by means of visual signals using hand-held semaphore flags. Those not yet in their teen years practiced marching with sticks and brooms for guns. One of us was the sergeant and yelled out commands as loud as we could, imitating the army maneuvers, we saw on Fletcher's field. Girls participated as well and marched right along with us. We even staged battles in backyards. We built slingshots from forked Y-shaped tree branches to which we attached rubber strips wide enough to hold a stone. We fired it by holding the wooden Y piece in the left hand while pulling back on the rubber with the stone in it with our right hand. We aimed and released the rubber to fire the projectile toward the target. We also assembled ourselves into two groups and barricaded by bric a brac in the back yards, we threw rocks, stones, bottles and what have you at each other across the yard. Some kids even had army helmets which were bought from the army surplus stores. We were extremely lucky that no one got seriously hurt. But that was not always the case. My friend had his bleeding head wound treated by an opposing friend's mother before going home. Thinking back it was a totally stupid thing to do; yet we managed somehow to survive. In winter we threw snowballs and imagined them to be grenades. The icy snowballs hurt the most. Ignorance can be educated, crazy can be medicated but there is no cure for stupid.

Shoe makers and shoe repair shops were found almost on every city block as were people with holes in their shoes in need of repair. Generally when people got holes in their shoes they lined the inside of the shoe with cardboard, from a cereal box, to cover the hole until they had saved enough money to get the shoe repaired or to buy a new pair. In the rain the cardboard got soggy and the feet got really cold. To get some relief in the evening people often heated a kettle of water and poured the warm water into a galvanized tin tub and soaked their feet. The soggy cardboard was replaced with a new piece and life continued. People relied on shoemakers to extend the lives of their shoes. Shoemakers were so busy that at one point they had to close their shops in the middle of the week just to catch up on work. Even into the mid-'50s, they were so overworked that they collectively petitioned for a five-day work week. It was a time when thrift and modest spending habits ruled the day. My parents bought my new shoes at the Yellow Sample Shoe Store on Mount Royal Street.

I often visited Witold's shoemaker shop with my father. It had many pairs of highly polished shoes in the window accompanied by several shoe stretchers. There were many shoe polish posters on the wall and a long counter separating the work area and the customer waiting area which had several chairs that greeted you upon entry. The shop was well equipped with hammers, tongs (pliers), awls, chisels, nails, a sewing machine, several shoe stands and a large assortment of electric buffing machines with wheels of horsehair to polish leather shoes. A pot bellied wood and coal stove heated the store in winter. Off to one side was a chair higher than all the rest where you could sit and have Witold or one of his helpers shine your shoes. The smell of shoe polish and glue permeated the air. I watched Witold drive nails into leather soles and rubber heels and I watched people come and go as my father and he discussed everything from politics to economics and more. Customers had Witold nail on taps or blaikes (a thin metal piece) on the toe and heel tips of their shoes for a dime each. Witold repaired anything made of leather including belts, boots and ladies purses. He also sharpened ice skates and made door keys. My Father had acquired a metal shoe stand and repaired all of our shoes at home; cutting leather soles, gluing them on and driving in nails. He also had good horsehair shoe brushes with which we regularly polished our shoes. Whenever Witold had a backlog of shoes to fix, my father helped him repair shoes and when our shoes required sewing we had them sown on Witold's sewing machine with very strong thread.

Shoemakers stocked a large variety of shoe polishes that were traditionally packaged in flat, round, 2-ounce tins, usually with an easy-open facility. The tins were small because you didn't need a lot of it for a shine and you didn't want the volatile ingredients, such as naphtha, lanolin, turpentine, carnauba wax, gum arabic, ethylene glycol and a colorant, such as carbon black or an azo dye to quickly dry out. The high amount of volatile substances meant that the shoe polish dried out and hardened after being applied, while retaining its shine. Lanolin, a hydrophilic grease from wool-bearing animals such as sheep or goats, acted as both a waterproofing wax and a bonding agent, giving the shoe polish a greasy feel and texture. It prevented the naphtha from evaporating until the polish had been spread and buffed into a thin film on the leather surface. The chemical substances in shoe polish could be inhaled or absorbed through the skin, so , it was suggested that when handling shoe polish, a person should wear gloves, and stay in a well-ventilated area which was seldom if ever done. Shoe polish had to be kept out of reach of children and animals. It could stain the skin for a protracted period of time, and could cause irritation to the eye if there was direct contact. Kiwi remained the predominant shoe polish brand. Nugget was used as a common term for solid waxy shoe polish, as opposed to liquid shoe polishes. Shoe shine parlors were very popular and shoe shine boys could be found at most hotels, train stations and even on city sidewalks. Shoe polish was applied to the shoe using a rag, cloth, or brush. Shoe polish was not a cleaning product, and therefore the footwear had to be both clean and dry before application. A vigorous rubbing action applied the polish evenly on the shoe, followed by further buffing with a clean dry cloth or brush, usually gave good results. Another technique, known as spit-polishing involved gently rubbing polish into the leather with a cloth and a drop of water or spit. This achieved the mirror-like, high-gloss finish sometimes known as a spit shine which was especially valued in the military. Polishes containing carnauba wax were used as a protective coating to extend the life and look of a leather shoe.

Once when we were visiting Witold's shop, I sat in the shoe shine chair while my father and four other men discussed the news of the day, Shlomo the baker came in with a pair of shoes to be repaired. He said hello to everyone and they all reciprocated. Shlomo was a really jolly sort of man with a double chin and a protruding belly. He insisted on telling everyone the story that he had heard. He said that this one mohel had retired after forty years of service and decided that he needed something to remind him of his long career, but what? Cleaning out his cupboard and finding a large cardboard box that once was used for shipping, filled almost full with foreskins, it soon became clear to him what it must be. So next day, he went to the local shoemaker taking the large box with all the skins he had saved over the forty years. He said to the shoemaker, "I vant you should make me a memento of my years as a mohel." The shoemaker was amazed at the quantity of foreskins in the box and assured the rabbi that something could be done and that he should come back next week to pick it up. The shoemaker worked diligently on the memento in addition to his already busy schedule and was ready when the mohel returned, excited and anxious to see what the shoemaker had fashioned for him, saying, "Nu, what have you got for me?" The shoemaker very proudly produced what he said was his greatest feat of workmanship and presented the mohel with a wallet measuring no more that six inches by eight inches and about an inch in depth. The mohel was shocked, grew pale as a ghost and shook like he was having a seizure and cried out in agony. "Oy Vey, I vork for 40 years and all you can make for me is a vallet?" The shoemaker very concerned replied, "Rabbi take it easy, I don't want you to have a heart attack, look carefully it's not just a wallet, it is a special kind of wallet. When you rub it, it becomes a suitcase!" All of the men including Witold laughed.

Then Witold had a story that he recounted, He spoke about a wealthy Polish merchant named Jan who was riding on a train sitting opposite a man named Wladek. After a while Jan leans over to Wladek and asks if he would like to play a game. Wladek just wants to take a nap, so he politely declines and rolls over to the window to catch a few winks. Jan persists and explains that the game is really easy and a lot of fun. He explains, "I ask you a question, and if you don't know the answer, you pay me $1, and vice-versa." Again, Wladek politely declines and tries to get some sleep. Jan, now more insistent , says, "Okay, if you don't know the answer you pay me $1, and if I don't know the answer, I will pay you $5," figuring that he was smarter than Wladek. This caught Wladek's attention and, figuring that there was going to be no end to Jan's persistence unless he plays, he agrees to the game.
Jan asks the first question. "How far is the moon from the earth?"
Wladek doesn't say a word, reaches into his pocket, pulls out a dollar bill and hands it to Jan. Now, Wladek's turn.
He asks Jan: "What goes up a hill with three legs, and comes down with four?" Jan looks at Wladek with a puzzled look. He thinks for a few minutes. Then he asks every single person on the train for help and no one knows. After over an hour, he wakes Wladek and hands him $5. Wladek politely takes the $5 and turns away to get back to sleep.
Jan, who is more than a little miffed, wakes Wladek and asks, "Well, so what is the answer!?" Without a word, Wladek reaches into his wallet, hands the merchant $1, and goes back to sleep! Everyone applauded and acknowledged that Wladek was the smarter one of the two.

My father and I chopped wood logs into firewood and kindling in the back lane. The wood was pitched up into the second storey of the shed where he neatly stacked it. After throwing sufficient pieces of split wood into the shed my father would climb up and stack the wood. On this one occasion after being told several times not to throw the pieces of wood into the shed while my father was up there stacking the wood, guess what, I did anyway! I hit him on the head. I know that it was not intentional but it still haunts me to this day. Did I deserve the rapid response punishment I received? Most definitely, but the lesson "Think before you act" did not sink in. This was the same shed where I had invented the flame thrower using a lit candle and an oil squirt can. Squirting the oil through the flame threw the fire a fair distance forward and into a metal pail. Luckily a neighbour spotted me playing with matches and in the midst of my flame throwing discovery I was caught by my mother who put a fast stop to the experiment. This was the same shed in which I broke every window pane in the winter double windows being stored in the loft by throwing pieces of coal from the coal bin. Did I deserve a good whack on my backside? You bet I did.

We had two pool rooms on St Lawrence Blvd. between Rachel and Mt. Royal streets. They rented tables by the hour and supplied a set of balls, a white cue ball, pool cues and chalk, etc. Each pool room had no windows and was spacious enough to allow from six to eight tables to be played at one time. There was at least a six foot clearance between the table and other tables or walls on all sides and at all corners of the table. The typical cue was between five and six feet long. Each pool table required enough space around it to accommodate the range of a stroke of the cue from all angles, while also accounting for benches and the storage rack. The pool tables had overhead lighting consisting of a multi-bulb light fixture; the older ones used incandescent light bulbs and were later replaced with fluorescent lights. The table itself was felt-covered and had six pockets. Mostly only men played pool.

Snooker was one of the most popular games at the time. Snooker was played with 22, unnumbered object balls, divided into two groups of 15 red balls, 6 balls of different colours and one white ball (the cue ball). Each ball had a different point value: red=1, yellow=2, green=3, brown=4, blue=5, pink=6, and black=7. Each player tried to score a higher number of points than their opponent by pocketing the balls. Sinking a red ball into one of the pockets earned the player an opportunity to go after one of the colored balls. Usually a coin was tossed to decide who played first. The cue ball was placed within the "D" marked on the table for the break. The first player had to make sure that the white cue ball made contact with a red ball. If he failed to do this, the other player tried. Players would often check their cues to make sure that they were not warped, bent or broken. Professional players often owned their own pool cues in special sturdy cases and handled them with great care making sure to keep them in a cool, dry place so that they would not get damaged by sunlight or humidity (heat and moisture).

After pocketing a red ball, the player could shoot at his choice of colored balls. If a colored ball was pocketed, it was re-spotted to its assigned spot and the player could attempt to pocket another red ball, followed by any colored ball. All red balls stayed down, but the colored balls were re-spotted immediately after being pocketed. Play continued this way until there were no red balls remaining on the table. When all of the red balls were cleared from the table, the remaining colored balls were pocketed in ascending order from where the cue and object balls lay. A player was awarded one point for each red pocketed, and the numerical value of each colored ball pocketed after his turn at the table was ended by a miss. If a player fouled, the opponent was awarded seven points (no points were deducted from the offenders score).

Men often gambled In the pool room, player against player and also spectators watching the game. I never gambled and never played for money; in short, I was not that good at Snooker. My brother Walter on the other hand was more of a pool shark and would come home proudly announcing how much money he won, even though my parents discouraged him from playing and most strongly against gambling. One evening he came home with a dress for my mother that he said he had won. At the time she was not happy that he had not listened to them telling him not to gamble. In later years she laughed about it.

I remember hearing a story about Mark Twain playing pool. Apparently, Mark Twain had been called upon to make a speech at a billiard tourney in the early 1900's and reportedly said, "The game of billiards has destroyed my naturally sweet disposition. Once, when I was an underpaid reporter in Virginia City, whenever I wished to play billiards I went out to look for an easy mark. One day I spotted a stranger in the billiard parlor. I looked him over casually. When he proposed a game, I answered, "All right."
"Just knock the balls around a little so that I can get your gait," he said; and when I had done so, he remarked: "I will be perfectly fair with you. I'll play you left-handed."
I felt hurt, for he was cross-eyed, freckled, and had red hair, and I determined to teach him a lesson. He won first shot, ran out, took my half-dollar, and all I got was the opportunity to chalk my cue.
"If you can play like that with your left hand," I said, "I'd like to see you play with your right."
"I can't," he said. "I'm left-handed."

The Main had many sewing machine stores and sewing accessory stores known as haberdashers. The sewing machine stores sold various models of Singer sewing machines and replacement parts. My mother had a Singer sewing machine with an elegant ironwork treadle that ran very smoothly and quietly. In one of the haberdashery stores people could find any kind of button, thread or fastening they needed for their sewing projects. The stores were a treasure trove of supplies including sewing needles, thimbles, thread, sewing tools, pins and accessories, tapes, cords and elastics, bias binding, edging and interfacings, fasteners, zippers, pin cushions, sewing machines, bobbins, patches, pads. dress forms, ribbons and buttons. The stores had walls of small drawers with buttons displayed on the outside indicating the content of the drawer. It didn't seem to matter how many buttons a person had when they didn't have the "right" one they went to the haberdashery shops. They also sold sewing patterns under the brand names of Butterick, Kwik Sew, McCall's and Vogue Patterns, The stores had a variety of pin cushions designed in fanciful shapes adorned with embroidery and glass beading, crafted from every material imaginable, including precious metals, bone, celluloid, wood, ivory, porcelain, fabric, and paper. There were novelty cushions resembling miniature boots and shoes and some modeled after various animals with velvet pinning-fabric mounted on their backs.

As long as human beings have needed to keep their clothing fastened, buttons have been there to do the work. Many people collected buttons as a hobby, all sorted by colour, material and type (shanked, two hole, four hole or other). There were buttons made from antlers, bone, glass, ceramics, painted, embroidered and carved buttons, buttons embellished with enameling or hand painted, pottery buttons, black glass Victorian era buttons, bakelite buttons, buttons made of metals, brass, stone, military buttons, flat buttons made of lead or pewter, two-part convex buttons, and buttons produced for officers.. There were "diminutive" buttons (less than 3/8" across) and large buttons (greater than 1 1/4" wide), Buttons either have a shank or don't. A shank is a loop that allows you to attach the button to an article of clothing. Shankless buttons are pierced with two, three, or four holes so that they can be sewn directly onto a garment. Many women collected thimbles besides the one that they used which made hand stitching an easier, and safer, activity. Thimbles were small and were always pocked and pitted leaving little space for any embellishments. Despite this thimbles had been made out of mother of pearl, sterling and plated silver, brass, porcelain, wood, carved stone, bone, and even gold. Some thimbles featured delicate filigree work around their sides; others were decorated with colorful enamel patterns or bands. Among the most legendary were the Fabergé thimbles from the 19th century; some with polished agates or other semi-precious stones set in their tops. Some women not only collected thimbles but also thimble holders and the little display cases that some of them came in.

People came together for family game nights and went to professional tournaments and enjoyed playing games with 'Bicycle' playing cards. In 1885 the first Bicycle Brand cards were produced by Russell, Morgan, & Co. which became The United States Playing Card Company after acquiring the Standard Playing Card Company (Chicago), Perfection Card Company (New York), and New York Consolidated Card Company (also New York) in 1894. In 1942 the United States Playing Card Company began producing Bicycle Spotter Decks to help soldiers identify tanks, ships, and aircraft from other countries. They also produced decks for POWs that pulled apart to reveal maps when moistened. Playing cards were inexpensive and affordable and people collected them for various reasons. Many people collected decks of playing cards to satisfy their collecting passion while others enjoyed the packs with their beautiful designs and clever artistry executed in many colours and gilding. Some people just loved the novelty of custom designs, and appreciated high end artwork and unique designs. They collected playing cards simply for their beauty and uniqueness. Some collectors kept decks of cards sealed in shrink-wrap, and never opened them. In any deck of cards the ace of spades usually contained the manufacturer's name, the place of manufacture and codes that were helpful in dating the cards. Prior to the 1870s, playing cards around the world were made without the numbers or face card letters in the upper and lower corners. Adding the indices was considered a major improvement in playing card history. Jokers were also first added to American decks around the same time. Until 1965 playing card decks were subject to "sin" taxes just like alcohol and tobacco products, and they had a revenue stamp on the packaging to prove it. Cards were taxed for the first time in 1892 during the U.S. Civil War as a funding measure.

Later taxes were imposed due to the association of cards with gambling and mysticism frowned upon by religious institutions. If the original stamps were still present, they could be used to date card decks. Some older cards were made with coarse paper and were unpolished; others included linen. Plastic coated cards were only produced starting in the 1940s. There were custom playing cards with train illustrations, Coca-Cola advertising, automotive shop advertising, insurance agencies and pin-up girl cards.

Many people collected postage stamps for their visual appeal and the simple joy and satisfaction they felt whenever they looked at their stamp collection. They admired the various pictures, designs, and colors and enjoyed the process of searching, locating and acquiring postage stamps, new and old ones or rare stamps that were needed to complete their stamp collection. They enjoyed the praise they received from family and friends; and from other collectors at stamp shows which gave them a sense of pride, success and accomplishment. Postage stamp collecting was a cheap and affordable hobby that many people enjoyed. For many of them it represented having a living history of their country. For many others it educated them about history, art, geography, architecture, mythology, music, religion, culture, science, modes of transport, sports, animals and plants, famous people and world events. Stamp collecting connected them to relatives, pen pals, and people from other countries all over the world. People collected stamps from letters, postcards and packages that they received in their own mail box. They tore the envelope with the stamps and then soaked the stamps off of the remnants of envelopes. The soaking was done in water for about 15 or 20 minutes which caused the stamps to float free from the paper. They then dried the stamps and added them to their collection.

Doing men's work in factories during WWII may have had an adverse effect on women's feminine self-image, but women still did their best to stick to their beauty routines keeping up their outward appearance for both their own morale and for those around them. Despite austerity measures experienced during the Second World War, looking good was still as important as ever to women. Cold creams and make-up removal creams disappeared off the market as the War continued. War manufacturing plants and military posts started operating beauty salons on their properties for the convenience of workers and members of the women's branch of the army. These salons provided services and cosmetics for the woman who's schedule made it more difficult to make it to her usual salon or to the department store. During the war, many products were hard to come by and women made do with whatever they could use from items found in the home. Instead of throwing away lipstick ends, they were melted down and re-used. When a lipstick ran out, solid rouge was used on lips. While playing with Sasha, the son of Dmitry, a steel worker and his mother Varvara; and Itzik, the son of Jacob, a mechanic and his mother Golda. We overheard Golda talking to Varvara about how rose petals steeped in water produced a liquid tint that was effective in colouring the cheeks. She also said that in the absence of cold cream, she had used a small amount of lard on her face to remove stubborn make-up traces.

The rationing of clothing and fabrics during World War II made women concentrate on making their hair as beautiful as possible. War greatly influenced how working women wore their hair. The armed forces enforced rules and hair had to be off the collar while on duty and a hat was part of the uniform. Women in the armed forces and those who worked in factories and in the fields needed hair styles that would not get in the way or be caught in machinery and wore scarves to protect their hair. Some of the hairstyles looked complicated and it was amazing to see what women did with just a few tools: bobby pins, hair elastics, curlers or a curling iron, a comb, and a hairbrush. Some women had the new electric curling irons that were being sold while others still used the short handled old hot curling irons heated on the stove to create waves. The longer handled curling irons were heated in the open fire. To dampen their hair before setting they used beer or sugar water because hair setting lotion was difficult to obtain. These hot curling irons were dangerous because heat was not distributed evenly across the iron rod and could not be regulated. Women sometime burned their hair or singed their scalp while using one of them. Others recalled the smell of their mother's singed hair filling the house. Hair in the 1940's was set in the most elaborate ways with pin curls, perfectly placed finger waves, and in a variety of hair styles such as updos, pompadours and bangs; all very super-stylish, flattering, glamorous and womanly. If their hair was shoulder length or longer, the updo was an easy option for bad hair days. All it required was a paddle brush, a comb, a hair elastic and bobby pins. An updo was a hair style that involved arranging the hair so that it was pointing up. It could be as simple as a ponytail, but was more commonly referred to more elaborate styles intended for special occasions. A favourite hairstyle for many was a bun hairstyle where the hair was pulled back from the face, twisted or plaited, and wrapped in a circular coil around itself, typically on top or back of the head or just above the neck. The bun was secured with a hair tie, barrette, bobby pins or a hair stick like a pen or pencil. Actress Veronica Lake made the peek-a-boo bang hairstyle famous and it was imitated by countless women worldwide. It was best described as cascading waves tumbling from a deep side part which allowed hair to fall seductively over one eye, partly hiding one side of the face.

I heard my friend Zoolie's mother Dinah, tell her daughter Hanna how to create an updo. Hanna grew up to be an enterprising hairdresser. Dinah said, "Brush your hair back and gather it into a low ponytail at the nape of your neck. Secure it with a hair elastic. Split the ponytail in two. Using a comb, tease each half. To do this, place the comb in the section of hair, about halfway down the length of the section, and then comb it *back* towards the elastic. Take one section, twist it under, and secure it with bobby pins. Do the same with the other side." It seemed so much easier for us boys who hardly ever even combed our hair. On another day Zoolie and I overheard Hanna and her friends talking about a peek-a-boo bang. Zoolie thought that it was another name for a pirate eye patch. The girls disagreed. Hanna's friend said that it was a charming hairstyle. Hanna said that it was super-stylish and explained how she would create the style. She said, "First you wash your hair and dry it leaving it warm and barely damp. Then you part your hair deep on one side and using a curling iron, you curl small sections of hair, beginning at the top. Each time, you do not unwind the curling iron, but open it up slightly and slide the curl off the barrel. Then you pin the curl in place with a bobby pin. You do this to all the curls and pin them in place. When your hair is cool, remove the bobby pins and with your fingers loosen the curls into waves. Because one side is parted so deeply, the other side has hair that partly covers one eye giving you the peek-a-boo effect over one eye. If you want to you can put a bobby pin in the wave over the eye so that you can see."

The hairspray can was not invented until 1943 during World War II, when aerosol sprays were used to kill insects. After the war, the beauty industry recognized the "power" of the aerosol containers, which were pressurized by a fluorocarbon, or liquefied gas. In 1950, Helene Curtis was the first to use "hairspray" for its newly developed aerosol product called Spray Net to keep hair in place. It quickly became women's favourite product. Companies found that aerosols also worked well with antiperspirants. When chlorofluorocarbon (CFC) aerosols were found to be detrimental to the ozone layer in the 1970s, countries began phasing them out. The beauty manufacturers found alternative approaches and in 1977, Alberto VO5 Hair Spray was the first to introduce an aerosol free of CFCs.

After the war, many products became available and hair permanents were all the rage. Perms lasted a long time and were much easier than setting with rollers. For many women the real joy was being catered to and getting groomed by stylists. Women spent hours in beauty salons with their hair bundled up into creepy heating wired machines to achieve a fashionable curled look. The beauty parlours featured permanent wave machines which offered hair permanent results using a combination of chemicals and electrically heated clamps. A permanent wave, commonly called a perm or "permanent", involved the use of heat and/or chemicals to break and reform the cross-linking bonds of the hair structure. The hair was washed and wrapped on a form and waving lotion or 'reagent' was applied. This solution reacted chemically softening the inner structure of the hair by breaking some of the cross links within and between the protein chains of the hair. The hair swelled, stretched and softened, then molded around the shape of the form.

The permanent wave machines looked very strange. A vertical metal pipe mounted on wheels held a circular unit, called a "chandelier" from which the bakelite heaters (curlers) were suspended on separate wires leading to each chemical-wrapped curl. The bottom of the pipe was mounted on a base with wheels which enabled the device to be moved easily between clients or to one side of the salon. The chandelier took some of the weight of the heaters and kept them tidy; it also facilitated the electrical connection. The heaters were tubular or like a bulldog clip called a croquignole heater. The trend was to replace some of the tubular heaters on the sides of the head with croquignole ones, to allow greater scope of styling. After washing, cutting or tapering, the hair was combed into sections or locks, a process known a sectioning or squaring off. Each lock starting at the bottom of the curler using the hair nearest the scalp was then wound on to the tubular curler which was basically a rod which stood upright from the head and the hair was wound spirally up the curler. The croquignole heater on the other hand fitted over the hair which had been previously wound on to a form or curler, rather like a bulldog clip. By 1930, the process of permanent-waving was well established. The majority of middle-class women had their hair set once a week and permed perhaps once every three months as new hair replaced the waved hair. Women with straight hair wanted permanent curls and waves, others with naturally curly hair wanted their hair straightened. The permanent wave dome-shaped helmet machine worked both ways although was somewhat impossible for consumers with excessively curly hair.

Hanna explained the technical considerations associated with perms by saying, "There were two parts to a perm; the physical action of wrapping the hair, and the chemical phase; both of which can affect the result. Concerning the physical, it's important to know what type of rod is used, how the hair is wrapped and how end papers are used. Rods can be straight or concave; each giving a different curl effect. The wrapping method is either spiral or croquignole, and various types and the positioning of end papers can be used with any combination of rods and wrapping methods. Smaller rods produce smaller, tighter curls and increase the appearance of shortening the hair. Regarding the chemical phase; the chemical solution used is determined by the client's hair type. Alkaline perms containing ammonium thioglycolate are used for stronger, coarser hair and they work at room temperature. Acid perms containing glycerol monothioglycolate are used on more delicate or thinner hair and they require outside heat application." She continued and said, "It is important when using chemicals that contact with the skin is minimized. A poorly performed permanent wave can result in temporary hair loss. Most perms require at least a couple of hours in the salon chair. Expect the results to last six to 12 weeks before you need to do it again or change your style."

Beauty parlours or salons were located in shops, rather than having the equipment at home, permanents made women's hair care into a social event rather than a private ritual. These shops brought the latest technology into the world of women's fashion and beauty, they were the most modern and many women wanted to try the new style. The beauty shops offered haircuts, styling, and permanent waves. These shops created places for women to gather and socialize while their hair was done. There was lots of activity in the place as customers were getting groomed on wrap around styling chairs by stylists while other women received a perm under the permanent wave machine; and while still others sat under the massive chrome metal hood shaped hair dryers which were standard in all hairdressing salons. The beauty salon was always a brightly lit place with pictures of different hairstyles on the pale baby blue painted wall, marble-topped sinks with hot running water; recliner chairs; and a shiny linoleum floor. There were dressing stations, geometric bevel-edged mirrors and sweeping curved reception desks with vases filled with fresh flowers and a faint fragrance of cologne permeated the air.

Some beauty salons offered women a manicure while they sat under a hair dryer. Others read magazines while they waited for their hair to dry. Many women found it difficult to apply nail color with a professional finish. Before applying nail color, the beauty salon made sure that the nails were free from grease. They used long straight strokes of the brush from the half moon to the free edge, covering the nail with as few strokes as possible and resisting the temptation to go back and retouch. They allowed plenty of time for varnish to harden as well as to dry. The hardening process took up to half an hour was hastened if the finger tips were put under the cold water tap when the varnish was dry. the manicure, followed by a harmonizing nail varnish and a final hand massage sent women out in to the streets floating a foot off the ground and feeling simply gorgeous. Certain beauty routines like the permanent wave and facial make-up grew increasingly elaborate when compared to the preceding decades.

Demand for female hairdressers, stylists and assistants outstripped supply and resulted in the setting up of technical training schools and employment bureaus specifically aimed at women. It was one that Hanna had attended and served an on-the-job apprenticeship in order to become a fully accredited, certified and licensed hairstylist. Hairdressers were expected to have an updated knowledge of hygiene, science and medicine. To reflect this they wore a white salon coat and maintained a high standard of cleanliness and neatness in their ordinary attire. It was no longer simply enough to be a hairdresser, they had to be versed in all branches of the profession, competent in the operation and understanding of newer, complex technologies as well as fundamental knowledge of skin and hair diseases. Apart from this knowledge, hairdressers were expected to be able to diagnose, prescribe and dispense chemical lotions and pomades for curative treatments of the hair and scalp, which they were required to mix themselves. A licensed professional stylist was the only person who could truly determine whether a person's hair was healthy enough for any type of treatment. If a woman's hair had been previously treated with color, bleach or relaxants, seeing a professional first was especially important. If the stylist decided that a particular treatment was an acceptable option for their hair type and condition, then they would discuss healthy cut and styling requirements in addition to the perming process.

By the 1940s, "cold waves," which relied only on chemicals and not heat for perms, gained in popularity. Home permanent kits also grew increasingly popular, but the threat of hair "disaster" remained ever present, causing many women to seek the expertise of a more experienced hairdresser in hopes of avoiding such catastrophes. Cold waves used no machines and no heat. The hair was wrapped on rods and a reduction lotion containing ammonium thioglycolate was applied. The chemical reacted with the keratin (the protein structure in the hair) affecting its elasticity. Next, hydrogen peroxide, an oxidation lotion, was applied and the hair took on the shape of the rod. The entire process took 6–8 hours at room temperature. In the 1970s, ammonia-free acid perms were used with glyceryl monothioglycolate in the place of ammonia. They were slower but gentler to the hair. Heat was usually added by placing the client under a dryer, after covering the wrapped head with a plastic cap. Today sodium thioglycolate is used instead reducing the time to only 15–30 minutes of exposure to the sodium thioglycolate solution before a neutralizer solution is applied.

The Hamilton Beach Co. had sold a hair dryer small enough to be held by hand but they were heavy, weighing in at about 2 pounds (0.9 kg), and were difficult to use. They required an increased amount of time to dry hair and they had many instances of overheating and electrocution. In 1951 consumers were introduced to the bonnet hair dryer. It came in a small portable box which was connected to a tube that went into a bonnet with holes in it that was placed on top of a person's head. The dryer worked by giving an even amount of heat to the whole head at once. In 1954 the design of the hand held hair dryer was changed moving the motor inside the casing. In 1956 portable hand-held hair dryers really caught on with the introduction of better electrical motors and the use of plastics making them more lightweight and allowed women to be their own hairstylist. With the new cold perm method and new portable hair dryers, do it yourself home perms rose in popularity.

Toni introduced a home permanent product during the early 1950s for women who wanted a permanent wave without the salon price. There were formulas for normal hair, hard-to-curl hair, fine hair, tinted hair, and damaged hair. Women could achieve a variety of looks, from tight curls to a body wave, by selecting the proper rod size. Permanent wave rods are what the hair is wrapped around when doing a home perm. The rods came in a variety of sizes; a small diameter rod created small, tight curls, while large rods produced a loose, wavy look. Rod sizes were mixed to give a combination of curl sizes. It took about three hours to complete a home perm and they lasted as long as a salon perm, about three to four months. Some women found the smell of rotten eggs and vinegar associated with a Toni Perm offensive. Unless the scalp started burning, when the timer dinged the perm was over and the towels were taken out to be boiled in hot water because they smelled also.

The use of home permanent kits decreased as the popularity of permanent waves decreased in the 1980s. It was interesting to note what women wore in their hair or on their heads during this time. Shiny bobby pins and slides were used to keep waves shaped and off the face. Combs and slides made from Bakelite and looking like tortoiseshell were used to keep rolls in place. Slides were used to keep the side hair pinned out of the way or to hold a wave in place, while adding a bit of decoration. Hairpieces, false braids and curls were popular throughout the 1940s and could be either someone's own long hair or added hair pieces. Some ladies with thinning hair or who had been badly burned at the hands of a 1940's salon perm wore wigs. Hairnets were used to keep the back of the hair neat. Colourful flowery head kerchiefs or headscarves were worn either like a turban by being folded into a triangle and tied on top of the head or simply worn around the head and knotted under the chin. They were used as decorative pieces, to keep the hair out of the face or to help keep hair protected from dirt. Ribbons were also worn tied around the head and finished with a bow on the top of the head or to the side. Other times a bow made of a bright ribbon would be pinned into the hair. Turbans were also worn. A turban was a length of material made from soft wool or rayon crepe. It was tied on top of the head and the long ends were then either simply tucked under, or rolled up first then tucked under to create a more defined U-shape.

Hats were a fun part of a woman's attire, with no single style or shape, everything was worn, from the smaller pillboxes and berets to the wide-brimmed fedoras. Hairstyles were easily adopted to fit the hat, or the hat to fit the hairstyle! A hat was easily changed by the addition of adornments like feathers, a veil, bows, beads, flowers or ribbons. Berets made from wool or rayon felt in a variety of plain colours were worn either to one side or pushed straight back off the face. Pillbox hats, stiff and round, were worn on top of the head or at an angle, held onto the head with a hatpin. Wide-brimmed felt fedora style hats with an indent in the top or smaller straw versions with a narrower brim were worn at an angle and were pinned on with a hatpin.

Magazines and the movies featured glamorous new role models to popularize the new "Modern" standards for beauty and heightened their importance to the morale of many women during those times. Magazine advertisements constantly linked beauty products and services to film star looks in a drive to promote their consumption. Women's interest in hair, cosmetics and fashionable dress increased, encouraged by Hollywood films and disseminated in a variety of women's illustrated magazines. In an effort to attain this aura of Hollywood glamour, women eagerly assimilated the appearances and gestures of their screen idols and then looked to magazines for the products and services to help them accomplish it. Hairdressing and especially the salon experience became integral to the attainment of a sophisticated and glamorous, feminine identity. Hollywood's female screen stars' made vibrant cosmetics acceptable in real life The attraction of these individual film star 'looks' greatly influenced female cinema-goers. The romanticism of Paris continued to captivate; whether it was a dress, a hat, perfume or hairstyle, whatever emanated from the French capital had a magical allure. The cupid-bow shaped dark lips and rosebud mouth, the seductive smouldering eyes, the long fluttering lashes, were all looks created by cosmeticians such as Helena Rubinstein, Elizabeth Arden and Max Factor. The film industry created a commercial demand for the cosmetics. Women reproduced the looks of their screen idols by buying or making copy outfits, purchasing make-up and altering their hairstyles to create their own version of a glamorous image. The rise in popularity for all sorts of new and complicated beauty rituals led to a huge growth in beauty salons.

Cold cream developed by Pond's, Elizabeth Arden, Helena Rubinstein and others formed the basis of every beauty regime. By establishing a daily regime, cosmetic companies hoped they could increase the usage of their creams and widen consumer consumption to entire product lines. Applying cold cream before sleep to remove the dirt, grime, and cosmetics of the day became a habit for many women. It cleansed the skin and, if not removed with soap and water, left a thin film with moisturising properties. As the use of make-up increased, cold creams were also promoted as a way to help remove face powder, lipstick, rouge, foundation and other forms of make-up. Pond's cold cream was marketed as a food and cleanser for tired pores to be gently massaged into the face, neck hands and arms each night on retiring. Because it supplemented the natural oil of the skin it helped in preventing and eradicating wrinkles around the eyes and mouth. Pond's began selling Pond's Extract Cold Cream and Pond's Extract Vanishing Cream in 1904. The marketing campaign promoted the use of each cream as part of a skin-care system; the cold cream as a cleanser, and for massaging the skin at night; the vanishing cream as a skin protectant during the day. Advertising stressed the need for both creams and gave detailed instructions on how they were to be used. For many women this was the first time they had a simple skin-care routine they could follow.

In the 1930s, Pond's introduced a series of hand cream formulations starting with Pond's Hand Lotion and Pond's Danya Cream Lotion (1937) followed by Pond's Angel Skin (1953) which was aimed firmly at the housewife with 'detergent hands'. In 1946, Pond's introduced their Angel Face compact powder. As a powder-cream it was applied with a puff rather than with the wet sponge needed for cake make-up. Then Pond's announced a completely different kind of new make-up, Pond's Angel Face, a foundation and powder all in one. It was not a cake make-up and not a greasy foundation and was applied with its own downy puff. A smoothing 'cling' ingredient made Angel Face go on evenly and to stay on longer than powder. Shades included were Blonde Angel, Ivory Angel, Pink Angel, Tawny Angel, Bronze Angel, Blushing Angel, Gypsy, Golden Angel. Their 1948 advertisement promised that "hours after a make-up with Angel Face, your skin still looks exquisitely fresh and velvety." In the early 1940s there were fewer shades of makeup and nail polishes, powder and lipstick was dry and flaky; shortages of alcohol meant more perfume and less cologne. Shortages of fat, oils and the complete absence of glycerine resulted in products with no emollients. Nail polishes were made with film scrap instead of nitro-cellulose. After the war, in the late 1940s lipstick shades became lighter and emphasis shifted away from the lips to the eyes.

Pan-Cake was the product that defined what came to be called cake make-up. It came in 6 shades and first appeared in 1947. It was water-based, containing a highly pigmented powder incorporated into a dehydrated cream made from triethanolamine stearate (a soap), lanolin and water, so it was regarded as a dehydrated powder cream. It was manufactured by adding fillers such as talc and pigments like iron oxides to oils and waxes that had been previously mixed in water with the aid of a dispersing agent. After blending the mixture into an even paste, it was dried and then pulverised into a fine powder. As the pigment particles had absorbed the oils and waxes they became water repellent, a quality they retained when pressed into cakes.

Commercially Pan-Cake by Max Factor was a tremendous success for Max Factor and this led to the release of similar products by other cosmetic companies. Loose face powder looked darker in the box than it did when spread on the face but after a while women learnt to match the colour of the bulk powder with their skin tone. As a good deal of pressure was required to lift powder from the tablet it was virtually impossible to use a 'swan's down' puff (actually made from gooseflesh) and puffs made from chamois, lamb's-wool or cotton (e.g., velour) were used instead, with synthetic materials coming into play at a later date. Although these were not as soft as down, they had the advantages of being less likely to spill powder on clothing and could be made very thin to fit into a small compact.

Flapjack' compacts became very popular. At 100mm in diameter they were up to twice the size of previous compacts. Although they were originally designed for use on dressing tables women carried them around to take advantage of the larger mirror and increased powder source. Although pressed powder compacts were popular and technical advances meant that compressed cakes became softer which enabled the use of softer puffs. Compacts containing loose face powder also underwent developments. Improved machine tolerances meant that lids and other parts fitted more snuggly, while advancements in metal and fabric filters, improved the delivery of loose powder to the puff. Progress meant that by the 1930s women could carry loose powder in a compact with little risk that it would spill.

During the 1950s, the range of face powders and foundations was matched by an equal variety of lipstick, eye shadow and nail varnish colours. Paler lipstick tints appeared designed to enhance and contrast with the beauty of a summer tan. With a large number of mid-tone colours, 'Italian Pink' was a favourite colour and 'Sari Peach' was the most popular shade. At the time, Woolworths produced a more affordable lipstick line at the lower end of the price scale. Softer coloured lip shades made the mouth less noticeable and attention was drawn toward to the eyes instead. Eyelash curlers began to appear as did artificial eyelashes, fluid eyeliner, cake eyeliner, eye shadow sticks, cream shadow and waterproof creme mascara. Eye make-up remover became available in pads. The upper lid of the eye was emphasised by a thick black line applied using the newly fashionable liquid eye liner. Natural brows were accentuated with dark pencil. The eye decoration resembled that seen in ancient Egypt. Eye shadows in a vast range of colours were sold in cream or compressed powder which were applied with water and brush. Some eye shadows resembled colour crayons and were sold in metal holders. Glitter eye shadows were created by adding fish scales to the powder. Violet mascara, blue eyeliner, silver eye shadow, copper mascara with green frost shadow were popular bold colour combinations.

The 1930's to the 1960's were the golden age for men's barbershops. During this time, men socialized in all male hangouts, and barbershops rivaled taverns in popularity. For some visiting the barbershop was a weekly, and sometimes daily habit. Men would stop in not only for a haircut and a shave, but also to fraternize with friends and to catch up on the news, discuss politics, cars, sports, and family. In between the banter and current events, jokes were told and laughs were had and everyone was involved; the barbers, the customers getting their haircut, and the customers waiting to get their haircut. Adding to the enjoyment was that a variety of men took part in the conversation; young, old, and middle-aged joined in the mix. I enjoyed getting a haircut and listening to the conversations. The barber used scissors to cut hair and he used hot lather and a straight razor to clean up the area on the back of my neck and around my ears. Barbers were trained to cut with clippers, the main tool in cutting a man's hair. Years later barbers used electric hair trimmers beside scissors.

Barbershops were classy places with marble counters lined with colorful glass blown tonic bottles. The barber chairs were elaborately carved from oak and walnut, and fitted with fine leather upholstery. The chair was fixed to the floor, with adjustable height (with a foot-operated jack). It could also rotate, or lean backwards (for hair washing). Everything from the shaving mugs to the advertising signs were rendered with an artistic flourish. Some shops even had crystal chandeliers hanging from fresco painted ceilings. Barbershops were homey and inviting with a memorable aroma of cherry, wintergreen, apple, and butternut flavored pipe and tobacco smoke mixed with the scent of hair tonics, pomades, oils, and neck powders filling the air. These aromas became ingrained in the wood and every cranny of the shop. The moment a man stepped inside, he was enveloped in the warm and welcoming familiarity. He was able to relax, and as soon as the hot lather hit his face, his cares simply melted away. Many fell asleep while getting a shave. Barbers were specially trained to give customers a thorough and quick shave, and a collection of straight razors ready for use was a common sight in most barbershops. Barbers always had interesting stories to tell. Clients felt at ease to say whatever was on their mind. Only a few barbershops remained during the 1980's. Hairdresser salons siphoned off the barbers' former customers and catered to both men and women. These salons became experts in styling, coloring, and perming; things a man has no need for. Men found it difficult to get a good haircut.

Most men shaved at home with a straight razor which was the most common form of shaving until the 1950s. To be most effective, a straight razor had to be kept extremely sharp and that required considerable skill to hone and strop and required more care during shaving. The hanging leather strop was handmade of full grain horse hide, bark tanned and finished in the ancient Cordovan process by the Horween Co. of Chicago, Illinois. Horween was the oldest and sole surviving horse hide tannery in the USA, and a major supplier of fine stropping leather since 1905. The front leather was smooth and designed for daily use. The leather on the back was hand embossed in a diamond (Russian) pattern for use when a razor began to pull. Due to the Cordovan process, water did not harm this exquisite leather. The strop maintained its beautiful iridescent color for generations and needed only a gentle massage between the fingers to keep the hide supple. The sharp edge of the blade was delicate, and inexpert use could bend or fold over the razor's edge. To unfold and straighten the microscopic sharp edge, the blade had to be stropped on a leather strop periodically. Care was taken so that the blade never rotated on the strop about the cutting edge so as not to damage the sharp edge. The blade was sharpened about twice a year by honing it with a sharpening stone. Most men had several razor sharpening stones made of silicon carbide to sharpen and hone their straight razors. The stones were very fast cutting even when used dry and produced an extremely sharp cutting edge.

Williams Mug Shaving Soap in a cup was used extensively. It was lathered and applied using a a shaving brush whose handle was made from ivory or tortoise shell and had silvertip badger bristles (the most expensive and rare type of badger hair). The "flared" bristles gave the 'silvertip brush a fluffy appearance and enabled the brush to hold a large amount of water. The more water a brush held, the moister and richer the lather was. Thicker and more emollient lather translated to less razor skipping and dragging. In the mid-1950s, aerosol cans were introduced, and the Barbasol Company changed the formula of its shaving cream from the thick cream in a tube to the soft, fluffy foam familiar in the aerosol cans today. The can design mimicked a barber's pole, and is still the trademark design used today. The shave was completed using as few strokes as possible, stropping sparingly if at all. A second shave with another razor in an alternate direction against the beard yielded an extremely close shave. A light steady touch was most effective at providing a close shave, preserving the edge and avoiding cuts. Rinsing with cold water and using an astringent or aftershave lotion constricted minor abrasions or cuts. More serious nicks were attended to with direct pressure for perhaps a minute with a styptic pencil which applied a form of alum, usually aluminum sulfate, or titanium dioxide to the wound. This caused the blood vessels to contract and stop bleeding and the spot would not be red since blood-flow to that particular area was constricted. The pencil promoted healing and removed most itches and irritation.

Straight razors fell out of fashion when a double-edged safety razor with replaceable blades was manufactured by Gillette. Shaving became less intimidating and men began to shave themselves more, the demand for barbers providing straight razor shaves decreased. Safety razors provided a less effective shave, yet were immensely successful due to advertising campaigns and slogans. Gillette's jingle for their blades went like this:
>To look sharp every time you shave,
>To feel sharp and be on the ball,
>To be sharp, use Gillette Blue Blades,
>It's the quickest, slickest shave of all!

In 1939, Gillette had purchased rights to the World Series. A special promotion of Gillette razors and blue blades sold four times better than company estimates and Gillette sought additional sports sponsorships. The Gillette Company sponsored the Cavalcade of Sports, a diversified field of sporting events, which officially began on radio in 1942. The radio sports programs spanned several different networks (including NBC, CBS, and Mutual) and grew to include not only ongoing sponsorship of the World Series and All-Star Game in baseball, but the annual Kentucky Derby in horseracing and football's Cotton Bowl Classic, Rose Bowl, and Orange Bowl; several golfing tournaments and the NHL's Stanley Cup playoffs and Friday night boxing on NBC from 1944 through 1960.

The new safety razors did not require any serious learning to use. The blades were meant to be thrown away after one use, and rusted quickly if not discarded. In 1957, Gillette introduced an "adjustable" razor enabling the blade to be adjusted to increase the closeness of the shave. In 1960 came Gillette's super blue blade. It had a silicon coating. It cut better than the blue blade, but it wore out fast. The same year, stainless steel blades that could be used more than once became available, reducing the cost of safety-razor shaving. The first such blades were made by the Wilkinson firm, famous maker of ceremonial swords, in Sheffield, England. Wilkinson's market share grew rapidly at the expense of Gillette which countered in 1963 with its own stainless blade which replaced the older blue blades in popularity. Soon Gillette, Schick, and other manufacturers were making stainless-steel blades. Wilkinson blades became harder to find and Gillette regained market dominance..In 1971 Gillette introduced it's two-edge blade followed years later by multiple-blade cartridges and disposable razors. For each type of replaceable blade, there was generally a disposable razor. Soon better electric razors also became available. On October 1, 2005, The Gillette Company was merged with Procter & Gamble and as a result the Gillette Company ceased to exist. Gillette continues as a brand of Procter & Gamble for safety razors, among other personal care products.

Men used Brilliantine, a perfumed and colored oily liquid as a hair-grooming product that softened their hair, beards and moustaches and gave them a glossy, well-groomed appearance. Men's wartime hairstyle of short back and sides was pretty-much standard until the early 1960's, with a little dab of "Brylcreem" sold in a tube that kept combed hair in place while giving it a shiny "wet" look. Brylcreem was de rigueur for many years and was heavily advertised on radio by this catchy jingle:
>"Brylcreem — A Little Dab'll Do Ya!"
>Brylcreem, you'll look so debonair.

Brylcreem, the gals will all pursue ya,
They'll love to run their fingers through your hair."

Men used Old Spice or Aqua Velva as an aftershave lotion containing denatured alcohol as an antiseptic agent that prevented infection from cuts. Barbers used Bay Rum Aftershave which was imported from Dominica, "The Nature Island of the Caribbean". Bay Rum was a masterful blending of the purest of alcohol, exotic herbs and spices, and the leaf extract from the Bay Tree. The aftershave lotions left the skin feeling clean, fresh, smooth and lightly scented. On June 18, 1941, I listened to the boxing match radio broadcast sponsored by Gillette between Joe Louis and Billy Conn in front of a crowd of 54,487 fans at the Polo Grounds in New York City. The fight was one of the greatest heavyweight boxing fights of all time with Joe Louis knocking Conn out with two seconds left in the thirteenth round.

In late autumn every year we stood with a crowd of people and watched the Eaton's Santa Claus parade on Park Avenue. In the winter my friends and I were busy with school homework but we did listen to the radio. There were dramas and mysteries: Inner Sanctum, The Shadow, Lux Radio Theater, The Green Hornet, Sergeant Preston and his dog King of the Northwest Mounted Police, Superman and Radio City Playhouse. Outdoors in the winter we played hockey on the street, built snow forts and threw snowballs. After a heavy snowfall, we built tunnels through the snow banks and played inside them.

My friends Georges (who later joined the Montreal police force), his brother André, Jacques, Pierre and I attended indoor sports activities including boxing, wrestling, basketball and swimming at the YMCA / YMHA on Park Avenue and Mount Royal respectively. There was also bowling and wrestling at the Loisirs de St Jean Baptiste on Rachel Street and Berri Street. Bowling was very popular during the period from 1940 to 1960 known as the golden age of bowling. Bowling alleys employed pin boys to set up pins that had been knocked down. In the late 1940s pin boys were being replaced by semi-automatic pinspotters and in the mid 1950s by fully automatic pinspotters with quicker delivery of returned balls. \

I received our first phonograph or gramophone (vinyl record player) in 1950 from our landlord's son in law. They were trading up to an electrically powered record player so I got their manual windup version along with a recording of Twinkle, Twinkle Little Star sung by Bing Crosby. The phonograph was a portable one and had a picture painted on the inside cover of a dog Nipper listening to a wind-up gramophone. The dog was listening to a phonograph cylinder and the words below the picture said "His Master's Voice". This Master's Voice trademark image was owned by the Victor Talking Machine Company which was purchased in 1929 by RCA-Victor. A few years later I purchased a standalone electric RCA-Victor phonograph and all of my vinyl records and because I enjoyed listening to harmonica music i acquired an album called "Jerry Murad's Harmonicats", a wonderful recording by an American harmonica-based group from Sinclair Radio store on the Main.

During the half century from 1930 an overwhelming majority of people smoked tobacco either in cigarettes, pipes or by sniffing or chewing. The significant health effects of smoking were not known at that time and cigarette or pipe smoking was cool, cheap, legal and socially acceptable. Hollywood stars made smoking look sensual and sophisticated and more than half of the population of industrialised nations smoked. Movies from the 1930s to 1960s, displayed men and women smoking cigarettes; men smoking cigars or with a pipe in their mouths. Turret Cigarettes were produced by Ogden's of Liverpool, a division of Imperial Tobacco Canada and were very popular in the 1940s as were the factory made (FM) cigarettes from MacDonald's Export A, Sweet Caporal, Camel, Lucky Strike, Pall Mall, Marboro and Players Navy Cut among others. These same companies also sold fine cut tobacco enabling smokers to roil their own (RYO). Fine-cut tobacco used to make RYO cigarettes were taxed at a lower rate than FM cigarettes favouring smokers who tended to have lower incomes and those who wanted to compensate price increases. People who rolled their own claimed that they used about half the tobacco as that found in FM cigarettes. They also claimed that after you go through the withdrawal of the chemicals in premade cigarettes, you actually enjoy your smoke more. I started smoking with cigarettes, graduated to smoking cigars and settled on smoking a pipe using Erinmore pipe tobacco mixture for several years. The tobacco was naturally sweetened bright Virginia premium tobacco hand blended with cool-smoking black Cavendish tobacco which produced the unique citrus fruit flavor and distinctive aroma of Erinmore. The mixture was a mellow, slow-burning, aromatic tobacco with a cool taste. Pipe smoking was really no different from cigarettes or cigar smoking as all three involved inhaling smoke produced by burning tobacco. Pipes were produced in several models. I had several and probably favoured the full bent briar wood pipe most.

PRINCE   ZULU   FULL-BENT

Beside different models, pipes were made from an assortment of materials including briar, clay, ceramic, corncob, glass, meerschaum, metal, gourd, stone, and wood. Perfectionists even discriminated by size of the pipe's bowl, saying that it depended on what was going to be smoked. Strong tasting, harsh tobaccos, the smoke from which is not intended to be inhaled requires a larger bowl. Milder tobaccos which are inhaled require smaller bowls. Pipe smoking was considered a manly art; it was as much ritual as it was relaxation. To smoke a pipe one needed a pipe, a pipe tamper tool to pack the tobacco into the pipe bowl, pipe cleaners, wooden matches or a pipe lighter and tobacco.

After World War II, major breakthroughs were made in epidemiological research. It was observed that there was a relationship between rising rates of lung cancer and the increasing numbers of smokers. It was always suspected that all tobacco products delivered nicotine to the central nervous system, However in the 1980s, scientists established that nicotine was extremely addictive. This was a confirmed risk of dependence. The tobacco companies publicly rejected such claims, even as they took advantage of cigarettes' addictive potential by routinely spiking them with extra nicotine to make it harder to quit smoking. More research uncovered that tobacco use was associated with a significantly increased risk of morbidity and premature mortality due to tobacco-related diseases. Further evidence uncovered that tobacco smoke contained carcinogens that increased a person's risk with increased exposure. Then, in 1994, the tobacco industry was sued in the largest potential class action suit in history. Thereafter efforts were undertaken to protect non-smokers from being exposed to second hand smoking leading to the 1995 ban on smoking in most enclosed places of employment. In 2004 a judge of the Federal District Court for the District of Columbia concluded that the tobacco industry had engaged in a 40-year conspiracy to defraud smokers about tobacco's health dangers. The majority of people including myself quit smoking.

On Mount Royal street east of the Main was D. Leonard Photo Studio where families went to get baby pictures, family portraits, graduation pictures, wedding photos, to record precious moments that held personal significance to them and their loved ones. All such portraits were precious and rare investments for many people which they mailed to and received from family across the seas. The studio had darkrooms and sitting areas featuring skylights and banks of windows that exploited the soft natural light that was controlled with a system of adjustable blinds. Mr. Leonard prepared sensitized plates for exposure and ducking under the cloth cape of his camera used them to take the picture after carefully directing lighting, obscuring shadows, and getting the right pose. He then developed the plates and several days later the people came back to view the proofs and selected the photos that they then bought. People did not have easy access to taking pictures or sharing them as they do today. Modern cellphone cameras have made professional portrait taking obsolete.

I had purchased an Eastman Kodak Hawkeye Brownie with attached flash camera from my earnings working in the summer at Steinbergs Groceteria Supermarket on St Denis Street. It was a simple black bakelite camera that used Kodak 135 film and had a fixed-focus lens and used flash bulbs. The bulbs yielded a bright flash but were fragile and could only be used once. After being fired the bulbs were too hot to handle right away. People were able to get their exposed films developed and obtained paper prints from a service offered by all drug stores. In 1954 many of my neighbours had a Leica 35 mm rangefinder camera which they all praised very highly. In 1963 Kodak introduced the immensely successful inexpensive, easy-to-load Instamatic cameras. They were the first cameras to use Kodak's new 126 format. The easy-load film cartridge made the cameras very inexpensive to produce. They were an instant success; more than 50 million Instamatic cameras were produced between 1963 and 1970. I took many photos and slides with this camera. In 1970 a new series of Instamatics was introduced to take advantage of the new Magicube flash technology which did not require batteries. In the 1970s I had a Polaroid SX-70 instant camera. It was a folding single lens reflex camera with a built-in flash that used a self-developing film to create a chemically developed print without chemical residue shortly after taking the picture. Pictures were quickly ejected automatically. The Polaroid SX-70 instant camera was the best-selling camera of the 1977 Christmas shopping season,

Films used for prints was generally a dangerously flammable Eastman Kodak nitrate-based nitrocellulose cellulose film which Kodak began replacing in 1949 with the safer, more robust cellulose triacetate-based "Safety" films. By 1952, all camera and projector films were triacetate-based. Most if not all film prints today are made from synthetic polyester safety base (which started replacing Triacetate film for prints in the early 1990s). Kodak had developed a digital camera in 1975, the first of its kind, the product was dropped for fear it would threaten Kodak's photographic film business. In the 1990s, Kodak planned a decade-long journey to move to digital technology. Consumers gradually switched to the digital offering from companies such as Sony and in 2001 film sales dropped.

CHAPTER 5 - Daily Living

Washrooms with toilets and less frequently with bathtubs started to become standard equipment in the homes of labourers. Before amenities of this kind were added, however, existing dwellings had to be connected to the municipal sewer system and have plumbing installed for cold running water. Cities ever so slowly were installing cold water piping replacing wells and sewer systems eliminating outdoor toilets, outhouses and latrines in the backyards. Hygiene took on greater importance thanks to the efforts of public health doctors and various organizations that made it a top priority and pressured the authorities to improve sanitary conditions particularly in poor neighbourhoods. Residential builders were required to meet increasingly strict standards respecting ventilation, drinking water piping and the elimination of waste water. Residential buildings in the neighbourhood consisted of either a duplex or triplex, (a two- or three-storey building) many with exterior winding stairs to the upper floors and with no front lawn. Homes tended to be small with a kitchen and two or at most four narrow rooms and a tiny toilet closet. Typically these homes had a two window bedroom in the front and another small windowless bedroom between it and the kitchen with a window at the back. On upper floors, the kitchen shared space with the stairs leading from the downstairs front door. The kitchen had a tiny little closet sized room which housed a toilet where aside from a toilet paper dispenser or nail on the wall impaled with tissues garnered from the fruit market or telephone book pages, there was a light and an overhead water box with pull chain attached to flush the toilet. There was no sink, no mirror, no towel rack, and no bathtub or shower. The kitchen sink served multiple purposes. Most flats had access to a gallery or a shed at the back of the home where double windows for winter and wood and coal were stored. Almost all of them had no central heating and no hot water. They were called cold flats because they only had cold running water. Hot water was only available to the tenants when they heated the water on their wood and coal stoves.

Full-scale domestic hot-water services, heating water centrally and piping it throughout the house, had been advertised since the 1920s, but by 1943 only a small percentage of households had a hot-water service and most of the households were still heating their bathwater on the stove. It was only in the mid 1950s that standard bathroom fittings for the home became available. By the early 1960s people no longer considered 'continuous hot water a luxury, but a necessity; where families could simply turn a tap to obtain a copious supply of hot water for washing, bathing, cooking and cleaning. Landlords were finding it more difficult to rent cold water flats and when costs of hot water systems declined there was an increase in the number of houses installing gas or electric hot-water services. The installation of a bathtub, hot water heater and plumbing in the relatively small cold water flats often posed major and expensive renovation costs for most landlords. Domestic hot water consumption heralded the rapid decline of the traditional bath-night. People could now take a bath or shower whenever they liked, without having to bring in a galvanized metal tub into the kitchen, heating pots and kettles with water on the stove; and filling the tub to take a bath and then having to empty the tub. Domestic hot water service laid the foundation for the introduction of other household appliances such as the washing machine and, later, the dishwasher. In the 1960s, architectural plans for new houses included separate shower recesses and in the 1970s, ensuite bathrooms were being planned as well. It was a far cry from the time when the bathroom was the worst decorated room in the house, just a utilitarian, cold and sterile room where people did their business. At that time it had no daring colour scheme, no wallpaper, no soft carpet and no comfort. In 1978 the bathroom was undergoing a 'revolution of thought although remaining structurally unchanged the bathroom was getting a touch of luxury.

There were some exceptions and in our neighbourhood during the 1940s and 1950s, some families were better off than others and rented houses that had more rooms, were equipped with hot water and had bathtubs. These flats with hot water heater radiators, central heat or hot water boilers and bathtubs rented for much more than the typical working class cold flat home. In order to meet the higher rent payments many renters turned them into rooming houses and rented out rooms. Some even became boarding houses, providing meals; others shared the kitchen and bathroom with their roomers. The recent and newly arrived families could not afford the heated, more appropriately-sized housing, so they often shared these relatively tiny cold flats with another family. It was common for children to share a bedroom and even a bed with their siblings. Some of the homes were very crowded, were poorly ventilated and lacked air circulation. Cold flats were heated with a cast iron wood and coal cooking stove with natural gas burners.
The centerpiece of every cold flat kitchen was the La Salle Belanger coal / gas stove with a lot of shiny nickel trim, built by the Belanger Foundry in Montreal.

Some had a warming oven about two feet above the stove top; others had a shelf on which people kept an alarm clock and a box of wooden matches. The stove stood over five feet high and almost three and a half feet wide and had a large cook top surface with four cast iron round lids on top where kettles and pots of water or soup were heated, In addition it had two top gas burners and a cook oven. Natural gas and electricity was supplied by The Montreal Light, Heat and Power Company (MLH&P) headquartered on Craig and St Urbain street near the streetcar terminus. It was nationalized in 1944 and was called the Quebec Hydroelectric Commission (Hydro-Québec) who ran the operation until 1957; at which point it's gas properties were sold to the Corporation de gaz naturel du Québec (Gaz Métropolitain).

Cast iron stoves easily handled the repeated temperature swings of hot and cold and when they got hot they radiated heat all around. Most of the homes kept a fire burning almost non-stop, throughout the winter months providing enough heat to keep the entire house warm and cozy despite the extremely cold outdoor temperatures. Children were told over and over again to never touch the stove when it was hot and often much to their regret they had to learn the hard way. Wood logs were ordered by the cord from the farmers in the market or from the wood and coal delivery man who dumped it into backyards or lanes so that the purchasers could chop the logs into manageable fire wood size and kindling. These were stacked on the wood pile beside the coal bin in the shed. Coal was ordered by the ton which the coal man delivered in sacks; bag by bag carried on his back, through the house and dumped into the coal bin in the shed.

Heating with wood and coal required lots of work. Wood and coal had to be brought in to feed the fire and ash had to be cleaned out, sifted through a large metal screen to remove unburned coal which was reused and the ash had to be disposed of daily with the garbage. This was the procedure followed by all of our neighbours until the switch to home heating oil was made in the 1950s. The stove was connected by an umbilical metal stove pipe to the chimney enhancing the draw for the stove and exhausting the smoke. Stove pipes typically ran across the kitchen and were hot to touch adding heat to the entire area. Coal burned best with a supply of air from below, so it was necessary to adjust the top and bottom air vents of the stove to regulate the fire. Often starting a fire in a cold stove on a very cold day was a frustrating and smoky experience. Twisted newspaper had to be burned first to generate a quick hot heat that warmed up the air in the chimney and created a better draft. Attention had to be given to the stove's fire chamber which was lined with insulating fire bricks that periodically had to be replaced. Chimneys used the pressure difference caused by a hot column of gas to create a draught and drew air over the hot coals or wood enabling continued combustion. During normal operation a layer of soot and creosote would build up on the inside of the chimney restricting the flow and making it necessary to have the chimney swept to remove the soot or the hot fire could end up in the chimney instead of in the stove. With the soot on fire, it could easily set the chimney and the building on fire. In order to avoid house fires chimney sweepers covered from head to toe in black soot, came around twice a year offering their services for a fee usually followed several days later by city inspectors. The chimney sweeps did not have vacuums or cameras and got real dirty performing their jobs knowing that the sound of a crackling fire on a cold winter day ensured warmth and comfort throughout the house. After cleaning the chimney, the chimney sweeps issued receipts which had to be shown to city inspectors. The chimney sweeps came with ladders and chimney tools such as round, oval, square and rectangular wire flue brushes that ranged in sizes from 5" to 14" in diameter. There were three that were commonly used; an oil tempered steel one, a stainless steel one and a polypropylene plastic brush. They carried U shaped wire hand brushes with attached scrapers and chimney rods used to push the brushes through the flue. They removed creosote deposits from the interior of the chimney along with bird nests, cobwebs and other blockages.

The alternative to taking a bath at home in the galvanized tub filled with hot water heated on the stove, was to use the Schubert Public Bath which still stands today at the corner of Bagg and St. Lawrence. It cost ten cents for admission and people had to bring their own soap and towel. Public health and hygiene officials together with progressive members of Montreal's upper middle class urged the City of Montreal to build a sanitary bath for every neighbourhood where local workers could go to wash up after a hard day's work. The situation prompted the construction of public baths and for them to be named for city councillors of the district. Our city councillor for the district known as the St Louis ward, was Joseph Schubert (1889-1952), a Romanian Jew, the district's first Jewish City Council alderman in the 1920s and 1930s. The Schubert Bath opened in 1931, offering hot water bathing to Montrealers who didn't have any hot water in their homes. According to city archives, Montreal built 23 public baths at the time. Thousands of Montrealers living in cold water flats who were deprived of indoor plumbing frequented these public baths in the pursuit of hygiene and health. Today, some of these public baths have been abandoned, others repurposed and some have been preserved. In 2000 the Schubert Bath underwent a $2-million renovation offering the citizens a place to relax with recreational swimming and for water sports training.

There was also the Colonial Turkish Steam Baths on Colonial Street near Napoleon which were preferred by many of the immigrants who were already familiar with this type of social bathing. These baths were more in the nature of a sauna or steam room and were frequented by almost all of our neighbours. The Turkish bath started with relaxation in a warm room that was heated by a continuous flow of hot, dry air, allowing the bather to perspire freely. Bathers could then move to an even hotter room with more steam before they washed in cold water. After performing a full body wash and receiving a massage, bathers finally retired to the cooling-room for a period of relaxation. Both bath houses had weekly days set for ladies only with most other days set aside for men only. Even with warmth supplied by the stove, people suffering with cold winter chills, arthritis and rheumatism swore that the Turkish Baths helped a lot. There were no heating pads so rubber hot water bottles filled with hot water and sealed with a stopper, were a must have in many of the homes. The rubber hot water bottles were readily available at drug stores and were used to provide warmth while in bed and to apply heat to a specific part of the body helping people suffering from arthritis and rheumatism. Today they have been replaced by better heated homes and electric heating pads and blankets.

In the cold flats the only source of water was the single sink in the kitchen which were made of porcelain enameled iron. They had to be cleaned with Bon Ami, a very gentle scouring powder, to avoid scratches which would lead to rust. Bon Ami was a regular dependable household cleaner whose slogan was "Hasn't Scratched Yet!" referring to its ability to clean without scratching porcelain plumbing fixtures. Most cooking pots were also porcelain enameled, although aluminum ware was just becoming popular. Nobody outside of a commercial setting had stainless steel kitchen fixtures. All skillets were cast iron and steel wool pads were used to scour these, along with kitchen cleansing powders like Old Dutch and Comet. Dishes were washed in the kitchen sink, usually with the same soap that was used for the laundry; flaked or chipped soaps like Rinso, Chipso, or Oxydol. These were all *soaps,* not detergents, so there was a lot of rinsing to make sure the dishes didn't end up scummy. In the late 1940s Vel liquid detergent soap made by Colgate-Palmolive was promoted as being milder for the hands, made for washing dishes and fine fabrics. Vel's new soapless suds required no hard scouring and removed grease faster, cutting dishwashing time in half leaving dishes and glassware gleaming without wiping.

Mondays on the street meant wash day involving a homemaker, her hair tied up with a kerchief; dressed with a full-length apron over her dress in a steam-filled kitchen, draped over a basin filled with soap and water, with a scrub board scrubbing clothes. In winter washday had the windows all steamed up with water vapour condensation running down the windows making every surface feel damp and filling the entire house with the smell of wet clothes. Hanging wet clothes in freezing weather or bringing them back in when they were dry was not much fun either and many complained of cold and chapped fingers. Bringing in frozen long woolen underwear (long johns) provided some merriment as they continued to stand in their frozen state until they were thawed out. Washday was incredibly hard work that had to be done each week, no matter what the weather or the season. Winter and summer washing was done by hand,. A round galvanised tin ribbed basin or tub about two feet high and four feet wide was brought into the kitchen from the shed. Besides being a wash basin it was the same tub that served as a bathtub on bath night. Some families used the tub during the week for anything that was dirty and needed washing, ready for wash day to come round. Pots and a kettle of water filled at the kitchen sink were heated on the wood and coal stove and on the gas range. The hot water was used to fill the wash basin. The dirty clothes were sorted into separate piles; one for those that required scrubbing; one for the whites, another for the coloureds and another pile for all the delicates. The whites were added to the tub of hot water and allowed to soak. The clothes that were the cleanest were washed first since the water was re-used for the next load.

Clothes requiring scrubbing were placed in a smaller tub of hot water along with the scrub board, brush and the old reliable Sunlight laundry soap made by Lever Brothers or lye soap, Socks, collars and cuffs of shirts that had particularly grubby areas were first treated to some intensive hand washing with the Sunlight soap and the scrub board with ridges on it. This treatment served two purposes, one it got most of the grime out before it went into the tub to be washed and secondly, it kept the water in the tub from getting dirty too quickly. More delicate items were washed by hand with soap flakes. The sheets, towels and tea-towels were constantly prodded and moved around with a laundry stick. A bluing agent was sometimes added to the whites to make them appear whiter. Dark clothes followed the whites. There were no Kleenex facial tissues or disposable diapers and instead cotton diapers and handkerchiefs were washed by hand.

After the heavy washing was done; the arduous task of rinsing the soap out of the washing began. First, as much as possible of the soapy water was wrung out of the washing by hand, the water going back into the tub to be used for the next load of washing. The wrung out clothes were piled on a wooden chair and were rinsed in cold water in the kitchen sink until the water ran clear and there was no soap left in the clothes. The clothes were then wrung out by hand again to squeeze out as much water as could be. Hand operated wringers were a great invention at that time. Tablecloths, hankies and men's white shirts were starched. The white powdered starch was mixed to a cream, then stirred with boiling water to a glutinous clear liquid in which the articles to be starched were then steeped for five minutes or so. During the 1940s soap manufacturers were engaged in a powerful marketing laundry soap campaign. Ivory laundry soap made by Procter & Gamble was marketed as the "floating soap" with all the fine qualities of a choice toilet soap, and was "99 and 44-100% pure." Another P & G product was Oxydol a laundry soap.

Very few people had carpeting. Most floors were wood or covered with linoleum. Some people had woolen rugs and some made their own by weaving bits and pieces of repurposed textiles braided into an oval rug. Twice a year, in the spring and fall, housewives hauled any rugs that they had out to the backyard or balcony. They draped them over the clothesline and beat all the dust out of them with a metal-wire rug beater. "Uptowners" frequently hired women to clean their homes and to wax their floors. The common cotton mop and wringer pail were usually found in every stairwell or broom closet; messy, but effective for general cleanup. The 1940s were the heyday of labor-saving household products, such as Johnson's Glo-Coat, the first one-step liquid floor polish -- "No Rubbing! No Buffing! You just apply -- and let dry!" Before such things housewives laboriously coated their floors with paste wax, rubbed it in, and then buffed it until the floor shined. These new products were meant to lessen or eliminate the hands-and-knees work, although "buffing mops" were sold. To combat household smells Air-Wick, was introduced as a major breakthrough in air-freshening products. It was a liquid solution, not a spray, heavily scented with pine oil, packaged in a glass bottle with a fiber wick extending into the fluid. The wick was pulled up and the bottle was left in the kitchen or bathroom allowing the fluid to disperse into the atmosphere by evaporation.

Electrically powered washing machines with wringer included as a powered attachment above the washer tub became widely available after Whirlpool Corporation had introduced the first top-loading wringer equipped machines in 1947. It was only in the early 1950s that most people acquired a brand new gleaming white enameled washing machine with powerful wringer rollers. In many cases, washday shifted to Saturday morning. The washing machine still had to be filled up with hot water but was able to be drained by a hose and pumped into the kitchen sink. Cold water rinses were easily accomplished in the machine as well. The greatest relief came from running the dripping clothes between two wringers and squeezing out excess water from the clothes. Electric washing machines with attached wringers were a blessing. The wringer was swung over the wash tub so that extracted wash water fell back into the tub and was reused for the next load. The wringers however were dangerous, especially if a person's fingers, hand, or hair became entangled in the laundry being squeezed. The tub of heavy semi wet clothes still had to be dragged outdoors for the clothes to be hung on the clothesline to dry. Every house had a clothesline or several of them crisscrossing the backyards and laneways. Even with a machine washday was still very labour intensive and demanded careful attention unlike the automatics of today. In the late 1970s, shortly after the invention of the first microprocessors, the first fully automatic washing machine was born which in time replaced washboards and hand operated wringers.

In the 1950s P & G introduced its popular heavy-duty synthetic laundry detergent Tide as a modern washday miracle with the slogan, "Tide's In, Dirt's Out". Tide became the leading detergent which cut into Oxydol's sales and the Oxydol soap formula was discontinued. Oxydol was transformed to a detergent product, with color safe bleach and was one of P&G's best sellers for years. Tide was especially well suited to the electric washing machines that were appearing on the market in the mid 1950s. Tide did not combine with the calcium and magnesium ions found in hard water to form an insoluble curd that turned clothes gray or yellow, left spots on dishes, or left an ugly ring around bathtubs. It was easier to rinse from clothes and dishware and Tide formed more suds, even in cool water. Housewives tended to equate suds with cleaning power. Tide captured nearly a 30 percent slice of laundry product sales.

During the 1940s Lever Brothers Company (later known as Unilever) marketed Rinso soap powder with the slogan "Rinso white, Rinso bright" which boasted that Rinso contained "Solium, the sunlight ingredient". P&G introduced Chipso and Duz soap powders. Duz was advertised as an amazing new kind of soap getting clothes as white as any soap made, yet being safer for colors, and for your hands than any of the other four leading granulated soaps. "You can trust even bright washable prints and pretty rayon undies to those fluffy DUZ suds!" Javel/Javelle or eau de Javel **wa**s a popular bleach which was strong and with improper use could lead to textile damage. Rinso was revamped in the early 1950s as a true detergent, with a bluing agent, and was rebranded as Rinso Blue with different packaging to differentiate it from the still available Rinso White which was still a soap, and not a detergent. By the mid-1960s the soap variation was discontinued; the detergent variation was again reformulated, and given a new name, Sunshine Rinso which eventually disappeared from store shelves by the mid-1970s. In the late 1980s P&G introduced Tide with Bleach, which again cut into the sales of Oxydol.

The textiles used for clothing in the 1940's was unforgiving, particularly clothing made from wool. A mistake made at the washing or ironing stage meant being stuck with the results. Woollen clothing washed in water which was too hot resulted in a matted shrunken miniature of the original which was impossible to return to its previous shape. If it was possible for another member of the family to squeeze into the item that had shrunk, then they would wear it. Even though a shrunken garment did not look particularly good it was still functional.

After the washing, rinsing and wringing out, all of the damp wash was hung out secured to one or two clotheslines with wooden clothes pins to catch the wind and dry. There were no electric dryers. The clotheslines were thin tough ropes strung between two wooden posts with pulleys for moving the line out and in. Most neighbours had two or more long ones from the house to the corner of a shed across a laneway or back yard and perhaps another shorter line on a small balcony. The weather was carefully watched. If the day was fine, the clothes were hung outdoors. The threat of rain saw homemakers rushing out to bring in the clothes, to be hung on clothes lines strung in the house. A windy day was a mixed blessing. It was fine for drying the clothes, but gusty conditions often wrenched the clothes off the line and onto the muddy gardens or dirty lanes below. The real disaster was when the clothesline broke, as it did about once a year. Not only did the whole lot have to be re-washed, but also a new line had to be set up. All the problems associated with wash day meant that clothes had to be kept clean as long as possible.

With the washing on the clothesline, close to noon on Monday, the kitchen was tidied up, dried out and lunch was being prepared. Fast food, apart from kolbasa sandwiches or cold meat with vegetables left over from Sunday, was unheard of and tinned food was not considered nutritious so there was no alternative. With no fast food available, food preparation occupied a considerable portion of a homemaker's day. There was little time to run errands when items were missing in the pantry. A favourite story that Max liked to tell concerned his neighbours Rivkah and Shlomo. Rivkah had said to her husband, Shlomo, "I'm short of some ingredients for the cake I'm baking, so could you please get some things for me from the grocery?" "Of course I can, darling," replied Shlomo. "What do you need?" "Please get one bottle of milk, and if they have eggs, get six." replied Rivkah. Putting his fedora on his head Shlomo quickly left. A short time later he returned with six bottles of milk. Rivkah looked unbelievably at him and said, " What did you do? Where are the eggs? As she continued she became more furious with him and asked, "Why on earth did you buy six bottles of milk?" Looking very puzzled, Shlomo answered, "Because they had eggs," No matter how he tried to explain he could not appease his wife.

It was considered almost a sin to waste anything. Especially food if it was still edible. So no food was discarded if it could be used in another dish. Before the electric domestic refrigerator became commonplace, ice boxes and ice delivery were part of daily life. Instead of going to the market every day for meat, fruit and vegetables, people could buy for more than one day and keep the extra food in their ice box. In the winter food in need of refrigeration was kept in containers outdoors. Lacking refrigeration, most homes had an ice box and in the summer people bought ice from the ice man who came by daily with his horse-drawn ice wagon, offering a single block of ice for 15 cents and a double for 25 cents. Iceboxes were good looking pieces of furniture, made of wood, they had hollow walls lined with tin or zinc and were packed with cork, straw or sawdust insulation. At the top of the box was the ice compartment where the block of ice was placed. Food was kept in the lower storage compartments where cold air from the melting ice kept the food cool. A drip pan under the ice box would fill with water from the melting ice and had to be emptied daily. Regular door-to-door deliveries of block ice was made depending on whether the individual tenants put out their ice sign for a single or double block of ice. The icemen used ice picks to break up the very large blocks of ice he received from the ice factory into ice box sized blocks and then used tongs to lift and carry the blocks. The iceman and his crew wore leather vests and a wet piece of sackcloth slung over the right shoulder with the ice in it to carry it into the homes. Once they slid the ice into the top of the icebox, they slipped the sacking off, were paid and departed ready for the next house. While deliveries were being made, children went up to the ice wagon and took chips of fallen ice and sucked on them as treats. A block of ice could last for as long as five days and of course for much shorter times during a heatwave. People tried to preserve the ice for as long as possible taking care not to run out by cooling hot foods before placing them in the icebox. Running out of ice resulted in food spoilage.

During the war years, even chicken fat (called schmaltz) was saved and used in cooking replacing oil and butter. Sandwiches with ham, egg salad, tuna, salmon, roast beef, salami, kolbasa, grilled cheese with lettuce and tomato were very popular as were a variety of soups such as vegetable, mushroom, borsch (beet soup), krupnik, barley soup, cabbage soup and chicken noodle (lokshen in Yiddish) soup. Other popular soup ingredients were kneidlach (matzo balls) and kreplach (dumplings). Pickled herring with onions, fried cod fillets, halibut, haddock, pike, carp and gefilte fish with chrain (horseradish) as well as beef, pork chops, liver, beef tongue and hard boiled eggs were popular also. Various types of bread, buns and bagels were consumed as well. Traditional breakfasts included eggs turned over easy with La Belle Fermiere pork sausages or bacon; bagel with cream cheese and lox; smoked salmon or whitefish; Evening meals often included pierogi filled with potato or cottage cheese served with sour cream; chopped liver or cabbage rolls. Dessert included compote or stewed fruit, applesauce, stewed prunes, baked apples, fresh fruit or Jello.

With all the clothes washed and dried it was time to iron them using the electric iron to remove creases. In the 1940s and early 1950s some homemakers used folding Ironing boards that had wooden frames while others used an old folded up blanket, with an old sheet on top, on the kitchen table or on a wooden board spanning two chairs. Ironing was harder and more tiring work than it is today. Fabrics like wool, linen and canvas were much harder to press than today's lighter synthetic fabrics and the irons were heavy. Accidents did happen when someone tripped on the electrical cord to the iron and pulled the hot iron down to the floor. Homemakers always started with the fabric type that needed the coolest temperature setting and worked their way up to the one that needed the hottest iron. Most fabrics were ironed on the wrong side of the garment preventing the fabric from acquiring a shine. This was particularly important for dark colors, silk, rayon, linen fabric and acetates. For fabrics like velvet, corduroy and textured fabrics, ironing on the wrong side prevented crushing or removing the texture. They usually found it best to iron clothes while the clothes were still slightly damp and sprinkled the clothes lightly with water to add dampness. When ironing shirt collars, cuffs, pockets or hems that had a double thickness of fabric, they ironed on the inside first and then on the outside to smooth out any final wrinkles. They never ironed over buttons or any decorations or zippers when these became in common use.

Freshly ironed clothes were immediately hung in the closet after ironing to help them keep a just-pressed look. When it came to ironing clothing made with cloth that they were not familiar with, knowing what ironing setting to use was really important because every fabric was different. They had to know whether to use high heat like on cotton, denim, muslin or calico or medium heat like on wool or silk to make sure they didn't damage the garment. They always used the lowest temperature first and tested on an inside seam when they were not sure what the fabric was made out of. I heard the terms "ironing" and "pressing" used interchangeably but was informed that they were actually very different dewrinkling techniques. When ironing, the iron is slid back and forth over the fabric. When pressing, the iron is placed on the fabric and is held on that one spot, lifting up and repeating the process until all the areas needing attention were smooth. Pressing is necessary to avoid stretching fabrics and using a pressing cloth such as a clean dishtowel or cotton pillowcase, helped to reduce unwanted shine on fabrics. I learned that to press a silk tie you laid it down on top of a pressing cloth right-side facing down. Then using a medium heat setting the dry iron was pressed on a particular area of the tie. The iron was then lifted and the process was repeated until the entire tie was smooth.

During the early 1960s permanent press garments were introduced where the fabric had been chemically processed to resist wrinkles and hold its shape; a fabric that never needed ironing! Alternative descriptions were used such as wrinkle resistant, wash and wear, no-iron, durable press, and easy care. Because of the finish, the fabrics did not fray or stretch, and they were easy to cut. However, women who sewed their own dresses using the treated fabric found it difficult to stitch and iron the fabric that had been treated to remain flat. If alterations were necessary such as lengthening skirts and trousers or letting out seams; they found that the crease marks remained and continued to show.

On occasion ironing was interrupted because of an electric power failure or by a blown fuse. All the fuses for a house were in a fuse box situated where the electric power came into the house. Before 1950, most homes had a 30-amp fuse panel with two screw-type plug fuses with a sight glass that showed if the fuse was blown or not, its rated capacity and a center contact point, to protect the branch circuits and a knife-blade switch to disconnect power to the house. This 30-amp service panel typically supplied only 120 volts to the home. There was no 220-volt service for large appliances like electric ranges and dryers. Today homes have circuit breaker panels which serve the same purpose; designed to protect the branch circuits from overloads and to trip in the event of a sustained short circuit. There was one fuse for each circuit and there were several sockets on any one circuit. Fuses blew if too many pieces of electrical equipment were turned on in the same circuit or from surges from faulty equipment. Often the situation was resolved by moving a piece of equipment to another less-used circuit, however, when a fuse blew, it had to be replaced with a new one with the same rating purchased from the hardware store.

Between 1950 and 1965, landlords had to upgrade to the 60-amp fuse panels to accommodate a 220 volt feed. This panel was mounted inside a gray metal cabinet and had two cartridge-fuse blocks and four sockets for plug fuses. Cartridge fuses were used for amperages over 30 amps, were cylindrical in shape and had the contact points at either end. The first cartridge fuse block held 60-amp fuses and was used as the main disconnect. The other was used as an appliance feed and held a 30-amp fuse. It fed power to an electric dryer, water heater, range, or other high-demand electric appliance. The four plug fuses served four individual branch circuits. In smaller homes with minimal electrical needs, this was often sufficient to power the home. However, these panels could not support more than one 220-volt feed or more than the four individual branch circuits. Certain equipment tended to take a larger current than when it was running, causing the fuse to blow. Fuses and today's circuit breakers are designed to interrupt the power to a circuit when the current flow exceeds safe levels.

If a fuse kept blowing, it meant that something more serious was wrong on that circuit and our neighbour Patrick, an electrician had to be called. Patrick always explained that a UL or CSA approval on equipment meant that the equipment itself should not cause a fire and the fuse actually protected the wiring in the walls from melting. Fuses contain a narrow strip of metal which is designed to melt (safely) when the current exceeds the rated value marked on the fuse such as 15 amp, 20 amp, 30 amp, and 40 amp. When a fuse blew it interrupted the power to the circuit. A fuse could only trip once, then it had to be replaced. Patrick often complained that older homes had only a few branch circuits where everything ran off of one or two fuses which created the problem of blown fuses all the time. He explained that people thought that the solution was to simply install a larger fuse which was an extremely dangerous thing to do because it created a dangerous overloading of branch circuit conductors, namely the wires in the wall. These wires or cables were conductors and were rated by how much continuous current they could safely carry. A #12 cable could carry up to 20 amps while a #14 cable could carry 15 amps. A 15 or 20 amp fuse protected a normal branch circuit containing lights and receptacles. By installing a 30 amp breaker or fuse on a 15 or 20 amp branch circuits people were exceeding the rating of the cable resulting in heat being produced which would melt the insulation covering of the cable and cause an electrical fire. He always told people that rather than installing larger fuses they should do it the right way either by breaking up overloaded circuits or by reducing the number of outlets on the circuit.

In the 1960s, newly constructed homes were built with circuit breaker panels instead of fuse panels and have remained the standard although much expanded ever since. The panel not only provided extra slots for adding circuit breakers, it also included both 120- and 220-volt circuits and a total amperage of 100 amps. The panel featured the main breaker and two rows of circuit breakers that were used for branch circuits. Today the standard for new homes and old homes with updated wiring is 200 amps and the 100-amp panels are the minimum allowed. These days' houses are wired much differently with circuit breaker panels housing 32 to 40 branch circuits and most older homes have had their old fuse panels replaced with a circuit breaker panel. The big advantage of circuit breakers is that they can be reset unlike fuses that had to be replaced when they blew.

In the early 1940's most clothes were custom made with dressmakers and tailors in high demand until the late 1950s. In the late 1940's fashions changed very noticeably from dull to more flamboyant colours and styles. People had strong opinions and expressed them very openly and honestly. They provided advice much of it never asked for but given freely and in a helpful manner. Criticism was always constructive. Honesty, truth and trustworthiness were always treasured. A person's word was their unbreakable promise. Neighbours respected each other and always tried to be helpful. On weekends they all dressed up smartly. At the end of the second world war clothes were full-cut again, with longer double-breasted jackets and wider trousers. People returned to traditional fashions for business wear, but looked for brighter colours and smarter styles like tweed sports jackets for casual wear. Worn out shoes and leather goods were repaired by shoe makers while dresses were adjusted by seamstresses. In those days clothes, like everything else, were made to last. The engineered, built-in obsolescence of the modern day generation had not yet started.

Neatness in dress and appearance were the stand out fashions. Tailors introduced woolen jackets that featured center vests and peaked lapels as well as single-breasted suits with notched lapels. Jackets with a loose fit, broad shoulders and heavily padded chests worn with wide flowing pleated full-length, loose cut trousers with or without cuffs. For business men the pinstripe suit was the universal uniform. Up until the 1960's, many companies applied dress rules that required male staff to wear a suit, a white shirt and a tie to work. Depending on their jobs, industrial workers wore casual clothes to work; some wore overalls, some wore uniforms and some wore more formal attire. Men often selected leather wing-tip shoes and cap toe shoes with laces in brown or black or two-tone colors. In the 1940s and 1950s boys wore baseball caps or far more fashionable were "beanies", a head-hugging brimless cap without a visor resembling a large skullcap, but with a small flipped up brim less than an inch deep forming a band all around, made from the felt of old fedoras. This band had a decorative repeating zigzag or scalloped pattern cut around the edge. It was also quite common for schoolboys to adorn their beanies with buttons and pins. My friends and I fashioned beanies out of old fedoras that we obtained from the passing rag men. The wide-brimmed fedora, a smart, strong, stylish men's hat was popular in cities and in the movies for its stylishness and ability to protect the wearer's head from the sun, wind and weather. I wore a charcoal gray Stetson fedora, manufactured by the John B. Stetson Company of St. Joseph, Missouri; the world's largest hat maker, producing over 3.3 million hats a year. They ceased manufacturing in 1970, then started again in the 1980's and finally went bankrupt in 1986. Stetson hats are now being manufactured by Hatco Inc, in Garland, Texas. My hat was made of ultimate suede finish fur felt with a black one inch grosgrain band around it and a small colourful feather. The hat had an inside leather sweat band and was satin lined. I bought it open crown, meaning that it was uncreased and was something that I had to do or have done. My father far more experienced than me creased my fedora so that it had a crease lengthwise down the crown and was pinched in the front on both sides making it ready to wear. Later in the 1950s, hat makers started blocking the various creases into the hats when they were made and continue this practice today. As the years passed by, hats slowly lost favour and more and more men were going bareheaded even to weddings and worship.

In the 1940s, men wore ties to express their individuality and showed off their style through their accessories. They favored wide, short ties that came in bright, colorful patterns with Windsor knots and accessorized them with decorative tie pins or tie clips. Shirts were held in place by cufflinks made of gold and onyx or mother-of-pearl and trousers were dressed up by suspenders, which were fastened to the trousers with buttons using leather tabs at the ends. Leather used to make belts was in short supply being reserved for the war effort. Suspenders, also called braces, made out of elasticized fabric, either entirely or only at the attachment ends, were worn over the shoulders to hold up trousers forming an X or Y shape at the back. They ensured that the trouser waistband did not slip below the bottom of the waistcoat (vest); they aligned the trousers' pleats with the waistcoat's points and they avoided the extra waistline bulk that resulted from wearing a belt. Suspenders were considered to be underwear and as such were never meant to see the light of day. This was the reason why a jacket was never removed at a formal function. Slowly it became acceptable for suspenders to be visible. Though the return of fuller-cut trousers in the 1940s revived braces, they did not dominate over belts again to the same extent as they had before the war. During the late 1940s and early 1950s belts became increasingly common as men began to view suspenders as being old fashioned. Suspenders and suspender pants were seen as being more appropriate for younger boys who wore clip-on suspenders that were easier to attach and detach and that didn't require separate buttons sewn onto the trousers.

Men's trousers had pleats and cuffs; but no belt loops and no zipper flys; instead the front fly had buttons and buttonholes and there were buttons on the waistband to attach braces. There were buttons on long john winter underwear with even a button on the rear flap or "trap door". Gradually suspenders and buttons were replaced and zippers began to make inroads in the 1950s as more clothing designers began to incorporate zippers into their fashions. Esquire magazine declared the zipper the "Newest Tailoring Idea for Men" and among the zippered fly's many virtues was that it would exclude "The Possibility of Unintentional and Embarrassing Disarray." Obviously, the new zippered trouser owners had not yet discovered the experience of forgetting to zip-up. The next big boost for the zipper came when zippers could open on both ends, as on jackets. Today the zipper is everywhere, in clothing, luggage, leather goods and countless other objects.

Everyone used cloth handkerchiefs to blow their noses. Cloth squares and cloth handkerchiefs were also incorporated into men's suits for an elegant look that added interest to what otherwise might be an overly dark, plain look. If you wanted to look sharp you explored variations in how to fold your handkerchief to display on your suit. At present, the use of a cloth handkerchief is occasionally considered old-fashioned or unhygienic, or both, mainly due to the popularization of disposable paper tissues.

Making a good first impression when meeting people, focussed on a person's appearance and how they dressed. A well groomed short hairstyle was the best choice. Beards were not acceptable and needed to be shaved off as were moustaches which were seen as negative. Fingernails had to be clean and trimmed. Wedding or college rings were generally acceptable but other rings were not. Deodorant was very important and men had to make sure that they did not smell bad. After shave lotion was very popular but perfumes and colognes were kept to a minimum. The ideal suit to wear was a conservative, two-piece dark grey or dark blue business suit. Next came a white, long-sleeved, neatly pressed, dress shirt with a plain colored, non-distracting, conservative dark blue or dark red necktie made of 100% pure silk tied with a thick, wide and triangular Windsor knot. A gold or silver tie bar ensured that the tie was held in place. Without a tie pin or bar, a person often ended up adjusting their tie several times, which made them look nervous. It was also very important to wear clean and well polished conservative black, lace-up dress shoes along with dark socks, black if possible. The belt was to match the color of a person's shoes, again black if possible.

Clothes particularly woolen clothes were stored with white semi-translucent moth balls about the size of marbles made of a pungent substance called napthalene which had its own unique smell to deter moths from eating small holes into the wool. Moth attacks were very troublesome on clothes that had been put away in storage for a while, like winter clothes over summer. The holes could be darned of course, and they usually were, but the darning never looked quite like the original fabric. Another more expensive and labour intensive solution was to have the damaged garment undergo invisible weaving which was an active industry in the 1940s through to the early 1970s repairing cigarette burns, moth holes and rips in any fabric. Reweaving meant rebuilding the fabric of a damaged garment or upholstery to mend the cloth making it look like new. A swatch of the fabric was taken from an unseen part of the garment or article such as a seam or hem and the threads were rewoven thread-by-thread into the damaged area. In weaving two terms were used to describe turning thread or yarn into fabric; namely warp and weft. The lengthwise or longitudinal warp yarns are held stationary in tension on a frame or loom while the transverse weft yarn is drawn through and inserted over-and-under the warp. All of the necessary warp and weft material needed for the repair was taken from the swatch of fabric. After the mender reconstructed the warp and weft using a long needle on the damaged area to exactly match the original weave the garment was pressed and the mended part was undetectable on the outside of the fabric. On the reverse side of the restored area there were long hanging threads where the re-weaving was done. These hanging threads occur because (unlike in darning work) invisible weaving was done without tacking, in case it deformed the fabric. Invisible weaving was labour intensive and very time consuming and many times people found it cheaper to replace the garment. Up until the 1970s, invisible mending was common practice, but today it is a fine craft associated with tapestry weaving and is a custom service that is still provided by some quality dry cleaners.

The larvae of moths were often found in the dark corners of wardrobes and drawers and they tended to feed off woollen or silk clothes. Because of this people turned to a remedy that had been used since Victorian times, namely napthalene or moth balls. People made sure that they used enough of them in drawers and cupboards where clothes were kept, always spreading them evenly The moth balls evaporated releasing a fumigant gas which was why they smelled so strongly. They had to be replaced before they had completely evaporated otherwise the moths came back and ate into the clothes. You could often smell when someone was passing by without even looking up. The smell of moth balls was common because everyone used them, and it stayed in clothes. People tried to get rid of moth larvae and eggs by vigorously brushing garments outdoors in bright sunshine particularly around cuffs, collars and other hidden places, or by having them dry-cleaned. They aired out their clothing thoroughly outside before wearing it or hanging it up in their closet again to try and get rid of the moth ball smell. They also found out that dry cleaning didn't eliminate the mothball odor either. With the development of synthetic fibres, and their popularity over wool, the clothes moth had less to feed on but it has not disappeared and you may still find unexpected little holes in your woollen clothes. Adult moths lay almost invisible eggs on wool, fur, silk and feathers and other items of animal origin. The eggs develop into larva that feed on the items and cause damage. Development from egg to adult is as little as a month.

Being in the bank one day to make a deposit, taking my wallet out from my jacket pocket, the bank teller and I were startled to see a buff gray color moth about 1/4 inch long take flight from the wallet. We laughed as someone in line remarked, "Well I would say that was old money, really old money. Adult moths are rarely seen because they tend to hide in the dark during daylight so it was quite a surprise. Moths were attracted to articles soiled by food, beverages, perspiration and urine, rather than the clean wool itself so people cleaned their homes often to prevent lint, dust or hair from accumulating and garments were thoroughly cleaned regularly before storage. Furs were professionally cleaned and placed in cold storage and the moths ate on. People used trunks lined with cedar and beautifully made cedar chests and treated them as good pest-proof containers and only kept clean fabric and garments with lots of moth balls in them. Cedar oil killed young larvae, but did not affect older ones and as the wood aged the oils were not as volatile. Light sanding every year or two helped release cedar oil but as the scent faded so did it's killing effectiveness. Older mothballs consisted primarily of naphthalene, but due to naphthalene's flammability, many mothball formulations used 1,4-dichlorobenzene. Both of them evaporated from a solid state directly into a gas and both had the strong, pungent, sickly-sweet odor of mothballs. US Health authorities consider 1,4-dichlorobenzene and naphthalene as possible carcinogens and have stated that exposure to mothballs can cause acute hemolysis (anemia) in certain people and they reported that exposure to mothball vapors had caused cataracts and retinal hemorrhage in humans. Mothballs containing naphthalene had been banned within the EU since 2008.

Most women's 1940s coats and jackets were made from wool and rayon-wool blends with linings made of rayon crepe or satin. Most coats were long, coming to just below the knee, and were frequently made in herringbone, tan, grey, dark green, navy and red among other winter colors. They were generally without decoration and all had large square shoulder pads. There were two predominant styles; namely, the box style and the swagger style. The box style coat was lightweight, cut very straight and oversized wide, in the shape of a box and hung down just to the mid hip. They were worn open or buttoned closed with large, covered buttons. The swagger style was a long version of the box coat. It fit wide and boxy but came down to below the knee. The back of the coat had flared swing pleats coming from the nape of the neck allowing extra movement and more room for clothing underneath.

Fur coats were a very important part of the 1940's wardrobe. When it came to luxury, genuine fur, puffy fox stoles, floor-length minks were very much admired and were an important status indicator. The most popular kinds of fur bought by the rich in the 1940s through the 1960s were blond mink, silver striped fox and red fox. Common animal sources for fur clothing and fur trimmed accessories included fox, rabbit, mink, muskrat, beaver, stoat (ermine), otter, sable, persian lamb, marten, seals, cats, dogs, coyotes, chinchilla, and opossum and common brushtail possum. Some of these were more highly prized than others, and there were many grades and colors. Furs were associated with glamour and lavish spending; and were widely embraced by Hollywood and the wealthy. Elegant ladies wore them over suits and kept the cold out. While quite desirable, real fur had the disadvantage of being expensive and in short supply.

Fur coats in the 1940s were designed and worn in the same shapes as fabric coats. They featured full-draped swaggers, wide-armhole sleeves, dramatic extended shoulders, turn back cuffs, cardigan necklines and saddle shoulders. The box coat and swagger style looked best with a thick fox, sable, and seal fur. Sleeves being wide with turn-back cuffs slid easily over suits. Fur coats usually had two or three buttons or clasps to keep the coat closed. Some box styles only had a single clasp at the neckline. Pockets were hidden slashes on the coat sides. Fur stoles with large round or square collars or long wraps like a scarf were used to accent winter wool coats. In the 1930s fur stoles worn by the rich had an entire animal complete with head and feet draped across the shoulders. This was largely out of style in the 1940s. Fur coats and stoles were crafted with pride and made to assure lasting wear. The pelts were typically hand selected by experts who had in-depth knowledge and chose furs that were full-furred, supple, strong, good in color and texture. Better coats were much sought after by those who could afford it; such as superior blending, matching of skins, use of more skins per coat, seams reinforced at points of stress, fine linings, interlining, quality trimmings and a good finish. A lot of women couldn't afford the most desirable furs: beaver, leopard, lynx, chinchilla, mink, etc. So they bought Mouton Lamb, a deep textured, dark silvery brown lambskin processed to resemble expensive sheared beaver that was rayon lined. In the 1950s they bought coats made out of faux fur. Fur is no longer the status symbol it used to be because of the proliferation of fake furs and public awareness campaigns orchestrated by animal rights groups,

There were many signs advertising cold storage along with many furrier establishments. Owning a fur coat was very desirable but was only affordable by the wealthy. A fur coat was an investment that never went out of style and had to be properly cared for. Most people stored their furs through the summer months, and brought them home when the cooler weather returned in the fall. Furs had to be stored properly in the off season in a cold storage facility since it was near impossible to duplicate in a home closet, the scientifically controlled constant temperature of 50-60F (10-15C) and 45-55% humidity ideal for preserving furs in a spacious professional fur-storage vault. People with fur coats made expert cleaning and cold storage a yearly habit. Fur storage costs were usually based on the value of the garments. Fur coats required annual professional cleaning to restore the natural brilliance and beauty of the fur; inspection to identify rips, small tears, dirty linings, missing buttons, broken clasps, worn elastics, worn spots or other damage and to have them repaired by fully qualified furriers before they became bigger and more costly problems.

The true modern faux fur or fake furs were not developed until the mid 1950s, with the introduction of acrylic polymers which provided the bulk required to imitate real fur without the weight associated with other fake fur fabrics. Later in the 1950s producers found that acrylic polymers produced even more fur-like and fire resistant fabrics, called modacrylics which became commercially available in the 1950s. By then, fake fur was more than just a cheap alternative. Faux fur was a fabric and not an animal-use product and were more durable and resistant to environmental assaults. They were much more affordable than real fur and faux fur coats were not affected by moths and they did not require cold storage to prevent deterioration. Historically fur was fashion's loudest signifier of identity and status and in the 1960s fake fur began to rival it. Today it is difficult to tell the difference between real and fake fur.

Throughout the 1940s until the early 1960s ballrooms and dance halls were the popular forerunners of the discothèque or nightclub. Every neighbourhood had at least one dance hall, that always featured live musicians playing a range of music from waltzes, tangos, sambas, foxtrot, jitterbug, swing and polkas. People wanting to meet others of the opposite sex had to learn to dance. Several of our neighbours had signed up and had taken dance lessons at Arthur Murray's in the 1950s. The Arthur Murray Dance Studios was a popular business franchise selling dance lessons which were advertised on radio and billboards. Arthur Murray's slogan was: "If you can walk, we can teach you how to dance", and the company guaranteed that the pupils would learn to dance in ten lessons. After the war, Murray's business grew with the rise of interest in Latin dance (tango, mambo, samba, conga) and he regularly taught and broadcast in Cuba in the 1950s. Murray went on television with a dance program called the Arthur Murray Party which ran from 1950 to 1960 hosted by his wife, Kathryn Murray. In the late 1970s there were more than 3,560 dance studios bearing his name. In 2007, only about 220 Arthur Murray Studios remained in operation.

The alleys and lanes of our neighbourhood formed a network of secondary streets, providing access to the backyards of the houses. They allowed wood and coal deliveries for heating, as well as garbage collection and access for firefighters if necessary. The alleys were a wonderful playground for many children, as well as a shortcut for pedestrians and cyclists. The back lanes had a mess of telephone and electrical wires crisscrossing the alleyways intermingled with clothes hanging out on the clothes lines. Some lanes had garbage piled up along the fences waiting to be picked up by the garbage men. Apart from cats and dogs running loose, we also had the occasional rat the size of some cats darting here and there. We even had one hiding in the wood pile in the shed that jumped out into the back lane as we were getting set to put more wood on the pile.

As children, we played kick the can, street hockey, hide and seek, throwing a ball against the brick exteriors and bouncing it to see how high we could make it go. We made a game out of flipping pocket-knives into the ground; every throw had to have the knife standing, blade stuck into the dirt. First one to miss was out of the game. We also played marbles where you won someone else's marbles, or lost most if not all of your own marbles. We played dodge ball, softball, soccer, tag, and even hop scotch. My friends Lionel and Danny had Daisy Red Ryder BB guns which were modeled after a lever action rifle and resembled the Winchester rifle of Western movies. It was a multi-pump pneumatic rifle capable of firing pellets or steel BBs at low velocities. We all took turns shooting steel BBs at little red bulls eye targets in Danny's back yard. We counted the holes we made closest to the center to see how good we were at aiming and hitting the target. The steel BBs were very prone to ricochet, especially off hard surfaces such as brick, concrete or trees. We were very careful not to have them ricochet and hit any windows. We never thought of wearing eye protection and I thank my lucky stars that we never got hit in the eye. We enjoyed visiting with Lionel where we played with his electrically powered "Lionel" miniature train set which had a whistle and gave off smoke as it went around the track.

Everyone on our city block listened to the hockey game radio broadcasts, read the sports pages in the newspapers and collected hockey player pictures by mailing in a number of Quaker Oats box tops. For street hockey we wore Montreal Canadiens red, white and blue hockey sweaters with a large crest made of a big letter C and a smaller H in the middle. The Montreal Canadiens were our professional ice hockey team. The team's nickname was and is the Habs, an abbreviation for "Les Habitants". They were part of the "Original Six" teams that were part of the National Hockey League (NHL) from 1942 until the 1967 expansion. The Canadiens played their home games at the Montreal Forum for seven decades and all but their first two Stanley Cup championships, a veritable shrine to hockey fans everywhere. The Canadiens enjoyed success in the 1940s with Bill Durnan in goal and the Maurice "Rocket" Richard, Toe Blake and Elmer Lach "Punch Line". From 1952 to 1960, they won six Stanley Cups, including a record five straight from 1956 to 1960, with a new set of stars that came into prominence such as Jean Beliveau, Dickie Moore, Doug Harvey, Bernie "Boom Boom" Geoffrion, Jacques Plante, and Rocket Richard's younger brother, Henri. The Canadiens added ten more championships in fifteen seasons from 1965 to 1979, with another dynastic run of four straight Cups from 1976 to 1979. In the 1976–77 season, the Canadiens lost only eight games in an 80-game season, setting a modern day record. During this time there was a new set of hockey stars such as Guy Lafleur, Yvan Cournoyer, Ken Dryden, Pete Mahovlich, Steve Shutt, Bob Gainey, Serge Savard, Guy Lapointe and Larry Robinson. Scotty Bowman, who later set a record for most NHL victories by a coach. He was the team's head coach for its last five Stanley Cup victories in the 70s. In 1996, the Habs moved from the Montreal Forum, their home during 71 seasons and 22 Stanley Cups, to the Molson Centre now the Bell Centre.

Girls had their own games one of which was jacks, played on the floor or sidewalk. They bounced a ball and then as swiftly as lightning, they scooped up jacks. Girls often drew hopscotch patterns with coloured chalk on the sidewalks to skip on. Almost daily a water truck came by spraying water and using huge circular electric brushes to clean the dirty streets and washed away all of the chalk marks. The girls drew new patterns the next day. Boys and girls ran alongside the truck and tried to jump over the spray without getting their feet and legs wet. But on hot summer days, that cold spray was refreshing. The girl's favourite activity was skipping rope where one or more of them would jump over a rope swung so that it passed under their feet and over their heads. Often you would see them taking turns or where two of them would turn the rope while one or more jumped. Sometimes they used two turning ropes which looked a lot more difficult and called that activity of jumping "Double Dutch". While skipping they would often chant some nonsense rhymes beginning when the skipper jumped in and ending when the skipper tripped up. My friends and I played street hockey all year round and the girls joined in as well.

On summer evenings after supper in the early 1940s, my parents and I frequently went to Mount Royal Park where I caught fireflies and put them in a jar. It was easy to be mesmerized by the flickering light from the fireflies and to associate them with magical fairies. Fireflies were also called lightning bugs or glow-worms; in fact they were beetles that produced a yellow or pale green light in their lower abdomen during twilight. I later learned that the chemical reaction producing the light was called bioluminescence. After admiring them in the jar I always let them go free and watched as they twinkled like stars while disappearing into the woods. On some evenings we joined a large group of people and listened to various military bands play at the band shell near Duluth and Park Avenue. I enjoyed the freedom of the outdoors where there was spontaneity, wonder, laughter and creativity and where life held the promise of a certain degree of magic.

On very hot summer days children would beg their mothers for a nickel so that they could buy a cold, refreshing "Popsicle" that came in several delicious flavors at the grocery store. Everyone had a preference orange, blue, red, grape or chocolate. Popsicles were made with twin sticks and a groove in the flavoured ice between the sticks so that each double sticked Popsicle could be split apart by pushing your thumbs in and pulling your fingers back. Popsicles were meant to be shared. Not only did the children want the popsicles, they also wanted the popsicle wrappers which every kid on the block saved. I kept my popsicle wrappers in a large paper bag. The wrappers had to be brought to a redemption store which was located on Marie Anne street way east of St Denis street. The store supplied a prize catalog which listed the number of popsicle wrappers needed to be redeemed and the different pictured prizes such as chess and checker sets, metal toy cars and airplanes, train sets, joke books, jumping ropes, toys, roller skates, wagons and even bicycles. The "Popsicle Pete" wrapper loyalty program was one of the oldest and longest-running child-targeted loyalty programs having been started in the 1930s with kids being encouraged to save the wrappers and to redeem them for merchandise, and was still going in the late 1970's.

In response to the fear that parents and the community at large had neglected young men and boys and to curb the rise in juvenile delinquency, the police established the Montreal Police Juvenile Club. To join, my friends and I went to the police station on St Lawrence and Laurier streets to register. We were fingerprinted (presented in an educational manner) but the Police had our fingerprints and we were issued a light blue membership card. The club was the only one in Canada and had a membership of 50,000 members under the age of 18. During the first three weeks 45,000 had signed up. The Police said that the club was a major factor in reducing the juvenile crime rate from 4,000 in 1943 to 1800 in 1948. The Police Juvenile Boys' Club, started by Captain-Detective Ovila Pelletier, had made a big difference. By providing youngsters who had few, if any, options in their leisure activities with the opportunity to learn, play and watch team sports, and to borrow the expensive sports equipment, he offered them a pleasing and acceptable alternative to delinquent behavior.

Det. Capt O. Pelletier headed the prevention bureau and his signature was on every official blue membership card. The Montreal Police Juvenile Club was a youth organization sponsored by the Montreal City Police with the purpose of combating juvenile delinquency by providing teenagers with ample recreational facilities. The police officers and civilian employees who built the organization did so voluntarily, including putting their money, their time and their love to achieve a noble goal enabling thousands of young men of all persuasions to have a better life; to appreciate sport, music, practice all kinds of group activities and to ultimately become better citizens. The club provided supervised sports facilities and sponsored activities such as baseball, hockey, basketball, volleyball, boxing and wrestling. The club encouraged better social attitudes and humanized the police force. Its programs involved "the sports solution" in which policemen acted as instructors and guides for hockey and basketball games, boxing matches, and music lessons. The club was active for 17 consecutive years. The extraordinary accomplishment of the Montreal Police Juvenile Club and beautiful story of love of neighbor, self-giving and social commitment ended on December 31, 1965.

In the late 1940s many of my friends and I became members of the Neighborhood House located on Clark Street between Marie Anne and Mt. Royal Streets. Neighbourhood House offered a variety of complementary activities, ranging from after-school programmes that included crafts, science, and technology classes to social groups for teenagers and babysitting services. The school board agreed to accommodate Neighbourhood House at its Mount Royal, Devonshire, and Bancroft schools, where volunteers ran Girl Guides, Rangers, Wolf Cubs, Boy Scouts, and athletic and recreational programmes. Schools also coordinated activities with organizations such as the YMCA and YMHA. Boys were taught art, notch and soap carving, woodworking, lino-cutting, and balsa wood model airplane building. Girls were taught skills such as art, dressmaking, cooking, hooking and braiding rugs, dramatics, and music appreciation. Girls also knitted hats, mittens, socks, scarves, and sweaters.

I built my first scaled model spitfire airplane from a kit manufactured by Guillows. The pieces were made from balsa wood, with the individual parts such as wing ribs and fuselage formers being cut from sheet balsa and strip balsa making up the remainder. Balsa is actually a hardwood and is ideally suited to model airplane kit construction because of its excellent weight to strength ratio. The

Spitfire was the most widely produced and strategically important British single-seat fighter of World War II, was renowned for winning victory laurels in the Battle of Britain (1940–41). It was a high-performance fighter with an armament of eight wing-mounted 0.303-inch (7.7-mm) machine guns. The actual plane had a wingspan of 36 feet 10 inches (11.2 metres), was 29 feet 11 inches (9.1 metres) long, and reached a maximum speed of 360 miles (580 km) per hour and a ceiling of 34,000 feet (10,400 metres). Even more-capable versions of the Spitfire were developed, driven by progressively more-powerful Merlin engines. The eight 0.303-inch machine guns gave way to four 0.8-inch (20-mm) automatic cannons, and by war's end the Spitfire had been produced in more than 20 fighter versions alone, powered by Merlins of up to 1,760 horsepower.

I used an X-acto knife to cut out the die cut balsa pieces as well as cutting and shaping stringers and other parts. Construction of the kit took place over a paper plan laid out on a flat wooden board. The balsa was kept in place with straight pins on the building board while the glue set. A rubber band was put in between a support at the back of the plane threaded through the center to the front and attached to the propeller which enabled the plane to be propelled. Fine grade sand paper was used for doing finishing work on the completed frames. After the final sanding of the airplane parts (wing, fuselage, tail etc...) was completed, clear Nitrate Dope was applied on the wood surfaces, then, the plane was covered with a colored lightweight tissue paper; the dope acted like a glue and sealed the tissue covering. After it dried any excess tissue was trimmed off and several coats of Nitrate dope were brushed over the entire covered surfaces of the model giving them a high gloss. This "shrunk" and tightened the tissue covering, removing all (or most all) of the wrinkles and made the plane's surface very smooth. The model was ready to fly. The propeller was wound up and unwinding it spun the propeller enabling the plane to fly.

Many years later I built my first gas model, a Fokker aircraft. which was built using balsa in the same way as I did building the spitfire except without the rubber bands. Instead the gas motor was attached to the front of the model along with lead wires to a wing of the plane attached to a hand grip. Butyrate Dope was applied over the entire plane to protect all the surfaces from fuel penetration. The Butyrate Dope made the entire airplane "fuel proof" from the heavy droplets of fuel that would come out from the engine exhaust. This prevented the fuel residue that eventually coated the surfaces of the plane when the engine is running from penetrating the tissue covering. I flew the model on Fletcher's Field one morning and after making several round trips and a near perfect figure eight, the plane nose dived perfectly straight into the ground smashing the fuselage and wings to bits. I salvaged the engine and kept it for quite some time but never built another airplane model.

In summer the Neighborhood House had a summer day camp held daily except weekends, in the backyard of their building from the end of June until the day camp closed on August 26 each year. In 1948 at least twelve nationalities and four religious denominations were represented among the 435 campers who registered in the non-sectarian city camp which operated under the Federation of Jewish Philanthropies and was supported by the Combined Jewish Appeal. It was not unusual to find Chinese and Japanese children playing among a group of French Canadians, Russian, Yugoslav, Jewish and Czech campers. We lined

up around the flag pole at Neighborhood House every morning at 9 a.m. for the flag raising ceremony and singing of our national anthem and God Save the King. We also ended each day lowering of the flag the same way except that we sang Taps:
>Day is done, Gone the sun,
>From the lake, from the hills, from the sky;
>All is well, Safely rest, God is nigh.

Ranging in age from three to 13, the campers were divided into fifteen groups, each with its own counsellor / supervisor. Each group planned their own activities, which the supervisors scheduled to fit in with the preferences of the other fourteen groups. Camp recessed at noon for lunch and rest before afternoon activities. The tiniest tots had a miniature swimming pool (a six-man rubber dinghy). When they were not building castles in the sandbox, the three and four-year-olds paddled around in the dinghy, while the other children made judicious use of a common garden implement, the hose. Folk dancing was a camp specialty since the children were encouraged to share their rich folk heritages. Crafts, sports and drama groups rotated constantly. A well-equipped kitchen was available for older children who wanted to try out hot weather recipes. Some campers interested in nature study had converted the shed used for ice skating in the winter into a local museum of natural history, with biological specimens gleaned from Montreal's three mountains, or from the countryside. Swimming excursions to beaches and pools in the area, as well as day long hikes and picnics took some groups away from the camp centre. Rainy day programmes included movies, travel, participating in drama groups, gymnastics, etc. The aim was not to have a child return home and say, "Look what I made" instead they wanted the campers to say "Look what I learned".

We were bussed to an outdoor swimming pool near the Blue Bonnets Race Track on Decarie Boulevard. We got into our bathing suits and ran into the pool. I not knowing which side of the pool was the shallow end jumped into the deep end. Not having a clue about swimming I sank to the bottom of the deep pool. Hitting bottom with my feet I pushed up and came to the surface, took a quick breath and sank down again. I did this three times. On the third bounce up I recalled someone saying that after three times you drown! Finding super strength from somewhere I lunged at a lady swimmer, caught her and held on for dear life. She got me to the edge of the pool, I coughed, spit out water and thanked her for saving my life. I got out of the pool with the help of the counsellors who were there. After that we all were paired up with a buddy, following the buddy system and in the shallow end of the pool we learned how to float. Years later I heard a story about a lady diving into a pool and when she surfaced she had lost the top of her bikini. With her arms crossed on her chest she got out of the pool and was rushing to the dressing rooms when a little boy stopped her and asked. "Miss if you are giving those puppies away could I have the one with the pink nose?" That little boy could have been me after I lunged at that dear unsuspecting lady who got me to the edge of the pool.

The Neighborhood House had counselors and supervisors who took us on field trips, taught us swimming, boxing, floor hockey, basketball and supervised our production of H.M.S. Pinafore a comic opera by Gilbert and Sullivan. We all rehearsed our roles over and over, prepared all of the stage props, perfected the lighting, tested the music, acoustics, etc. and performed at the end of the summer for the members and invited guests of the Dalse Welfare Club. The performance was staged in the gymnasium / auditorium before a very well attended audience. We all participated as the crew in the many songs and enjoyed one particular song. The song starts with Sir Joseph saying: "I am the monarch of the sea, The ruler of the Queen's Navee, Whose praise Great Britain loudly chants. To which his cousin Hebe replies, " And we are his sisters, and his cousins, and his aunts!". It continues:

> When I was a lad I served a term As office boy to an Attorney's firm.
> I cleaned the windows and I swept the floor,
> And I polished up the handle of the big front door.
> I polished up that handle so carefullee   That now I am the Ruler of the Queen's Navee!
> Be careful to be guided by this golden rule--
> Stick close to your desks and never go to sea,
> And you all may be rulers of the Queen's Navee!

We all worked hard to ensure that the costumes and sets were as realistic as possible; the caretaker helped with the carpentry and we all painted the props. Our performance was nothing less than spectacular as "we polished up the handle of the big front door; we polished up the handle so carefully that now we were the rulers of the Queen's navy." We received accolades and a gift box filled with cookies and candies and ribbon with the Dalse slogan "Help unto others" stamped on it. The Dalse Welfare Club was a very important sponsor of the Neighborhood House. The Dalse organization started in 1929 and in 1942 decided to become a Service Club called "The Dalse Welfare Club." Over the years, Dalse was involved with many hospitals, institutions, groups and individuals. Dalse Welfare ceased operations in 1999 and donated its archives to the Canadian Jewish Congress (CJC) Archives.

The Montreal Royals was the team that my friends and I followed. We listened to radio broadcasts of their baseball games and attended several games sitting in the bleachers of the Delorimier Stadium also known as Montreal Stadium, Hector Racine Stadium and Delorimier Downs which was the Montreal Royals home stadium. It was a 25,000-seat open air sports stadium at 2101 Ontario Street East, near De Lorimier Avenue just up the street from where St. Sophie's Ukrainian Greek Orthodox Cathedral was located at the time. The Montreal Royals were an International League baseball team, top farm club of the Brooklyn Dodgers Major League Baseball team from 1928 to 1960 who had enjoyed great success and launched the baseball careers of Sparky Anderson, Gene Mauch, Roberto Clemente and the man who broke Major League Baseball's color barrier with the Royals in 1946, second baseman, Jackie Robinson. He became the first African American to play in the major leagues. There were many other great players of the Royals' such as Duke Snider, Don Drysdale, Chuck Connors, Walter Alston, Roy Campanella and the pitcher with the most wins in the history of the team, Tommy Lasorda. It was reported that one of Tom Lasorda's favourite memories of the Delormier Downs stadium was when they had a day for hockey players. Tom said. "I remember The Rocket, Doug Harvey, Toe Blake, Butch Bouchard and Jean Beliveau. One time I was eating with goalie Jacques Plante in a restaurant called the Chicken Coop and he was drawing something on a napkin. I said, 'What's that?' He drew the first hockey mask. He said, 'I want a mask like your catchers wear." Plante, in 1959, became the first goalie to regularly wear a mask. On September 13, 1960 Dodgers President Walter O'Malley announced the end of their affiliation with the Montreal Royals team and the team folded. In 1951, several British football (soccer) teams toured North America. Glasgow Celtic played an exhibition match at Delorimier Stadium on May 20th against Fulham. In 1957 Glasgow Celtic returned to Delorimier for a June 9th exhibition match against Tottenham Hotspur. Delorimier Stadium was also the site of a number of professional boxing and wrestling matches. After the Montreal Royals disbanded in 1960, the stadium saw limited use and was demolished.

In the early summer evenings, my friends and I attended the amateur baseball games played at the baseball diamonds on Fletcher's Field. There were several smaller baseball diamonds where softball teams sponsored by local businesses played on a regular schedule. Softball was played with a larger ball (11 or 12 inches in circumference) on a smaller field. The softball diamond baselines were about 65 feet and the distance from the pitcher's mound to home plate was about 50 feet. Each team had to have 9 players to play. Bats had to be official softball bats and no metal cleats were allowed. Pitching had to be underhand, in other words the pitcher had to deliver the ball on the first forward swing of the pitching arm past the hip while having one foot on the pitcher's plate. The usual baseball rules of 4 balls constituting a walk and 3 strikes constituting a strike out applied. Softball games were limited to 7 innings instead of nine.

One particular baseball diamond was well suited for hard ball games and had several rows of elevated seats behind a fenced in area along the first and third base lines. Our favourite was the Montreal Wanderers hardball baseball team. The game is played with a smaller ball (9 inches (23 centimeters in circumference) which has a hard rubber center with yarn wound around it and covered in white cowhide, with red stitching. Players wear gloves called baseball mitts made of padded leather some with webbing between the fingers as an aid in catching and holding onto the ball. There were also regular soccer games between such teams as Italia and Polonia played on the soccer field on Fletcher's Field. People would stand three or four deep along the sidelines to cheer and watch the games. The soccer field doubled as an ice rink in winter.

Our preteen and teen years were filled with many activities. We played hide and seek, baseball, touch football, soccer and we drove our tricycles and bicycles and raced around on our roller skates. A pair of strap-on roller skates allowed a person to quickly equip himself with a cheap method and faster than walking-type of transportation, which was usable on streets within the city. Roller skates in the 1940's were adjustable, nickel-plated roller skates which fit over regular street shoes and each skate was clamped to the front of the shoe, and attached around the ankle with a leather strap. We had a skate key attached to a ribbon which we wore around our necks. We used the skate key to adjust the length and to tighten the clamp part of the skate. Skates had two parallel sets of wheels, one pair under the ball of the foot and the other pair under the heel. The four ball-bearing wheels were made of steel. Since the roller skates were a strap-on version, the shoes themselves did not need to be switched, enabling you to quickly put the roller skates on while on the street. Several of us skated up and down the streets and sidewalks for hours at a time, ever watchful for horses and cars while making a racket and lots of noise throughout the neighborhood. Many pant knees were torn from falling down.

As part of our daily routine, we roller skated down St Dominique Street from Marie Anne to Rachel and raced around the block. On occasion we attempted a much larger route by going up St Dominique Street to Mount Royal and then east to the predominantly French speaking St Denis Street, south to Rachel and then north back to St Dominique. Going west on Rachel we passed the St Jean Baptiste Church. We watched as men saluted or tipped their hats when passing the church. Some days we covered an even wider route; either skating around Fletcher's Field or going south on the Main. The Sherbrooke Street hill on St Lawrence Street was a mark of passage and would be boasted about for a long time. Looking back at it, the sheer thought of going downhill on a very steep hill hearing only the click, click of the roller skates as the wheels went over the dividing lines in the concrete sidewalk, passing everything and everyone at blinding speed was nothing short of madness. The skates had no brakes so flying off the curb unto Ontario Street (now President Kennedy Blvd) into oncoming or passing traffic or streetcars was a very frightening experience bordering on insanity. Being hit by a streetcar, truck or vehicle was a definite possibility. We had someone above looking after us for sure because we all survived several of these outings with many stories of near misses that we recounted and boasted about later. Wearing T shirts and short pants in summer we often arrived home with bruised arms, elbows and knees. There were no protective pads or helmets to be worn those days. As autumn approached we wore long pants, britches or jeans. The worst was going skating with a brand new pair of britches and coming back about an hour later with a gaping hole at the knee. My concern was more about the pants than my bleeding bruised knee. Pants were patched with knee patches but it took time to heal the bruises. We listened to the lectures and we went skating again. Parents had a formidable job and exercised incredible patience. Mt friends and I, in retrospect, were quite the handful.

In time the adjusting screws at the front of the roller skates wore out, and by then the wheels were worn down also. The skate was taken apart into the front two wheel section and the two rear wheel section. These were nailed separately unto a two by four piece of wood of about four or five feet in length. Then a wooden orange crate was nailed on the front end and a scooter was born. These we raced up and down the street as well. One could at least stop the madness by hopping off and letting the scooter crash into whatever by itself. Not quite as much fun as the roller skates were by themselves but it led to some great artistic expression. We customized our scooters by painting them, naming them and even putting old vehicle license plates on them. Flashlights were taped on them and hand air pump horns were attached to them. The thrill was in the ride. In the late 1940s we left roller skates behind and rented bicycles to go further afield.

Most parents felt that in addition to English and French, arithmetic, geography, etc. which we were learning at Mount Royal Elementary School, learning their ancestral language would be beneficial for their children. My friends attended various parochial schools. Some went to Jewish schools; others to Polish, Hungarian and Slovak schools. We had Karem Israel Synagogue and school on our street where my Jewish friends went to learn the Hebrew language, the Bible, Jewish history, prayers, and selected portions from the Talmud. The synagogue was on the ground floor while the school was on the second floor. Parochial schools were organized on a parish or church basis and were supported by voluntary offerings from the parishioners and by charging tuition fees. Jewish schools however were not tied to specific synagogues.

My parents followed the same tradition of having children learn the ancestral language and I was enrolled in Ukrainian school which was held in the basement of St Sophie's Ukrainian Greek Orthodox Church on Delorimier St south of Ontario street. I travelled there by streetcar every Tuesday and Thursday afternoon. My Father arrived there after work on those evenings to pick me up and we would take the streetcar home for supper. The school held classes from grade 1 to 7 and even had dance classes on Saturday. Classes for grades four and up were held just once a week. I learned the Cyrillic alphabet, to read, write, count and sing with emphasis on Ukrainian traditions and history. The school held several concerts, plays, dance and choir presentations particularly on Easter, Mother's Day and at Christmas every year. All members of the school were encouraged to join a dance group or church choir. Before Ukrainian Christmas (Julian calendar, usually January 7) I along with other students went caroling ("koliada") visiting people's homes for Christmas following an ancient tradition. I was in the school choir and we sang at concerts staged in the church basement and on major occasions at the Monument National Theatre on the "Main". All of these activities helped to foster a strong sense of Ukrainian community.

We learned about the history of the Ukraine and about its literature and memorized some of the writings and poems of Taras Shevchenko and Ivan Franko. I often took part at concerts reciting long poems by Taras Shevchenko that I had to memorize. My mother sat with me for countless hours while I repeatedly struggled to memorize through repetition, over and over, of the famous writings. My emotional delivery at the poem recitals on Mother's Day always received thunderous applause. My mother and father always encouraged me and I always tried not to disappoint them. I participated in plays, sang as part of the youth choir and danced as a Cossack doing deep knee bends.

In grade three of Ukrainian school, one particular afternoon remains etched in my memory. Having arrived early for class which started at five p.m. and ended at seven p.m.; some four of us decided to go and see the Jacques Cartier Bridge thinking that we could be back before class started. The church and the approach to the bridge were not that far apart. We not only saw the bridge, we got carried away and actually went on the bridge, almost half way to St Helen's Island when we decided to turn back and return to school on the run. We came in with quite a clatter just as the clock struck six thirty. I quickly glanced to the back and saw my father standing at the back of the room with some of the other parents. I thought that I had seen a smile on his face, probably one of relief. We were marched to the front of the class, seriously lectured to and collectively apologized for being late because we had no watch and really thought that we had enough time. We must have sounded convincing enough because we were not assigned extra work but were warned to really know the lesson that we had missed. I promised my father that I would not attempt anything like that again.

Chapter 6 - Historic Beginnings

I tagged along with my friend André as he frequently visited a friend of his family and teacher. Let us call him Frère Marcel, because I no longer remember his name and at the time we simply addressed him as Mon Frère. Frère Marcel was a Jesuit brother (un frère jésuite), at the St Jean Baptiste Church on Rachel and Henri-Julien streets. André and I were both curious about some of the origins of the area since both of us were born and raised in the Paroisse de Saint Jean Baptiste. André was interested in the early train history since alot of the New France history had been covered in his classes at school. I was interested in the origin of street names and in the history of Montreal which was only covered in one chapter in our History of Canada class somewhere in elementary school. We were both very amazed at the detail knowledge of Montreal's history that Frère Marcel recounted and we both scribbled notes as Frere Marcel spoke. It was thankfully for these tattered old scribbled notes that the foundation for this chapter was formed. Frère Marcel started telling us about Jacques Cartier searching for a passage to Asia and reaching what is now Montreal in 1535. Jacques Cartier named the Saint Lawrence River in honour of the Deacon Lawrence, one of the seven deacons of the city of Rome, Italy, under Pope Sixtus II in 257 AD. Laurentius is called the archdeacon of Rome a position which took care of the wealth and treasury of the Church and the distribution of alms to the poor. He was martyred in the persecution of Christians ordered by the Roman Emperor Valerian in 258 AD. Where Montreal stands today, Cartier found a village he called Hochelaga. He was prevented from going further by boat because the Lachine Rapids made it impassable. Cartier climbed up the mountain and named it Mont Royal which is also how Montreal got it's name. The Lachine Rapids were named Sault St Louis and the lake where the Saint Lawrence and Ottawa Rivers meet at the western edge of the island of Montreal were named Sault-Saint-Louis and Lake Saint-Louis in 1611 by Samuel de Champlain who also named Saint Helen's Island in honour of his wife.

We had to curtail our discussions with Frère Marcel often having to bring him back to talk about what we wanted to know rather than embark on a detailed history lesson even though that in itself was very interesting and we did not wish to show any disrespect to him. He stopped and laughed many times realizing that he had ventured off track when we stopped writing notes on our note paper. Frère Marcel told us about François Dollier de Casson who was responsible for the first survey and street layout of Montreal which at that time was still called Ville Marie. François Dollier de Casson (1636 – September 27, 1701) a priest belonging to the Society of the Priests of Saint-Sulpice (Compagnie des Prêtres de Saint-Sulpice) arrived in Quebec in 1666 and served as military chaplain with Marquis Alexandre de Prouville de Tracy (c. 1596 or 1603–1670) lieutenant-général of the Carignan-Salières Regiment and acting governor of New France. Prouville de Tracy had initiated a brutal war and defeating the Iroquois attacked the Mohawk nation and seized all the Mohawk lands in central present-day New York in the name of the king of France. He forced the Mohawk to accept the Roman Catholic faith and to adopt the French language as taught by the Jesuit missionaries. A mission village for Mohawk Catholics, Kahnawake, was set up south of Montreal. Marquis Alexandre de Prouville de Tracy died in Paris, France on April 28, 1670. François Dollier de Casson became superior of the Sulpicians in New France in 1671. He wrote a "Histoire du Montreal" and drew up the plan for the construction of the church of Notre-Dame which was started in 1672 and completed in 1683. In 1672 he ordered the first survey of Montreal and laid out the planned first streets with the help of Bénigne Basset Des Lauriers, (1639 - August 4, 1699), a notary, clerk of court, and surveyor at Montreal. François Dollier de Casson undertook to negotiate with the owners of the lots and forced acceptance of his work by refusing to let the inhabitants sow crops where he had laid out these streets. The layout included three main streets parallel to the river (St. Paul, Notre Dame and St. Jacques) cut by seven others of varying lengths and widths. He named one of the streets "Saint-Lambert" which descended from Notre-Dame Street to the Petite rivière Saint-Martin, which flowed in the area of today's rue Saint-Antoine. On the other side of this river, a path in the forest became the main road to the Faubourg St Laurent (suburb St Laurent). That trail later became Saint-Laurent Boulevard and led north to the parish of Saint-Laurent. Le Faubourg Saint-Laurent was a suburb north of the fortified city of Ville-Marie. The area bordered on the east by Saint Denis Street, on the south by Saint Antoine Street, on the West by Saint Laurent Boulevard, on the north by Dorchester Street (today's René Lévesque Boulevard).

Because of clashes with the Iroquois in 1687 the settlers reinforced the palisade around Ville Marie with cedar piles 3.65 meters high. The village of Ville-Marie was officially renamed Montreal in 1705 and Place Royale was designated as a marketplace. On the north side of the wooden palisade there was the St Laurent gate, that led to the Saint-Laurent trail which now was a road that led into the Sulpician interior of the island of Montreal. Even as late as 1710 the area was mostly uninhabited and was covered with a dense forest of trees and bush. Settlers from within the fortified village of Ville Marie got their firewood and lumber for building their homes from the area helping to slowly clear the land from what they called Le Faubourg Saint-Laurent. Faubourg is a French term meaning suburb (now generally called banlieue), a term traditionally given to an area formed around a roadway leading outwards from a city gate. Le Faubourg Saint-Laurent slowly evolved east of what is now Saint-Laurent Street to Saint Denis Street. Further north beyond the Faubourg Saint-Laurent all the way north to near what is now Jean-Talon Street was a large area they called Coteau Saint-Louis. Remember that most of the area north of what is now Mount Royal Avenue, was blanketed with a thick forest of trees, bushes, creeks and water filled streams.

Meanwhile Montreal was growing and had several tanneries processing hides established s a major industry. To eliminate the offensive odours that the curing of hides generated, tanneries were being forced to relocate away from the city. This was also being done in order to permit development of Craig Street (now Saint-Antoine Street). In 1710 Jean-Louis Plessy Bellaire, installed his tannery in the Coteau Saint-Louis countryside, along a stream that descended from the mountain. The Belair Tannery (Tannéries des Bélair), the first industry in the sector, was located at the intersection of Chemin des Tanneries and Rabain Street, later Robin Street, (today's Mont-Royal and Henri-Julien avenues) just west of Saint-Denis Street. Chemin des Tanneries (Mount Royal Avenue) was built from St Lawrence Street to the tanning facilities of the Bélair family. Tannery workers decided to settle close to their place of work which resulted in them forming a small hamlet nearby on rue Rabain (Robin and now Henri-Julien). The hamlet grew into a village that became known as the "Village de la Tannerie des Bélair". It was the first village to emerge north of Faubourg Saint-Laurent. Quarries soon opened in the area with the discovery of gray limestone hard rock excellent for construction. Quarry workers streamed into the area accelerating the growth of the village and Coteau Saint-Louis became a source of limestone as the industry attracted the settlement of workers and artisans. Tannery Street led to the newly created Carrière Street further north. Its route followed the winding boundaries of the various quarries which were successively exploited. The tannery area was incorporated into the Municipality de la Cote Saint-Louis, commonly known as Coteau Saint-Louis, on October 20, 1846. Gilford Street led to the village of Côte Saint-Louis (north of present day Laurier Street) from Tannery Street.

The Saint-Laurent road was temporarily named Cote St. Lambert in honour of Raphael-Lambert Closse. The road was the dividing line between a farm given to Sergeant Major Lambert Closse in 1658 and the estate owned by Jacques Archambault from 1651. A stream ran down the route from the mountain to the St. Martin River, now St. Antoine. Raphael-Lambert Closse (1618-1662) a fur trader, notary seigneur, sergeant-major of the garrison of Ville-Marie and acting governor of Montreal had landed in Quebec (New France) in 1647. He rescued his wife Elisabeth Moyen from the Iroquois in 1657 and they got married on August 12, 1657. In February 1658 he was granted land by M. de Maisonneuve consisting of 100 arpents, beginning 10 rods from the big river, by 40 rods wide beginning at Saint-Laurent Street. Lambert Closse was killed by a band of Iroquois on February 6, 1662. On June 27, 1672 land was granted to Mrs Moyen, widow Closse. It was a narrow strip of land of 2 arpents over 45 arpents, located along the main street (Saint-Laurent Street) of the faubourg Saint-Laurent, east of it, and from the small river extending to the north. An arpent is a unit of length, about 58.47 metres (approximately 209 feet), while a perche (rod) is 5.847 metres (approximately 16 and a half feet).

Jacques Archambault (1604 – February 15, 1688) a French colonist had landed with his wife Françoise Tourault and family in Quebec City in 1645. He is commemorated with a plaque at the back of the Pointe-à-Callière Museum for having dug the first water well in Montreal on October 11, 1658 near today's Place-d'Armes at the request of Paul de Chomedey de Maisonneuve. In 1654 he received a concession of land to settle in Ville-Marie from Governor Maisonneuve. His wife, Françoise Toureau, died in 1663. After three years of widowhood, Jacques Archambault remarried in 1666 with Marie Denot de la Martinière, widow of Mathieu Labat, whose descendants created the famous brewery. Jacques Archambault died in 1688. The road was actually named Saint-Laurent Street in 1720 and sidewalks were constructed in 1804. It had its phone lines buried in 1961. Cabbages and potatoes grew alongside the hill below Sherbrooke until 1830. Horse-pulled streetcars required an extra team of horses to tackle the same hill until 1892 when electric trolleys replaced the horses and sped up development of the area. In 1905 the Main (Saint-Laurent Street) became the division between east and west addresses in the city. In the early days, Cars drove both ways on the Main until 1972, when the flow was directed one-way north.

Construction of a road called the Chemin du Roi (King's Highway) connecting the settlements along the north shore (Laval) of the St. Lawrence River, between Quebec City and Montreal began in 1731 and was completed in 1737. The Chemin du Roi was 7.4 metres (24 ft) wide and over 280 kilometres (170 mi) long, and crossed 37 seignories; it required the construction of thirteen bridges and enabled people to travel from one city to the other in four days. In 1910, the portion of the Chemin du Roi on Montreal Island was renamed by the District and County of Montreal as Gouin Boulevard in honour of politician Lomer Gouin (1861-1929), the thirteenth premier of Quebec (March 23, 1905 – July 8, 1920). Gouin Boulevard is the longest street on the Island of Montreal, stretching 50 kilometres (31 mi) across the north side of the island from Senneville in the west to Pointe-aux-Trembles in the east, where it intersects with Sherbrooke Street.

In 1713 fearing the threat of a British attack Michel Bégon de la Picardière (March 21, 1667 – January 18, 1747) the intendant of New France, decided that stone fortifications of grey crystalline and black limestone stonemasonry should replace the wooden palisade. These were constructed between 1717 and 1738; and Montreal became an enclosed stone wall fortified city. The perimeter of the stone ramparts totalled approximately 3,500 metres, and like the stockade that preceded them, the new ramparts consisted of strongholds and curtain walls forming defensive fronts. The main wall, or enceinte, was roughly six metres high and included eight large doors, some with drawbridges and eight posterns, or side entrances. The fortifications correspond roughly with present-day Berri Street to the east, Rue de la Commune to the south, McGill Street to the west, and Ruelle de la Fortification (Fortification Lane) to the north.

As we listened to Frère Marcel I remembered my drawing in grade four or five, which the school kept, of the fortified city of Montreal copied from an old map obtained from the school library. I found it very interesting to hear Frère Marcel describe fortification engineering using terms such as the glacis which was an artificial slope in front of the counterscarp of a rampart (the main defensive wall of the fortification) constructed of earth as a temporary measure or of stone for a more permanent structure. The counterscarp and scarp were the outer and inner sides of a ditch or moat. Attackers had to descend the stone counterscarp, get across the ditch and ascend the stone scarp. The combination with the ditch was an obstacle designed to slow down or break up an attacking force and to give no cover to the attackers making advancing or retreating more difficult while exposing them to defensive fire from the defenders on the parapet or bastion wall of the fortress. A bastion was the wall of the fortress projecting outward, most commonly angular in shape and positioned at the corners. The fully developed bastion consisted of two faces and two flanks with fire from the flanks being able to protect the fortress wall and the adjacent bastions. The fortress walls were supported and reinforced with buttresses and had posterns often located in concealed locations which allowed the defendants to come and go inconspicuously. In the event of a siege, the posterns which were secondary doors could act as a gate, allowing the defenders to make a sortie on the besiegers.

The stonemasonry wall built on the side facing the St-Laurent River was mounted with a parapet, pierced with meurtrières, or gun sites. It was reinforced in some places by a supporting wall and a terreplein, or sloping bank. A similar wall was built on the land side to protect the enclosure from small cannon fire. The glacis, or forward slope, counterscarp, ditch and scarp together formed a defensive barrier over 25 metres wide. Many craftsmen including stonemasons, stonefitters, haulers, carpenters, blacksmiths, sawyers, locksmiths, roofers and labourers worked alongside soldiers to construct the fortifications. The fortified city was dotted with nearly 400 large buildings, many belonging to religious communities, landscaped with great walled gardens. With its fourteen bastions and its adjoining stone walls at a height of more than six meters and an average thickness of 1.22 meters at its base, the fortifications of Montreal stood as a symbol of French resistance to Amerindian, English and American threats. On the north side only one door, the Saint-Laurent Gate, was used for security reasons. Northward from the gate leading to the back river was St Lawrence Street which was renamed St. Lawrence Boulevard in 1905. The road opened by the Sulpicians in 1717 made the area accessible and in the 1740s improved communications with the newly established farms which expanded the urbanized area of Montreal beyond its fortifications and into the central portion of the island of Montreal.

In 1754 the Notre-Dame-de-Bon-Secours Chapel within the fortifies city was destroyed by fire. Two years later, war between Great Britain and France erupted and was extended into North America along the frontiers between New France and the British colonies. It resulted in La guerre de la Conquête (the War of the Conquest) of 1756 - 1763. The French colonists were supported by France and by various native first nation tribes; namely, the Wabanaki Confederacy in Acadia; the Abenaki in Quebec, the Maritimes and in New England; the Algonquin Ojibwa, Ottawa and Wyandot in Quebec. The British colonists were supported by Great Britain and as well as the Cherokee and Catawba in the United States and the Iroquois Confederacy which included the Mohawk in Quebec and the Onondaga Cayuga Oneida and Seneca in New York. In 1759 the British army commanded by General James Wolfe defeated the French under General Louis-Joseph, Marquis de Montcalm on a plateau owned by Abraham Martin, a farmer, just outside the walls of Quebec City and the battle was said to have been fought on the Plains of Abraham. In accordance with the Treaty of Paris (1763) France ceded Canada and its territory east of the Mississippi River to Great Britain. France retained the islands of Saint Pierre and Miquelon. France's ally Spain ceded Florida to Britain in exchange for the return of Havana, Cuba. France ceded French Louisiana west of the Mississippi River, including New Orleans, to its ally Spain in compensation for Spain's loss of Florida to Britain.

In 1774 the British Parliament passed the Quebec Act formally known as the British North America (Quebec) Act 1774 allowing public office holders to practice the Roman Catholic faith, by replacing the oath sworn by officials to the British monarch without specifying any reference to the Protestant faith. This enabled French Canadians to legally participate in the provincial government without having to renounce their faith. It allowed Jesuit priests to return to the province and allowed Quebec to keep the French Civil Code to govern civil matters while English law prevailed in matters of public / criminal law. The American Revolutionary War (1775–1783), also known as the American War of Independence began with the Boston Tea Party in 1775, as a conflict between Great Britain and its Thirteen Colonies which declared independence as the United States of America. The first major military initiative by the newly formed American Continental Army led by major general Richard Montgomery (December 2, 1738 – December 31, 1775) and general Benedict Arnold (January 14, 1741 – June 14, 1801) was the Invasion of Quebec in 1775 aimed at gaining military control of the British Province of Quebec and convincing French-speaking Canadians to join the revolution on the side of the Thirteen Colonies. The British defenders of Quebec City led by General Guy Carleton defeated the Americans ending further confrontations.

In 1781 the Coteau Saint-Louis land area was shared by twenty owners including the Sœurs Grises, (Gray nuns, sisters of charity) and their neighbours Dumeyniou, Lepailleur, the Caron estate, among others. In the western area, near the mountain, the Religieuses Hospitalières of Hôtel-Dieu owned a one hundred fifty arpent property known as Terre de la Providence, or Mont Sainte-Famille. The religious orders still lived within the walled city and used these properties in Coteau St Louis primarily as woodlots. These lands at this time with the exception of two orchards, were mostly uninhabited, uncleared bush with some cropland but were mostly used as woodlots. To the east, across present day Saint-Laurent Boulevard, the Plessis-Bélair and Robrau-Duplessis families had eight properties and five tanneries near the "Village de la Tanneries des Bélair". In addition, Montreal bourgeoisie such as Bagg, Beaubien, Cherrier, Cadieux, Clark, Drolet, Boyer, Logan, Lafontaine, Foretier, Papineau, Guy, Viger, Villeneuve, as well as wealthy businessmen and industrialists such as Redpath, McGill, McTavish, etc. controlled large tracts of land.

In 1792, Montreal had expanded northward and established its official limits about two kilometers around the original fortifications, reaching north to where Duluth Street is. On December 20, 1792 the first post office was opened in Montreal and mail service between Canada and the United States was established on a fortnight (every two week) basis. Meanwhile the Napoleonic Wars in Europe (1803–1815), a series of major conflicts between the French Empire and its allies, led by Napoléon Bonaparte (August 15, 1769 – May 5, 1821) against a variety of European powers was taking place. With the wars came a demand for large amounts of squared timber for shipbuilding. Montreal was able to fulfil the demand which expanded its economic base considerably. The grey limestone from the Plessis-Bélair family quarries in Coteau Saint-Louis was used on most Montreal commercial buildings, houses and public buildings including the Montreal courthouse (1803), the Bank of Montreal (1818), the Bonsecours Market (1845) and the construction of the Notre Dame Cathedral on Place d'Armes. It was important to the growth of Montreal.

On April 26, 1803 the Soeurs de la Charité (the Grey Nuns), had sold land to Jean-Baptiste Boutonne Larochelle and Joseph Chevalier who on May 30, 1804 resold the land to John Clark (1767-1827) a butcher, born in England. John Clark erected and operated a tavern known as "Mile End" located at what is now the northwest corner of Saint-Laurent Boulevard and Mont-Royal Avenue. He was the first to use the Mile End name to designate the crossroads where his inn was located because the inn was located a mile beyond Sherbrooke Street, the outer limit of Montreal's built-up area at the time. The Mile End crossroads was strategically located at the junction of three roads. First was St-Laurent St., the main road to the north; the second was Côte St. Catherine Road and the third was Tannery Road. These last two are now parts of Mont-Royal Avenue. In his will, Clark called his property "Mile End Farm" and he called his own house located near to what is now the intersection of Saint-Laurent Blvd and Duluth Avenue, "Mile End Lodge". Part of his Mile End Farm, extended from Duluth to Mont-Royal, between Saint-Laurent and Saint-Urbain. Together with the Soeurs Hospitalières de Saint-Joseph, Clark was one of the main property-owners of the land north of Sherbrooke Street, from the slopes of Mount Royal to Saint-Lawrence Road.

Listening to Frère Marcel we were slowly getting closer to the area where our city block was located. Stanley Bagg (1788-1853) had left Massachusetts around 1795 together with his brother, Abner, and their father, Phineas who was a widower, farmer and in debt fleeing his creditors by emigrating to Canada. In 1810, Phineas and his son Stanley, then aged 22, signed a five-year lease with John Clark to rent the tavern and farm, known as "Mile End" today's northwest corner of Saint-Laurent Boulevard and Mont-Royal Avenue. Also in 1810, Stanley Bagg and a partner obtained a contract from the British Army to demolish the old citadel and to enlarge the Champ-des-Mars, on the edge of what is now Old Montreal. This first contract with the army led to a series of others; such as transporting weapons during the War of 1812, and construction of the fort on Île Sainte-Hélène. In the spring of 1811, Phineas and Stanley sublet a part of the farm, called The Quarry on the left side of the road to the Montreal Jockey Club and created the first horse racetrack in Lower Canada. The straightening of Côte Sainte-Catherine Road that had wound its way through the property of John Clark and his neighbours, helped to free space for the race track. Part of it later became the site of Jeanne-Mance Park, located between what is now Park Avenue and Saint-Laurent Blvd. On August 7, 1819, Stanley Bagg married Mary Ann Clark, daughter of John Clark. Stanley and Mary Ann had a son whom they named Stanley Clark Bagg. Stanley Bagg and his brother Abner became businessmen and were involved in several commercial projects: construction, brewing, wheat export, and even owned one of Mile End's quarries. Stanley Bagg also rented the land around Mile End Tavern so that cattle destined for John Clark's butcher shop were able to graze on the grasses there.

On June 18 1812 the United States president James Madison (1751-1836) who served in office from 1809 to 1817, declared war on Great Britain because Great Britain had imposed a number of trade restrictions disrupting American trade with France with whom Britain was at odds at the time. With Great Britain's naval superiority in control of the seas, the United States in order to strike at Great Britain, focused on expelling the British from Canada, then a British colony hoping to claim more territory to expand America's borders. The British navy's dominance of the seas was reflected in their conduct; where they boarded merchant ships bound to and from the United States, kidnapped the seamen and forced them to serve in the British navy. The practice was called impressment. On July 11, 1812 U.S. troops invaded Canada and faced a well-managed defense coordinated by Major-General Sir Isaac Brock (October 6, 1769 – October 13, 1812) a British army officer and colonial administrator in charge in Upper Canada (modern Ontario). The American army under General William Hull (June 24, 1753 – November 29, 1825) Governor of Michigan Territory (1805–13); invaded Canada at Sandwich (present day Windsor).

On August 13, 1812 Brock with a small body of regulars and York Militia volunteers arrived at Amherstburg at the western end of Lake Erie facing Hull's position at Detroit. There he was joined by Tecumseh (March 1768 – October 5, 1813) a Native American Shawnee warrior and chief, who had allied his forces with the British army and they prepared to launch an attack on Detroit. Even with his First Nations allies, Brock was outnumbered approximately two to one. He decided to lay siege to Fort Detroit from established artillery positions across the river in Sandwich and to use tricks to intimidate Hull. He dressed his militia volunteers in uniforms from his regulars, making it appear as if his entire force consisted of regular British infantry. Tecumseh had his approximately 400 warriors parade out from a nearby wood and doubled back under cover to repeat the maneuver, making it appear that there were many more men than was actually the case. Brock did the same with his men giving the appearance of having more numerous forces. Brock then sent Hull a letter demanding his surrender. In the letter he had stated that he did not want to be in a war of extermination making Hull aware that once hostilities commenced the large, raucous, barely controlled group of First Nations warriors would be beyond Brock's control. Brock then hammered the fort with cannon fire. On August 16, 1812 the day after receiving Brock's letter, Hull surrendered in fear of a massacre and withdrew halting the invasion.

The capture of Detroit and Hull's army wounded American morale, and eliminated the main American force in the area as a threat, while at the same time boosting morale among his own forces. Brock took the American supplies at Detroit and used them for his own. Brock's success at Detroit, earned him a knighthood and membership in the Order of the Bath. Tecumseh was made a brigadier general in the British army as the commander in chief of its Indian allies. The capture of Detroit led to British domination over most of Michigan Territory. Lieutenant General Sir George Prevost (May 19, 1767 – January 5, 1816) the military Commander in Chief in British North America (Canada), arranged an armistice with his counterpart, American Major General Henry Dearborn. However, President James Madison decided to continue the war, The pause gave the Americans time to regroup and prepare to invade Canada again on October 13, 1812 near Queenston when the Americans attempted to establish a foothold on the Canadian side of the Niagara River. The Battle of Queenston Heights was the first major battle in the War of 1812. It was fought between United States regulars and New York militia forces led by Major General Stephen Van Rensselaer; and British regulars, York and Lincoln militia and Mohawk warriors led by Major General Isaac Brock and Major General Roger Hale Sheaffe. Despite their numerical advantage the Americans, stationed in Lewiston, New York, were unable to get the bulk of their invasion force across the Niagara River due to the work of British artillery and inexperienced American militia. American forces were forced to surrender; however, Major-General Sir Isaac Brock was killed during the battle. The loss of Brock was a major blow to the British since it was he who had inspired his own troops, the militia and civilian authorities in Upper Canada by his blustering confidence and activity.

The victory at Detroit and Queenston Heights was short lived and on September 10, 1813 American Commodore Oliver Hazard Perry (August 23, 1785 – August 23, 1819) fought a successful naval encounter and defeated a Royal Navy squadron in the Battle of Lake Erie. It was the first time in history that an entire British naval squadron had surrendered. William Henry Harrison (1773-1841) mounted a successful defense of Fort Meigs, in Perrysburg, Ohio. Both of these events created a staging area for the recapture of Fort Detroit. Harrison went on to become president of the United States. He was the first U.S. president to die in office having served just one month in office, from March 4, 1841 to April 4, 1841, before dying of pneumonia. His tenure in office was the shortest of any U.S. president. The loss of the British squadron directly led to the critical Battle of the Thames on October 5, 1813 near present-day Chatham, Ontario. Harrison's army routed the British forces and killed Tecumseh which broke up the Indian alliance. Tecumseh had sought continued British support in order to defend tribal lands against the Americans. Harrison then retook Detroit. The British had burned all public buildings in Detroit and retreated into Upper Canada along the Thames Valley. With the defeat of Napoleon's armies in April 1814, Britain turned its full attention to the war in North America. British forces raided Chesapeake Bay and on August 24, 1814 captured the U.S. capital in Washington, D.C. and burned the White House. On September 13, 1814, Baltimore's Fort McHenry withstood 25 hours of bombardment by the British Navy. The following morning, the fort's soldiers hoisted an enormous American flag, a sight that inspired Francis Scott Key to write a poem he titled "The Star-Spangled Banner" which became the national anthem of the United States. Britain moved for an armistice after the failure of their assault on Baltimore. In the negotiations that followed, the United States gave up its demands for Britain to end impressment (the recruitment by force which the British navy used forcing unwilling individuals into service); while Britain promised to leave Canada's borders unchanged and abandoned efforts to create an Indian state in the Northwest. The Treaty of Ghent signed on December 24, 1814 ended the war between the United States and Britain restoring relations between the two nations with no changes to the pre-war boundaries.

The idea of circumventing the Sault-Saint-Louis (Lachine Rapids) goes back to the founding of Ville-Marie which was the hub for the fur trade. François Dollier de Casson, superior of the Séminaire de Saint-Sulpice de Montréal, reintroduced the idea in 1680 but attacks on Lachine by the Iroquois forced the work to be abandoned. The Montréal Sulpicians tried repeatedly to relaunch the project but they lacked financial resources in order to move ahead. In 1819, seven Montréal businessmen, founded the Company of the Proprietors of the Lachine Canal, however again their efforts to finance the canal failed. It was only in 1821 that the federal government took over the task and established a commission of ten men to supervise construction so that work could finally begin. The lowest bid was submitted by a group headed by Stanley Bagg who got the contract for the excavation and construction of the Lachine Canal. The group was awarded the contract, not only on the grounds of price, but because they offered to dig the whole canal of which one third of its entire length was composed of extremely hard igneous rock which would have to be blasted lose with gunpowder, whereas others offered to excavate only sections. The official breaking of the ground ceremony took place on July l7th, 1821, at Lachine with speeches, music and four large kegs of beer which were quickly emptied, by the labourers, most of whom were already internally reinforced with rum which was offered for sale nearby from Stanley Bagg's store. After the letting of contracts early in July, operations began almost immediately and Stanley Bagg brought in his father-in-law, John Clark, by making him the meat supplier to feed the men constructing the canal. The Lachine Canal, 14.6 m wide, 13.4 km long and 1.4 m deep was inaugurated four years later, in 1825.

The naming of Montreal streets is rather an interesting subject because the city includes a multitude of saint streets as their names but they do not refer to actual saints. These saint-streets occur where men are circumventing the Vatican to immortalize themselves in Montreal's collective memory. Many of the non saint names are self-serving street names named after the developers, their family or friends. Often they were used to honour people and even members of a land owner's family. In 1834, the heirs of notary Jean-Marie Cadieux de Courville (1780-1827) subdivided his land and laid out eight streets bearing the names of members of the Cadieux family: The notary and his wife Marguerite Roy (1787-

1857) had two sons Pantaléon and Hippolyte Cadieux de Courville and two daughters, Rachel and Henriette Cadieux de Courville. Both daughters were married. They were wives of the very patriotic brothers Jean-Baptiste Chamilly de Lorimier and Thomas Chevalier de Lorimier.

Rachel Street which runs east and west from Mount Royal mountain (Jeanne Mance Park or Fletcher's Field), past the Saint-Jean-Baptiste market and the Saint-Jean-Baptiste Church and past La Fontaine Park; is named in honor of the notary's daughter Rachel Cadieux de Courville (1814-1879). Her husband, the lawyer Jean-Baptiste Chamilly de Lorimier, was a member of the very patriotic Sons of Liberty and he participated in the patriot rebellion of 1837-1838 with his brother François-Marie-Thomas Chevalier de Lorimier. Her husband escaped imprisonment by taking refuge in the United States, until 1843. His brother François-Marie-Thomas Chevalier de Lorimier on the other hand was captured and was executed.

Henriette Street ran parallel to Marie-Anne street and disappeared with the rapid development of Marie-Anne street, was named in honor of the notary's daughter Henriette Cadieux de Courville and wife of the patriot Thomas Chevalier de Lorimier, brother of Jean-Baptiste Chamilly de Lorimier (Rachel's husband). Marie-Anne Street which starts at Jeanne-Mance Park and runs about 3 kilometers ending at D'Iberville Street where it changes its name to Hogan Street is named in honor of the notary's sister-in-law, Marie-Anne Roy, wife of Hippolyte Cherrier. The section of Marie-Anne Street west of Saint-Laurent Boulevard was ceded by Stanley Clark Bagg's estate on November 27, 1875.

Roy Street is named in honor of Marguerite Roy (1787-1857), wife of the notary Jean-Marie Cadieux. Napoleon street is named in memory of the notary's grandson, Jean-Guillaume Napoléon, son of Jean-Baptiste Chamilly de Lorimier and Rachel Cadieux de Courville, who died as an infant in 1833. De Lorimier avenue is named in honor of the patriot Thomas Chevalier de Lorimier, (husband of Henriette Cadieux de Courville), who was executed by hanging in Montreal on February 15, 1839 for his part in the rebellion of 1837-1838. Prince-Arthur was originally called De Cadieux Street and De Bullion Street was previously called De Courville in honour of the notary. City Hall Street (Hôtel de Ville) was once named Pantaléon Street and Coloniale Avenue had been named Hippolyte Street in honour of the notary's two sons.

The Pied-du-Courant Prison on DeLorimier Street, near the Saint Lawrence River and the Jacques-Cartier Bridge was opened in 1836 replacing the prison at Champ de Mars. It was built to hold over 276 prisoners, but held over 1500 prisoners from the 1837-1838 rebellion and was the site of the many executions by hanging following the Lower Canada Rebellion in 1838. The prison operated from 1836 to 1912 as a city prison and was replaced by Bordeaux Prison built in 1908 to 1912, located at 800 Gouin Boulevard West in the borough of Ahuntsic-Cartierville with a maximum capacity to hold 1,189 inmates. The Pied-du-Courant Prison was vacant from 1912 to 1921 at which time it was acquired by and became the headquarters of the Société des alcools du Québec, the provincial-owned liquor board in Quebec.

The Lower Canada Rebellion (La rébellion du Bas-Canada), the Patriots' War (la Guerre des patriotes) was an armed conflict in 1837–38 between the rebels of Lower Canada (now Quebec) and the British colonial power. There was a simultaneous rebellion in Upper Canada (now Ontario); both rebellions were motivated by frustrations with political reform. Their shared goal was responsible government. Louis-Joseph Papineau (October 7, 1786 – September 23, 1871), son of Joseph Papineau, a politician and lawyer was the leader of the reformist Patriote movement before the Lower Canada Rebellion of 1837–1838. He was the grandfather of the journalist Henri Bourassa, founder of the newspaper Le Devoir. His role in the 1837 rebellions against British rule forced him into exile until ne was granted amnesty and returned in 1845.

Louis-Joseph Papineau elected as speaker of the legislative assembly of Lower Canada in 1815 founded the Patriotes movement in 1834. He and members of the Parti patriote had drafted Ninety-Two Resolutions which were a series of demands for political reforms in the British-governed colony. Under the Constitutional Act of 1791, the government of Lower Canada was given an elected legislative assembly, but members of the upper houses were appointed by the Governor of the colony. The resolutions called for them to be elected rather than being appointed. On February 28, 1834, the Legislative Assembly approved Papineau's Ninety-Two Resolutions which together with a petition signed by 87,000 people was sent to the British House of Commons in London for consideration and adoption. The resolutions were ignored for almost three years; meanwhile, the Legislative Assembly did all it could to oppose the un-elected upper houses while avoiding outright rebellion. British Colonial Secretary Lord Russell eventually responded informing them that all of the Legislative Assembly's demands had been rejected. Most of Papineau's supporters were strongly opposed to the British parliament's rejection of the Patriote party's demands for reforms. They threw themselves into the resistance movement and took up arms. There were many skirmishes and casualties. Two major armed conflicts occurred when groups of Lower Canadian Patriotes, led by Robert Nelson (August 8, 1794 – March 1, 1873) an Anglo-Quebecer physician, crossed the Canada–US border attempting to invade Lower Canada and Upper Canada. They wanted to drive out the British army and establish two independent republics. A second revolt called the Battle of Beauharnois was fought on November 10, 1838 where François-Marie-Thomas Chevalier de Lorimier commanded five hundred armed Patriote men. They were crushed by the British colonial government forces and while attempting to seek refuge in the United States were captured and arrested near the border.

One hundred and eight rebels were taken to the Montreal Pied-du-Courant prison where a trial was held on January 11, 1839. Having failed to capture the principal leaders of the rebellion, the authorities eager for blood in an atmosphere of violence, fell back on the most prominent of the captured rebels. At the end of the trial on January 21, the accused were all found guilty of high treason. Fifty eight of the Patriote rebels were deported to Australia. The rebels Joseph-Narcisse Cardinal (February 8, 1808 – December 21, 1838) a notary and leader for the Patriote army at Châteauguay and Joseph Duquet (September 18,

1815 – December 21, 1838) a notary, captured at Kahnawake when they attempted to get weapons from the native people were executed on December 21, 1838. On February 15, 1839 Chevalier DeLorimier, Charles Hindelang (March 29, 1810 – February 15, 1839) who fought the Battle of Odelltown, and Amable Daunais, François Nicolas, and Pierre-Rémi Narbonne and others were executed by hanging by the British authorities at the Montreal Pied-du-Courant Prison. In 1882 the Montreal city council changed the name of Avenue Colborne to Avenue de Lorimier in honour of François-Marie-Thomas Chevalier de Lorimier (December 27, 1803 – February 15, 1839), a notary who fought as a Patriote and Frère chasseur (Hunter Brothers a paramilitary organization for the independence of Lower Canada - Quebec) in the Lower Canada Rebellion.

During this time Jacques Viger (May 7, 1787 - December 12, 1858), served as the Montreal island road's inspector (1813-1840). He was the first mayor of Montreal (1833-1836). The eastern portion of Mile End was dominated by active quarries and for purposes of road management was called the Saint-Michel division. It was bisected by Saint-Michel Road, better known as Tannery Road and Carrière Road. Maintenance of the roads linking the village at the quarries to the city was a major issue keeping road repair work brigades very busy because of the heavy loads of stones being transported to the city. At Viger's suggestion, to reduce congestion on St-Laurent Road, toll barriers were installed on Victoria Road (today's Papineau Avenue) which was used for a horse-drawn tramway to haul stones from the quarry. This in effect, was assessing a tax on the quarries requiring users to pay a fee in order to use the road.

The Act of Union known as the British North America Act, 1840 was enacted in July 1840 and proclaimed on February 10. 1841 abolishing the legislatures of Lower Canada and Upper Canada and instead establishing the Province of Canada which was divided into two parts: Canada East and Canada West. The Governor General remained the head of the civil administration of the Province of Canada appointed by the British government, and responsible to it, not to the local legislature. He was aided by the Executive Council who reviewed legislation produced by the elected Legislative Assembly.

In 1808 a cousin of Jacques Viger, Denis-Benjamin Viger (Aug. 19, 1774 - Feb. 13, 1861), lawyer, journalist, essayist, and politician who represented the county of Montreal East in the House of Assembly of Lower Canada married Marie-Amable Foretier, the 30-year-old daughter of Pierre Foretier, a seigneur and former fur trader. Through his mother, Périne-Charles Cherrier, daughter of François-Pierre Cherrier; a Cherrier of Saint-Denis-sur-Richelieu, Denis-Benjamin Viger was related to the Papineau's. On his mother's death in 1823, Viger inherited the family fortune, which included five houses and 47 acres of land in the faubourg Saint-Louis. Mme Viger inherited her father's, Pierre Foretier's property, the Île Bizard seigneury. From then on Viger was one of the most important landed proprietors of Montreal.

Another beneficiary of Pierre Foretier was Dr. Pierre Beaubien (1796-1881) a medical doctor and politician: a graduate of the Sorbonne, and one of the founders of Montréal's Francophone school of medicine over the opposition of McGill University doctors who wanted to maintain their monopoly over the field. On July 23, 1842 he inherited one-fifth of the estate of Pierre Foretier and his wife, consisting of two large properties: the terre de Sainte-Catherine (in the heart of what is now Outremont) and the terre des carrières, a long narrow strip in Coteau-Saint-Louis: its boundaries correspond to what is now Mont-Royal Avenue (on the south) de Castelnau Street (north); St.-Laurent Blvd (west); and Coloniale Street (east). In 1844, Pierre Beaubien with Louis-Hippolyte Lafontaine, future Prime Minister of the United Province of Canada and Joseph Bourret, then Mayor of Montreal, and others acquired land located north of Saint Catherine Street, up to the Saint-Laurent parish and bounded by what is now Henri-Julien Street.

Beaubien was one of the largest landowners in Montreal, holding large properties in Côte-Sainte-Catherine, Côte-Saint-Louis and Côte-des-Neiges (the site of the Catholic cemetery). At the time, the land owned by Beaubien north of today's Mont-Royal Avenue was deserted and not very inviting for agriculture. The soil was shallow, rocky and parts were marshland. However he had a stone quarry located between what are now the streets of Laurier, Colonial, Saint-Joseph and Henri-Julien. The area was home to the tiny hamlet where quarry workers lived, known as Pierreville. The largest quarries were located further east in what is now Sir Wilfrid Laurier Park bordered by Laurier Avenue East to the south, De Brébeuf Street to the east, Saint Grégoire Street to the north and De Mentana Street to the west. That was where the main core of the village Coteau Saint-Louis was located. Back in the 1840s the town had installed a toll booth on Saint-Lawrence and Mount-Royal, as St Lawrence Street was still the only North-South axis on the island.

The tannery area was incorporated into the Municipality de la Cote Saint-Louis on October 20, 1846. Le Coteau-St-Louis was one of the first villages founded north of Montreal in 1846. It grew around the Chemin des Carrieres, (present day Berri Street) which began at the Belair Tannery on the corner of Sanguinet and wound its way northwards to various stone quarries. This street is now called Gilford, but retains its old name above the tracks in Rosemont. The area around Laurier park was a quarry then and had been inhabited for decades by "pieds-noirs" (black feet) quarrymen, whose drinking, singing, feuding and fighting habits were legendary. The area became quickly populated because of increased economic activity from the quarries and tanneries. It was helped in 1864 with the introduction of a horse-drawn tramway that facilitated commuting with downtown Montreal. Believing that the establishment of a church was a sure way to increase the value of adjacent properties, on November 3, 1849 Beaubien donated a series of lots adjacent to his Pierreville quarry to Bishop Bourget to build the Enfant-Jésus Church on Beaubien Avenue (today's Saint-Dominique Street) between St Joseph Boulevard and Laurier Street. Until the early 1900s it was the heart of the community. In 1905 the town built an extravagant, chateau-like hotel-de-ville just across the street, which became the current police and fire station on what is now the corner of Laurier and St Lawrence Street.

Frère Marcel knowing that I was attending the High School of Montreal at the time thought that I may be interested in its history since I already knew that it had been founded in 1843 as an English-language high school for boys. In 1801 the

Royal Institution for the Advancement of Learning (RIAL) had been created by the Legislative Assembly of Lower Canada under an Act for the establishment of Free Schools and the Advancement of Learning in the Province. When James McGill died in 1813, he bequeathed his "Burnside estate", a 19-hectare (47-acre) tract of rural land and 10,000 pounds to the Royal Institution for the Advancement of Learning who were charged with administering the bequest. The will specified that the land and funds had to be used within 10 years of his death for the establishment of a private, constituent college or university bearing his name; otherwise the bequest would revert to the heirs of his wife. Marie-Charlotte (1747-1818), the widow of Joseph-Amable Trottier Desrivières (1732-1771) whom he had married in 1776. On March 31, 1821, after protracted legal battles with the Desrivières family (the heirs of his wife), McGill College received a royal charter from King George IV. The Charter provided that the College should be deemed as a University, with the power to confer degrees. McGill College was inactive until 1829 when the Montreal Medical Institution, founded in 1823, became the college's first academic unit and Canada's first medical school. In 1833 the Faculty of Medicine made history awarding the first medical degree in Canada when it granted its first degree, a Doctorate of Medicine and Surgery. The Faculty of Medicine remained the school's only functioning faculty until 1843, when the Faculty of Arts began.

In 1816 the RIAL was authorized to operate two Royal Grammar Schools, one in Quebec City and one in Montreal. In 1846 the Royal Grammar School in Quebec City was closed. In 1853 the RIAL took over the High School of Montreal from the school's Board of Directors and merged the Royal Grammar School that it was operating in Montreal with it. From 1853 to 1870 it was called the High School of McGill College and the RIAL continued to operate it until 1870 when control of the school was transferred to the Protestant Board of School Commissioners. After which the sole remaining purpose of the RIAL was to administer the McGill bequest on behalf of the private college. The RIAL continues to exist today; it is the corporate identity that runs the university and its various constituent bodies, including the former Macdonald College (now Macdonald Campus), the Montreal Neurological Institute, and the Royal Victoria College (the former women's college turned residence). Since the revised Royal Charter of 1852, The Trustees of the RIAL comprise the Board of Governors of McGill University. Girls were first admitted in 1875 to a separate division called the High School for Girls, and a new building shared by both the High School for Girls and the High School of Montreal was opened in 1878. In 1915 the shared school moved to University Street near Sherbrooke Street, close to the McGill University campus. Girls and boys were taught in separate wings of the building and were also apart for school sports. The school aimed to develop both body and mind believing in the principle of "mens sana in corpore sano" (a healthy mind in a healthy body) the University Street site had its own swimming pool, two gymnasiums, a library, an auditorium and a planetarium with a large dome-shaped projection screen onto which scenes of stars, planets, and other celestial objects were shown simulating the motions of the night sky from any point of latitude on Earth. In the late 1970s, with the school under the control of the Protestant School Board of Greater Montreal, the decision was taken to close it with effect from June 1979, largely the result of a decline in the English-speaking population in the area. The building was sold and today is used by the mostly French-speaking Fine Arts Core Education School.

In 1845 the territory around the city or parish of Montreal was organized as one large municipality called Hochelaga. On June 9, 1846, Hochelaga was subdivided, and the village around the Bélair tannery, together with the surrounding area, was incorporated as a municipality, called the Village of Côte-Saint-Louis. The boundaries of the Village of Côte Saint-Louis commonly called "La Tannerie de Bélair" included the area of the Sulpicians' Coteau Saint-Louis outside of Montreal's city limits including the locations of major quarries north to the Sault-au-Récollet Parish, east to Papineau road and west to the village of Côte des Neiges. In1847 within the parish of Montreal, there were two municipalities; namely, the city of Montreal itself, and the Village of Côte-Saint-Louis. Côte Saint-Louis was divided several times later as land promoters among the largest landowners of the district such as the Bagg family on the west side of Saint-Laurent Boulevard and the Beaubien on the east established residential towns; all of which were annexed by Montreal in 1893.

In the 1840s, the city of Montreal acquired and developed several parcels of marshland on which Viger Square was created (present day bordered to the west by Saint Denis Street, to the east by Saint André Street, to the north by Viger Street and to the south by Saint Antoine Street). Prior to 1851, a hay market and public weighing scale operated on the site on the east side of Saint Denis Street. The hay market moved a few times on the site, but was always to the east. Viger Square was inaugurated on September 11, 1860. In 1865, greenhouses were added.

In Feb 1849 Louis LaFontaine introduced the Rebellion Losses Bill to compensate Lower Canadians whose property had been damaged during the Rebellions of 1837-38 (totalling about £100,000). The Bill was modelled on and was similar to legislation for Upper Canada passed by Baldwin that was based on a claims report approved in principle in 1846. LaFontaine saw the bill as a step towards responsible government and as a symbolic means to stem the growing influence of Louis-Joseph Papineau (October 7, 1786 – September 23, 1871), leader of the reformist Patriote movement and the 1837 rebellions against British rule who having been granted amnesty had returned in 1845. The Tories who were largely Anglophones and supported British rule and economic links with Britain, felt threatened by the French Canadian influence in government. They saw the Rebellion Losses Bill as a sign of French domination of the union and their own loss of power; they criticized it as payment for disloyalty. The bill was signed into law April 25, 1849 confirming responsible government in Canada. It meant an executive or cabinet that was dependent on the support of an elected assembly, rather than on the monarch was vital to good governance. Further it meant that laws were made and taxes were levied by a body that had some accountability to the citizens it governed. Granting royal assent to the bill sparked riots in Montreal and people were summoned to a protest meeting that night, April 25, 1849.

That evening a crowd of over 1,000 loyalists gathered around 8 p.m. on the Champ de Mars (a former military parade ground) and were whipped to a frenzy by orators who led them to the seat of Parliament at the St. Anne's Market. The mob broke the windows of the House of Assembly, which was still in session despite the late hour. The members of the House ran for cover while the mob broke in and vandalized the building. Lit torches were thrown, which ignited coal gas (used to fuel gas lamps) leaking from broken pipes. The fire was set by loyalist rioters attempting to disrupt an ongoing Assembly session and was in retaliation for passing the Rebellion Losses Bill. The fire spread rapidly. Rioters ran outside carrying the Parliamentary Speaker's ceremonial mace. Firefighters arrived, but the mob stopped them from fighting the flames. The building was totally destroyed within two hours. The fire destroyed the Parliament's two libraries, and part of the archives of Upper and Lower Canada, along with other public documents. It was reported that out of 23,000 books in the libraries, only about two, along with the portrait of Queen Victoria, were saved. An invaluable collection of historical records were lost forever in the fire.

Parliament reconvened the following day, April 26, at the Bonsecours Market. Less than a month after the riots it was decided that the seat of government should no longer be Montréal, which was considered too susceptible to ethnic tensions. The capital of the Province of Canada was moved to Toronto at Front and Simcoe Streets and reconvened on May 14, 1850. Political reforms followed the rebellions and the burning of Parliament as Canada was of vital strategic interest to the British Empire. The British could not afford to lose the rest of North America, especially after the results of the War of 1812 and so they acquiesced to what gradually evolved into full legal national sovereignty.

By 1850 Montreal was already two hundred years old, having been founded as Ville Marie on May 17, 1642. It was the biggest city in British North America, a business metropolis and major port. Thousands of English and French speaking people kept arriving in the city from the rural countryside hoping to improve their lot and found work for wages in industrial shops and factories. They settled in the suburbs outside the city limits of Montreal; such as the villages of Saint Jean Baptiste and Saint Louis du Mile-End to the north, Hochelaga to the east, and St. Gabriel, Ste. Cunégonde and St. Henri to the southwest. A huge number of new dwellings to accommodate a greater density of population were built. Developers came up with an architectural innovation; a two-storey building with one flat on top of another. It was called a wooden duplex and it became the standard model for Montreal housing. Rows of duplexes were built right up to the edge of the sidewalk with staircases inside. After the 1860s duplexes evolved into triplexes which housed up to five or six dwellings. In the 1880s, wooden duplexes and triplexes were replaced with brick and stone and were built further back from the sidewalk with staircases outside. Further innovations to commercial buildings followed such as steel structures and elevators which made it possible to build taller buildings, new warehouses and Victorian style office buildings in Old Montreal.

On July 8, 1852, Montreal suffered a great fire that destroyed almost half of the city's housing. 11,000 houses on the eastern side of the city had burned leaving as many as 10,000 people homeless. The fire happened when the city's reservoir, located at the site of today's Saint-Louis Square, was drained and closed for repairs. The fire had started in a wooden house and quickly spread to a tavern on St. Lawrence Boulevard. Fanned by strong winds and hot, dry summer weather the fire engulfed the entire block in between Saint Denis Street and Craig Street (now Saint Antoine Street). The flames enveloped the Saint Jacques Cathedral, the hospital on Dorchester Street and the Theatre Royal. Within hours, one quarter of Montreal had been destroyed.

On June 18, 1853 the Grand Trunk Railway (GTR) started running trains between Montréal and Portland, Maine, whose harbour was open year round. It was the first cross border railway in North America. Portland was the primary ice-free winter seaport for Canadian exports. In 1856 GTR began passenger service between Montreal and Toronto and GTR built Canada's largest railway shops in Point St. Charles, southwest of Old Montréal, which hired over 2,000 workers.

On July 12, 1856 in the village of Saint-Jean Baptiste, Joseph-Octave Villeneuve (1836-1901) rented from Stanley Clark Bagg, the two-storey stone Mile End Tavern with stables, sheds and two gardens as well as a one-arpent lot fronting on Saint-Laurent Street, just across from the tavern on the southwest corner. On that land Villeneuve constructed a building with a 32-foot frontage and an 18-foot depth complete with butchers stalls which served as his J.-O. Villeneuve & Co. wholesale grocery store selling to retailers and to wholesalers (large families, who grouped together and bought their provisions by the sack). In 1857 the Saint-Enfant-Jésus du Mile-End Church was completed.

During the construction of the Lachine Canal and Notre Dame Church the Montreal Mechanics' Institute was founded in 1828, a time when the building trades were expanding rapidly. In 1833 with John Redpath, a builder, as president, a public lecture program was established and night classes were created having a syllabus which included mechanical and architectural drawing, details of engines and other machinery and practical geometry. This was one of the first organized efforts in Canada to encourage adult education, and it continued for nearly thirty years until the classes were taken over by the government sponsored Board of Arts and Manufacturers in 1868.

Beginning in 1843 small industrial exhibitions called the Mechanics' Festival were held annually in Bonsecours Hall by the Mechanics' Institute presenting to the public the scientific advances being made by various industries in the city. The exhibitions were focused on local rather than international industrial advances. The Bonsecours Market, which opened in 1847, provided an ideal venue. The vast market building was used for a manufacturing and industrial show in 1851, for an exhibit by the Natural History Society of Montreal in 1855 and, later that year, for a preview of exhibits bound for the London Industrial Exhibition of 1856. The shows were Victorian affairs and very popular Montreal social events and included vocal and instrumental music. In 1845, the Mechanics' Institute of Montreal was incorporated and in 1855, they opened their own building with a large lecture hall, library and reading room, at the corner of St. James and St. Peter streets (now St. Jacques and St. Pierre).

The Board of Arts and Manufactures for Lower Canada was created in 1857 by the Quebec government who were anxious to promote Provincial exhibitions and the Board undertook the construction of the "Crystal Palace", an exhibition hall, which was built for the Montreal Industrial Exhibition of 1860. It was built at the foot of Victoria Street (one block west of University) between Sainte-Catherine and Cathcart Streets. Its design inspired by the famous glass-and-steel structure of the Crystal Palace built for the Great Exhibition in London in 1851, the Montreal version like the London building was suggestive of an enormous greenhouse, although far less glass was used in Montreal's exterior walls and none in its barrel-shaped roof. It was well lit by tall, rounded windows, and the ornamental woodwork on the outside made the structure look especially exotic. Montreal's Crystal Palace was constructed in 20-foot modules, but was constructed with shorter transepts, reducing its dimensions to 180 x 120 feet. Its main facades were of iron and glass. Its side walls were of white brick with rose-coloured contrast, with the iron and wood elements painted to match the brick. Its bays were subdivided by three arches, with only the centre arch glazed. It had an iron framework, a tinned barrel-vaulted nave and two galleries, each twenty feet wide, extending all the way around the interior.

On August 25, 1860 Albert Edward, the Prince of Wales and future King Edward VII, while visiting Montreal officially opened Victoria Bridge that had just been completed and after arriving by horse drawn carriage at the Crystal Palace, he declared the exhibition of industry and the arts open. As part of the exhibition the Art Association of Montreal, the future Montreal Museum of Fine Arts, organized a display of Canadian art. The crowds attending saw paintings, furniture, clothing, machinery, iron work, tools and crafts, displays of minerals (including a seam of coal 12 metres long), native woods, seeds and grains, preserved birds and fish, oils and foodstuffs, textiles and leather goods and a collection of furs and skins.

In subsequent years, the Crystal Palace served not only as an exhibition hall but also as an auditorium, a concert hall, a military drill hall and even a hostel. In 1874, accommodation was provided for 844 people in town for the St. Jean Baptiste Day celebrations. In winter the large open space of the exhibition hall housed a natural ice skating rink and was one of the first indoor skating rinks in Canada. The skating rink was used by McGill University students to play ice hockey and housed the Crystal Skating Club and the Montreal Crystals Hockey Club which played men's senior-level amateur hockey in the Amateur Hockey Association of Canada.

The crystal palace was owned by the Board of Arts and Manufacture while McGill University owned the land on which the crystal palace was built. In 1877 when the board and the university couldn't agree on a price for the property, the Quebec government bought the building on behalf of the board for $80,000, dismantled, moved and re-erected it in 1878 on the newly established fairground on Fletcher's Field (Champ de Fletcher) at the eastern foot of Mount Royal between Mont-Royal Avenue and Saint-Joseph Boulevard. The fairground was situated on land which ran from the summit of the mountain to Esplanade Avenue, between Pine Avenue and Mount Royal Avenue which included Fletcher's Field, that the city of Montreal had acquired to be used for parkland.

Fletcher's Field was named after a farmer near the property and was used as a military parade and training ground and by the lacrosse and football clubs as well as the Royal Montreal Golf Club.

No exhibitions were held from 1884 to 1890. Organizing exhibitions resumed only after new owners, the Montreal Exhibition Co., took over the building and refurbished it and revived the provincial fall fair in 1891, which had been suspended for seven years. The Crystal Palace was the fair's centrepiece. In the morning of July 30, 1896, fire broke out at the fairgrounds and strong winds quickly spread the flames to the Crystal Palace where its tinder-dry wood made the firefighters' task next to impossible. Although the fire brigade from the St. Louis du Mile End fire hall were fast in getting to the fairground, the fire was even faster. Before reinforcements could arrive from other stations and from St. Pierre St., it was effectively all over and the Crystal Palace was a smoldering ruin. Insurance covered most of the loss but the crystal palace was never rebuilt. Several years after the fire the site was developed for housing. With William Rutherford as president of the Mechanics Institute, the St. James Street building was sold during the 1910s and a new building was constructed at the corner of Atwater and Tupper streets. By 1940, the library boasted one of the finest technical reference libraries in Canada, and had a total of approximately 45,000 volumes. In 1962, the library changed its name to the Atwater Library of the Mechanics' Institute of Montreal.

Adjacent to the rich limestone deposit quarries in Côte Saint-Louis and next to Montée-Saint-Laurent (St Lawrence street) was a vast rural property owned by the Comte family. The Mile-End Road (Tannery road today's Mount Royal Avenue) located at the southern limit of the incorporated village of Saint-Louis-du-Mile-End led eastward to the tanneries and quarries. A toll gate had been installed at the corner of St. Lawrence and the Mile-End Road and it became a crossroad stopping point with the Mile End hotel and Hotel du Parc situated there; one mile from the city boundaries of the day. This was a favourite stopover place for farmers from further north to sleep before entering the city or to stop there after a day's work. To the west the road was populated with shady poplar trees conferring a solemnity to the path leading to the Protestant and Catholic cemeteries which were interconnected atop Mount Royal mountain at that time.

Montée-Saint-Laurent (St. Lawrence Street), the main road north, crossed the entire island of Montreal from the old city to the Rivière des Prairies (the Back River) and divided the village of Saint-Jean-Baptiste between east and west. On the east lived Francophone Catholic labourers and artisans, near their place of work primarily in the quarries. Further west was an agricultural zone, which was primarily used for rural recreation by the Anglophone élite, owners of country homes, orchards and hunting grounds. Until 1886 present-day Duluth Street was the northern city limit of the city of Montreal; north of which lay the village of Saint-Jean-Baptiste. St. Lawrence Street saw the passage of wagon-fulls of cut stone, cartloads of produce, and stagecoach loads of travellers stopping at the hotels alongside the farmhouses and the tradesmen's workshops. The arrival of the tramway disrupted this bucolic tranquillity, transforming the old villages into neighbourhoods teeming with activity.

With the influx of population from rural areas and from immigration, in 1861 the village of Saint Jean Baptiste was detached from the village of Coteau-Saint-Louis and became the Municipality of Saint Jean Baptiste. Joseph-Octave Villeneuve became mayor of the municipality and focused on developing it as a residential suburb for workers who needed housing. He welcomed the arrival of the streetcar making travel easier for the thousands of workers attracted by employment in the new factories. He continued as mayor until the annexation of Saint-Jean Baptiste with Montreal in 1886. When Louis Beaubien left politics in 1886 Joseph-Octave Villeneuve succeeded him as representative of Hochelaga in the provincial legislature. In 1861, Denis Benjamin Viger left his fortune and some land located in the municipality of Saint- Jean-Baptiste to his cousin and lawyer, Come Séraphin Cherrier (1798-1885) who in 1869 Cherrier gave to the Municipality of Saint-Jean Baptiste, two areas along the Saint-Laurent Road; namely, the market square at the corner of Rachel and St Lawrence streets, and a residential square, Vallieres Square (the current Portugal Park) at the corner of the Marie-Anne and St Lawrence streets. Cherrier's neighbor to the east was notary Jean-Marie Cadieux de Courville (1780-1827). A market building was built on the market square and was opened in 1870 named as the Marche Saint-Jean-Baptiste. Set up in the heart of the city it was the nerve center being the central market and the civic centre for the municipality of Saint-Jean-Baptiste. The building contained various butcher and gardener stalls. The ground floor housed the Hôtel-de-Ville and a large auditorium, which was used by the community for cultural purposes and for political gatherings. The construction of the first Saint Jean Baptiste Church at the corner of Rachel and Drolet occurred between 1872 to 1874 and it was rebuilt in 1912 to 1914. The municipality of Saint Jean Baptiste was annexed by Montreal in 1886. The market square (today's Parc des Amériques and yesterday's Rachel street market; namely the St Jean Baptiste market) continued to be the heart of the area with Vallière Square (now Parc du Portugal) at the other end of the city block.

In the 1930s during the depression, a period of economic crisis, the municipal authorities decided to put the many unemployed people to work on a public works program. After sixty years of use, the old Saint-Jean-Baptiste market was completely rebuilt; its architecture inspired by Art Deco, with floral motifs and more well defined horizontal lines. In 1931 the neighborhood had a brand new market. It was a two-storey building, with a protected sidewalk to align the farmers carts. In 1955, the carts gave way to trucks. There were stores located with entrances on the perimeter of the building and a fish market in the basement. The market was closed in 1961 considered to be old and unhealthy and was demolished in 1966. The St. Jean Baptiste Market and its 75 merchants on the northeast corner of Rachel and St Lawrence, an institution since 1870, was a victim of the wave of demolitions Mayor Drapeau ordered prior to Expo 67. The city beside incurring demolition costs also reportedly had to pay the descendants of Come Seraphin Cherrier because the 21,000 square-foot lot (today's Park of the Americas), was given by Cherrier to the city under the condition it be kept as a market in perpetuity. It was replaced by a parking lot. In 1990-1991, the park of the Americas was built in honor of the Latin American community,

Chapter 7 - Early Development

The Montreal streetcar network began in 1848 with the horse car era of the Montreal City Passenger Railway when the first horse-drawn omnibus (tramway) link was established in between Bonaventure Station and the Longueuil ferry landing. On May 18, 1861 the Montreal City Passenger Railway Company (MCPRC), was granted a license by the City of Montreal to operate an animal drawn streetcar in the city. It was the city's first public transportation company. Construction began on its six mile (10 km) network on September 18, 1861 and a first horse-drawn streetcar line was put into service on November 27, 1861 in the business district along today's Notre-Dame Street from Rue du Havre (Harbor St) to McGill Street. In winter the horse-drawn streetcars were replaced by horse-drawn sleighs. A second line was inaugurated a few days later on Saint-Antoine Street. Each horse-drawn tramway had two employees: the driver and the conductor, who sold the tickets and collected the five-cent fare. Workers, who earned less than a dollar per day at the time, couldn't yet afford this service which was reserved for a certain elite group. People simply hailed the tramway to have it stop and pick them up, and they could even ask the driver to wait a few minutes for them. In its first year, the company logged a million trips. Three types of cars were used: the summer tramway, which had open sides, the winter or sled tramway, which was very useful when the rails were covered with snow and ice, and the omnibus, a wheeled vehicle used when the rails were impassable, such as during the spring melt.

In 1861 St. John the Evangelist Anglican Church was founded by Father Edmund Wood. The church was built in 1877-1878, dedicated in 1878, and consecrated in 1905. The church is well known in Montreal as the "Red Roof Church", which is also the headquarters of St. Michael's Mission which provides food, clothing, and support to the disadvantaged in the area. Inside the Church, there is a large stone rood screen with a crucifix flanked by statues of Our Lady and St John. There is a side chapel dedicated to St Anne, mother of the Blessed Virgin Mary. The church's orientation is Anglo-Catholic referring to beliefs and practices within Anglicanism that emphasise the Catholic heritage. St. John the Evangelist Anglican Church is the only Anglican locale in Montreal to practise this tradition, known as High Church which uses a number of ritual practices associated in the popular mind with Roman Catholicism. While High Church is referred to as Anglo-Catholic, the opposite is Low Church which media prefer to call evangelical. High Church Anglicanism tends to be closer than Low Church to Roman Catholic and Eastern Orthodox teachings and spirituality; its hallmarks are relatively elaborate music, altarpieces, clergy vestments and an emphasis on sacraments.

The Constitution Act / British North America Act of 1867 was passed by the British Parliament receiving royal assent on March 29, 1867 whereby the Province of Canada ceased to exist at Canadian Confederation on July 1, 1867, and was divided into the Canadian provinces of Ontario and Quebec, each province having its own Legislative Assembly, as well as representation in the Parliament of Canada. On July 20, 1871, British Columbia entered Confederation as Canada's sixth province after having been promised that a railway would be built from Montreal to the Pacific coast recognizing the importance of having an Intercolonial Railway extending across the nation. The last spike of the Canadian Pacific Railway track was hammered in the BC Kootenays on November 7, 1885 fulfilling the promise.

The chain of mountains north of Montreal called the Laurentians were sparsely colonized with only a few villages until the second half of the 1800s. During the winter these villages were completely isolated and the roads were completely impassable. François-Xavier-Antoine Labelle also known as Curé Labelle (November 24, 1833 – January 4, 1891) a Roman-Catholic priest was principally responsible for the settlement (or "colonization") of the Laurentians. He hoped to promote colonization of his parish in the Laurentians by initiating the Montreal Colonization Railway with a branch line between Montreal and St-Jérôme in 1869, and was determined to encourage industrial development in order to attract more residents to the area. In January 1872 Labelle arrived in Montreal which was then in the grips of a severe cold spell and running short of firewood and sold his idea of providing the city with a steady supply of firewood to Montreal businessmen, all he needed was a rail line to carry the fuel. He received financial support in the form of a grant of a million dollars from the city of Montreal on the promise of delivery of firewood to the city. The plan was for Montreal Northern Colonization Railway to create a rail line connecting Québec City with Ottawa with a branch line to St. Jerome on the north shore of the Saint-Lawrence River. The line started from the Harbor near the foot of Jacques Cartier Square, and ran to Craig Street, then east of St. Denis Street, to Cote de Baron (Sherbrooke St.) then north to the Back River, crossing it and going in the direction of St. Martin and St. Eustache then toward the Ottawa River at Carillon, and crossing various small streams following its north shore to the Village of Hull, then over the river into the City of Ottawa. Fulfilling the dream of Curé Antoine Labelle, the railway was nicknamed "le petit train du nord".

Louis Beaubien (July 27, 1837 – July 19, 1915) son of Pierre Beaubien represented the riding of Hochelaga in the Legislative Assembly of Quebec from 1867 to 1896 and one of the founders of the district of Outremont was one of the founding shareholders of the Montreal Northern Colonization Railway Company when it was incorporated on April 5, 1869. He and his group of businessmen saw it as a chance to compete with the Grand Trunk Railway who had a monopoly at the time. The route adopted by the company placed a train station in a sparsely inhabited area on land owned by Beaubien, less than a kilometre away from the cluster of institutions around Saint-Enfant-Jésus Church and the Institut des Sourds-Muets on Saint-Dominique Street and Laurier Avenue that the Beaubien family had created. On March 26, 1876, Doctor Pierre Beaubien submitted to the registration office a subdivision plan for lots in Côte Saint-Louis village, between the train station and the church, with many of the streets named after members of his family: Lauretta, Alma, Casgrain, de Gaspé, Beaubien and Maguire. The railway line and station were built and the company ran out of money, not having enough finances to complete the project.

At the time financing came from London and the British owned Grand Trunk Railway (GTR) lobbied secretly against the project and financing was denied. Although Quebec was already well-served by rail connections to Ontario and to some New England states, the province's regional network was sparse with Industry and politicians clamoring for more railways. The Quebec government purchased the Montreal Northern Colonization Railway Company as it headed toward bankruptcy in 1874. The government joined it in December 1875 with another project, the Quebec North Shore Railway who had planned a rail line along the north shore linking Quebec City and Montreal, and renamed the merged line the Quebec, Montreal, Ottawa and Occidental (QMO&O), and assumed responsibility for costs of construction. QMO&O began as a "colonization railway" built to serve regional needs and to open new territories for industry and development. The Montreal - Hull line opened in 1877 and the Montreal - Quebec City line, two years later. The Quebec government's commitment to the QMO&O ended with its completion and it officially became part of the Canadian Pacific Railway (CPR) in 1884. The line remained in operation until the 1990s, when the CPR abandoned or sold all its routes east of Montreal.

On October 16, 1876, the QMO&OR opened a railway line between Hochelaga (corner of Ste-Catherine street and Harbour, Montreal) and St-Jérôme. After the sale of the assets of the Montreal Northern Colonization Railway Company, its charter was used to restart a company in the Laurentians under the name of Montreal & Western Railway on May 25, 1883. On September 1, 1892, the St-Jérôme to Ste-Agathe line (30,5 miles) was opened and reached Labelle on December 4, 1893; the CPR leased the line from 1890 to 1897, then bought it on March 25, 1897. On July 10, 1899, the Compagnie de Chemin de Fer de Colonisation du Nord (Northern Colonisation Railway) was formed and extended the railway to Mont-Laurier which was reached in 1909; the railway was leased by CPR for 999 years.

In the 1870s, a group of four ambitious promoters accelerated residential development in the Municipality of Saint-Jean-Baptiste. They viewed the vast partly deforested territory to which a large number of workers and laborers had been attracted to as a lucrative opportunity. The vast rural Municipality of Côte-Saint-Louis had been divided into large estates of English and French Canadian notables who had built their mansions, cultivated the lands, tended apple orchards and operated a horse racing field. Ferdinand (Fernand) David, Severus Rivard, Michel Laurent and Gustave-Adolphe Drolet (respectively entrepreneur, lawyer and future mayor of the city, architect and lawyer) formed a real estate company and acquired land belonging to Benjamin-Godfroi Comte which extended from Duluth Street to Mont-Royal Avenue between the avenues of the City Hall Street (Hôtel-de-Ville) and Chateaubriand Street; and land belonging to Louis-Paschal Comte which was located from the mountain and the fields owned by the Hôtel-Dieu in the west and extended through the village of Saint-Jean-Baptiste east of lands owned by Cadieux de Courville all the way to Papineau Street in the east. They subdivided the territory into 1,298 residential building lots.

Gustave-Adolphe Drolet (February 16, 1844 - October 17, 1904) was an entrepreneur, a knight of the Legion of Honor by the French government in 1878, and a knight of the Order of St. Gregory the Great knighted by Pope Pius IX. in 1877. Sévère-Dominique Rivard (August 7, 1834 – February 4, 1888) was a lawyer and served as the Mayor of Montreal between 1879 and 1881. He was a member of the Legislative Council of Quebec from 1886 until his death. Gustave Drolet and Sévère Rivard had built their reputation as Papal Zouaves (an infantry force formed in defence of the Papal States), who had defended the Pope against the forces fighting to unify Italy. Ferdinand-Conon David (May 30, 1824 – July 16, 1883) was a building contractor and a member of the Legislative Assembly of Quebec from 1871 to 1875. He served on the Montreal city council from 1861 to 1877. He was vice-president of the Saint-Jean-Baptiste Society at Montreal, president of the Société de L'Union Saint-Joseph de Montréal and the Société de Colonisation de Montréal, and a director of the Montreal Northern Colonization Railway. Michel Laurent (1833-1891), was a busy architect who did the bulk of his work with the city of Montreal. Early in his architectural career he designed the City and District Saving Bank building fashioned from gray stone on 266 Saint-Jacques Street at the southwest corner of Saint Jean Street. The building housed many notable tenants including Montreal's first telephone exchange in the 1880s. He achieved the apex of his design work in the 1870s, while in his forties; he designed five warehouse stores of Montreal gray stone in similar Romanesque styles for the Gray nuns on the northeast corner of Saint-Pierre Street and Place D'Youville. The commercial spaces were occupied by merchants, commission agents and small manufacturers. The properties were repurposed for residences in the 1970s.

In 1872 after subdividing the property, they donated 20 lots measuring 15 x 200 feet, on present day Rachel, Drolet and Henri-Julien streets to Monsignor Ignace Bourget (1799-1885) for the construction of the church of Saint-Jean-Baptiste which was built thereon two years later. The developers firmly believed that having a church in the area would attract households to the area. The church, dedicated to the patron of French Canadians, was inaugurated in 1874. The current church is the third to be erected on the site, the first two were destroyed by fire in 1898 and 1911. The group marketed the remaining residential lots in the La Minerve newspaper and sold them all. Drolet street and Rivard Street were named after the developers. Drolet Street was named after Gustave-Adolphe Drolet, who financed a project which he named "Place Comte" in honour of the former owner of the farm. It consisted of 45 small row cottages located on Drolet Street south of the church. The houses were assembled of wood with a façade of brick and carved stone. The assembly type of construction enabled a rapid building process and changes to the facade allowed for a variety of architecture, which suited the diversity of the market resulting in increased sales at advantageous prices. The developers were also responsible for the construction in 1875, of the Marie-Rose Academy of the Congregation of the Sisters of the Holy Names of Jesus and of Mary for the education of young girls; and in 1894, the Auclair Hospice which offered services to the poor of the parish, including children and the elderly. Rachel Street followed the development from east to west, and became the main artery of the Municipality of Saint-Jean-Baptiste.

In 1878, Joseph-Octave Villeneuve's cousin, Leonidas Villeneuve (1849-1913) opened a large lumber yard located on land leased from the Bagg family, just behind Mile End Tavern on St Lawrence street. The two cousins became partners in Leonidas Villeneuve & Co, Dealers in Lumber which was the prime destination for fire wood and construction wood transported by the railway that Louis Beaubien had created. The Company also owned woodlots in the Laurentians and a sawmill in Saint-Jérôme. Léonidas was elected councillor or mayor of Saint-Louis du Mile End for almost the entire period between 1883 and 1900. By 1900 most of the Italian and Jewish immigrants that had arrived in Montreal in the 1880s had moved to Saint-Louis du Mile End to be near working people and jobs related to the rapidly expanding railways and grey stone quarries. Leonidas Villeneuve holding office did not prevent his company from benefiting from contracts received from the city; such as supplying materials for the construction of sewers for the municipality of Saint-Louis du Mile End.

In 1874, landscape architect Frederick Law Olmsted (April 26, 1822 – August 28, 1903) designed Mount-Royal Park which was inaugurated in 1876 as a healing environment enabling people to recover their spirit and to better withstand city life. Many recreational activities were developed on the eastern slope of Mount-Royal including the first golf course in Canada, the Royal Canadian Golf Club which had opened in 1874 just east of Hôtel-Dieu, on land purchased from the Bagg family. Tobogganing and skiing on the slopes in winter became a favoured activity. The Mountain Park Funicular Railway was built and officially opened in 1885 as the Mount Royal Funicular Railway bringing sightseers to the top of Mount Royal. The mountain consists of three peaks: Colline de la Croix (or Mont Royal proper) at 233 m (764 ft), Colline d'Outremont at 211 m (692 ft), and Westmount Summit at 201 m (659 ft) elevation above sea level. As the designer of Mount Royal Park, Olmsted was opposed to the funicular. Instead of being whisked straight to the top by a machine, he believed in a slow progression to the summit. He favoured people taking a leisurely stroll up the mountain along the winding path that began near the Sir George Étienne Cartier Monument that allowed for a greater variety of perceptual experiences and enjoyment of the views along the way.

The funicular steam-driven cable car ride cost 5 cents for adults and 3 cents for children. It took people from the corner of Park and Duluth directly to the top of the mountain on the south-east side, above Duluth street in a matter of minutes and provided easy access to the east-end lookout. It offered Montrealers a spectacular view of the city and of Mount-Royal Park. The funicular railway consisted of a horizontal section that brought travellers from the ticket house, located near what is now the George-Étienne Cartier Monument, to a transfer station at the base of the mountain, where riders boarded the funicular cars. Both sections were steam-driven, with cars pulled by cables. The funicular cars were attached to each other by a cable, which ran through a pulley at the top of the slope and a second pulley at the bottom of the incline. The cars counterbalanced each other; with one going up and one going down thereby minimizing the energy needed to lift the car going up. Winching was done by an electric drive that turned the pulleys. The cars ran on two parallel straight tracks, four rails, with separate station platforms for each vehicle. The tracks were laid with sufficient space between them for the two cars to pass each other. It was a welcome alternative to climbing the mountain along the paths or ascending using the wooden staircase. The Mount Royal Funicular Railway also known as the Mountain Park Funicular Railway operated from 1885 until 1918 when it was declared structurally unsafe due to the weakening of its frail structure. It was shutdown in 1918 and dismantled in 1920.

In 1870, Viger Square was the only public place in Montreal to hear live music. Ernest Lavigne (December 17, 1851 - January 18, 1909), a Quebec musician, composer, conductor and publisher was solo horn with the Roman Zouaves in 1869. As a soloist, he won several honors, including two gold-plated horns. In 1885, he opened the Jardin Viger free concerts in Montreal where his performances made him a star. In 1881 Ernest Lavigne joined Louis-Joseph Lajoie and formed the firm of Lavigne & Lajoie publishing and distributing hundreds of works by various composers. Lavigne created a symphonic orchestra and directed his orchestra in Viger Square from 1885 to 1889. In 1889 the firm of Lavigne & Lajoie acquired a vast tract of land on the edge of the St. Lawrence River between the former Water and Salaberry streets and Notre-Dame and Panet streets, in the eastern sector of the city of Montreal. Ernest Lavigne developed that location as Sohmer Park, an amusement park, which was inaugurated on June 1, 1889 by a concert of classical music. Sohmer was the name of a piano brand of which Lavigne was the dealer. Sohmer Park had many attractions including concerts, military marches, operetta singing, rides and other attractions. The park was so popular that a pavilion for 7000 people was erected in 1893, so that activities could continue in the winter. On March 24, 1919 , a fire completely destroyed the pavilion and several major installations which led to the permanent closure of the park. Today the space is occupied by buildings owned by the Molson Brewery.

In 1892, at the request of citizens, Viger Square was enlarged. The cattle and hay market near Saint André St. was demolished and the area experienced a boom with the construction of prestigious buildings such as Place Viger (700 Saint Antoine Street) in 1898. Many of the French-Canadian elite moved near the square. In 1874 the City of Montreal inaugurated Logan Park a 34 ha (84 acres) park located on the grounds of the old Logan farm (present day La Fontaine Park) used since 1845 to house soldiers of the British garrison and for military practice. The area around Rachel Street continued to grow. The city of Saint-Jean-Baptiste was not annexed to Montreal until 1886 and consisted of the area bounded by Duluth, Mont-Royal, Park Avenue (Du Parc) and Papineau streets. In 1888 Fire Station 16 on Rachel Street across from Logan Park was built. In 1889 Panet Street, now known as Calixa-Lavallée Street, was extended to the park and the Victorian greenhouses from Viger Square were moved to Logan Park where flowers that adorned the city were grown until 1952.

Most of the park's neighbouring streets were residential, but on the south side, (the Sherbrooke Street side) was the colonnaded municipal library building (now known as the Édifice Gaston-Miron and headquarters of the city's art and heritage councils) and further south was the Notre-Dame Hospital. The park itself was home to several buildings such as the École supérieure du Plateau and the Calixa Lavallée pavilion. In 1895 construction had started on the gray stoned Immaculate-Conception Catholic Church of Montreal on the corner of Rachel and Papineau Streets. It was consecrated on June 5, 1898. In 1900, the city dug two basins at different levels, in the center of the park. They were separated by a waterfall over which a bridge was built. In 1901 during the Saint-Jean-Baptiste Day parade, Logan Park was renamed La Fontaine Park (Parc La Fontaine) in honour of Sir Louis-Hippolyte Ménard La Fontaine the first Francophone Canadian to become Prime Minister of the United Province of Canada.

There were two roads from Rachel to Sherbrooke through the park. The road closest to Papineau street was Avenue Emile Duployé and the road further away was Avenue Calixa Lavallée. In 1929 an illuminated fountain commissioned by the Westinghouse Electric Company was erected in the north basin. A few years later, La Fontaine Park was completely redesigned and a chalet restaurant was built. It was destroyed by fire in 1944. In the 1930s and 1940s the Park had a small fenced off municipal zoo in the summer with bears, turtles, birds and farm animals on the north west side of the park near Rachel Street. In the late 1940s, a new gray stone chalet with a restaurant and public washrooms was built. Walking down the stone steps on the building's exterior brought you to a lower level where you could rent a rowboat or canoe and enjoy rowing it about on the ponds or enjoy strolling on the walking path around both lakes. There were large motor driven crocodile gondolas and swan shaped boats that accommodated groups of people. Gradually the canoes were replaced by row boats perhaps because of the number of paddlers that had capsized and had to come out of the pond walking pitifully in their wet clothes.

In 1950 La Fontaine Park was completely refurbished. The greenhouses, caretaker's house, the waterfall and the Grenelle-built bridge were demolished. A new chalet-restaurant replacing the previous one destroyed in the 1944 fire was opened in 1953 by Camillien Houde, the Mayor of Montreal. A central pavilion, a band shell for symphony concerts, an amphitheater with a capacity of 4,000 seats and a new bridge were built and modifications were made to the two ponds. The amphitheater called Le Théâtre de Verdure was inaugurated on July 8, 1956. For over 50 years, the outdoor open-air theatre offered, free cultural programming and outdoor theatrical performances in a natural setting. A small urban miniature zoo, its buildings inspired by fables and tales, called the Garden of Wonders (Jardin des merveilles) built by the city, was opened on July 5, 1957. It was a children's zoo with farm animals and some, more exotic creatures such as an elephant and sea lions. It was dismantled in 1989. Some animals were relocated to Angrignon Park and others to the Granby Zoo.

On November 7, 1885 the last iron spike was driven into the Canadian Pacific Railway (CPR) track at Craigellachie, British Columbia by Donald Alexander Smith (Lord Strathcona) a principal financier of the C.P.R. and of the Hudson's Bay Company, in whose honour a beaver was chosen as the railway's logo. The first Trans Canada passenger train departed from Montreal's Dalhousie Station, at Berri Street and Notre Dame Street at 8 pm on June 28, 1886, and arrived at Port Moody, 20 kilometres from the small town of Granville, at noon on July 4, 1886 after travelling for five days, 19 hours. By that time, however, the CPR had decided to move its western terminus from Port Moody to Granville, which was renamed "Vancouver" later that year. In 1887 the first railway station was built in Vancouver, which quickly became Western Canada's main seaport.

On June 21, 1886 the Montreal City Passenger Railway Company (MCPRC) changed its name to the Montreal Street Railway Company (MSRC) after signing a new 25-year agreement with the City. At this point it had 1,000 horses, 150 streetcars, 104 sleighs for winter use, and 49 omnibuses. Electrification of the streetcar system began in 1892 and by mid-September, a one-way loop line of about five miles encompassing Bleury, Park Ave., Mount Royal Ave., St. Lawrence, Rachel, Amherst and Craig St. was ready for operation. On September 21, 1892, Montreal's first electric streetcar named the Rocket made its maiden voyage. By October 1894, the City's entire 75.15-mile streetcar system was officially electrified and the last horse-drawn streetcars and sleighs were withdrawn from service.

The construction of the Montreal Street Railway headquarters building at 750 côte de la Place-d'Armes was completed at the end of 1895. In 1911, the Montreal Street Railway Company was integrated into a new company, the Montreal Tramways Company, that encompassed all of Montreal's urban transit companies. In 1929, the Montreal Tramways Company moved to its new headquarters on St. Antoine Street and the Place-d'Armes building was sold.

Construction of Windsor Station (Gare Windsor) a Canadian Pacific Railway (CPR) station and headquarters was started in 1887. It was bordered by Osborne Street (today Avenue des Canadiens-de-Montréal) to the north, Windsor Street (today Peel Street) to the east, Saint Antoine Street to the south and the Bell Centre to the west started. The Romanesque revival style building with Montreal quarried gray limestone walls was completed in 1889. In 1916, a fifteen-storey tower dramatically enhanced the building and altered Montreal's skyline.

In 1893 the Royal Victoria Hospital was established through donations by two public-spirited cousins Donald Smith, (Lord Strathcona), and George Stephen, (Lord Mount Stephen) who had announced in 1887, a joint gift of Cdn $1,000,000 for the construction of a free hospital in Montreal and purchased a site on Mount Royal for a further Cdn $86,000 on which the hospital was built. During 1897 and 1898, Smith and Stephen gave another Cdn $1,000,000 between them in Great Northern Railroad securities to establish an endowment fund to maintain the hospital. Stephen and Smith attached one caveat to their generous contribution to the City of Montreal; namely that the hospital's land and its buildings must only ever be used for healing. The founders intended the Royal Vic to be for the use of the sick and ailing without distinction of race or creed, and when it opened in 1893 it was hailed as the "finest and most perfectly equipped (hospital) on the great American continent". In 1920, the hospital became a medical research institute through the McGill University Faculty of Medicine. In 1929, Dr. Wilder Penfield established the Montreal Neurological

Institute adjacent to the hospital. Today, the Royal Victoria Hospital is part of the McGill University Health Centre. Over the years the hospital achieved global recognition as a major centre of healthcare and learning.

Canadian Car and Foundry (CC&F) was also known as "Canadian Car & Foundry," and as "Can Car" was established in Montreal in 1909 after an amalgamation of three companies, namely:
- Rhodes Curry Company of Amherst, NS - founded 1891
- Canada Car Company of Turcot, QC - founded 1905
- Dominion Car and Foundry of Montreal, QC

In 1911 Can Car purchased Montreal Steel Works Limited at Longue-Pointe, the largest producer of steel castings in Canada, and the Ontario Iron & Steel Company, Ltd. at Welland, ON, which included both a steel foundry and a rolling mill. These two companies were reorganized as Canadian Steel Foundries Limited, a company that Canadian Car & Foundry Co. had formed to take them over. Since inception, the company was the largest railway freight car manufacturer and the largest single factor in railway passenger car production and in electric street car production in Canada. The earliest passenger cars produced by this company were all-wood cars for the Grand Trunk and Grand Trunk Pacific with vestibules and double windows having arched upper sash, designed by the Pullman Company. Canadian Northern passenger car orders also came in 1910, when ten sleepers, five baggage and four dining cars were built for that road. Intercolonial passenger cars were first built in 1912 and Canadian Pacific passenger cars in 1913, when 15 wooden tourist cars and 20 wooden baggage cars were built. Canadian Car & Foundry Co. had built passenger cars for all major Canadian railways.

They constructed the first steel tank cars, the first steel frame box cars and the first steel twin pocket hopper cars built in Canada. Until 1920 Canadian Pacific favoured building their own cars in their own shops. In 1920 C.P.R. Angus shops ceased building cars in volume but continued to finish the interiors of C.P.R. passenger cars after the passenger car frames were delivered to Angus in skeleton condition. Can Car also built the frames for six palatial Canadian National business cars constructed in 1959, which were completed and outfitted at the CN's Point St. Charles shops. Can car also manufactured buses and later aircraft for the Canadian market. In 1957 control of the Canadian Car Co., Limited or "Can-Car", as it had by then become known, passed to A.V. Roe Canada Limited, a branch of the large British aircraft concern of the same name, which was seeking to diversify its interests. The company, now is a division of Hawker Siddeley (Canada) Ltd., a large British aircraft concern and holding company which had taken over A.V. Roe. The Turcot plant was closed and sold in 1958, and the new owner sublet parts of it to a wide variety of industries. The main, or Dominion plant of the company at Ville St. Pierre, Montreal last produced passenger cars in 1961 when the plant closed and is now used temporarily for storage purposes by outside firms, and is for sale. Production of motor buses and coaches at its Fort William plant ceased in April 1962. The Longue Point foundry continued operating under the name of Canadian Steel

Foundries Limited, a unit of the Hawker Siddeley organization. Today the remaining factories are part of Bombardier Transportation Canada.

Place Viger was built in 1898 for the Canadian Pacific Railway in the château-style common to railway hotels built by the Canadian Pacific. It was both a railway station and grand hotel. The railway station was housed in its lower levels and a luxurious hotel occupied the upper floors. Place Viger was named after Jacques Viger, the first Mayor of the city. Constructed in proximity to the financial district, the city hall, the port and the court house near what was then in an area central to the French Canadian élites, in contrast to the rival Windsor Hotel to the west, which was perceived to cater to the city's Anglophone classes. It served as the rail station terminus of the CP passenger rail lines running into downtown Montreal from the north and east; while Windsor Station served as the terminus for CP passenger rail lines running into downtown Montreal from the south and west.

Place Viger enjoyed an enviable setting adjacent to the gardens of Viger Square, allowing both railway travellers and hotel guests to stroll along the garden paths. The economic depression of the 1930s, proved disastrous for Place Viger and the hotel was closed in 1935. In 1951, the railway station was also closed, and the building was sold to the City of Montreal. The interiors were gutted and transformed into nondescript office space, and the building was renamed Édifice Jacques-Viger. The Viger Square gardens were destroyed in the 1970s to allow for the construction of the Autoroute Ville-Marie highway. After the highway was completed, a new poorly designed, desolate and underused Viger Square was created on the concrete deck covering the highway. For decades, the old Place Viger station sat isolated and neglected, a striking historic building surrounded by parking lots and concrete.

The Hôpital du Sacré-Cœur de Montréal was founded on June 1, 1898, the day of the Feast of the Sacred Heart by a group of women to care for a dozen ill individuals deemed the "incurables". In 1902, the administration of the hospital was taken over by the Sisters of Providence, a religious institute of Roman Catholic sisters founded in 1843 by Mother Émilie Gamelin. A new building known as Hôpital des Incurables with 375 beds was built on Décarie Boulevard. The building was destroyed by fire in March 1923, and in 1926 a new building was built on Gouin Ouest Boulevard in Cartierville, where it still stands today and the administration reverted to using the original name, Hôpital du Sacré-Cœur de Montréal. Considered a sanatorium, the new hospital initially focused on the treatment of tuberculosis and became an important teaching hospital for pulmonary illness. In 1931, Édouard Samson founded the orthopedics department, which eventually became the largest institution for training orthopedic surgeons in the province of Quebec. In 1973, the Hôpital du Sacré-Coeur de Montréal was affiliated with the Université de Montréal as its medical and health-sciences teaching hospital. The Albert-Prévost Institute merged with the hospital to form a centre for psychiatric patients. The Hôpital du Sacré-Cœur de Montréal is one of the largest teaching hospitals in Quebec

Between 1899 and 1901 thousands of immigrants from Russia, Romania and other Eastern European countries, many of them Jewish; poured into Montreal. The newly-arrived immigrants settled around St. Lawrence Boulevard and there was a rapid increase in Jewish schools, synagogues, charities, stores, delicatessens, tailors, newspapers, social groups, clubs, and other organizations. The west and east of the neighborhood around the Rachel Street market developed rapidly with massive migration and immigration of new arrivals to Canada linked to the industrial boom that was happening in the city. Between 1890 and 1920 many Italian immigrants had moved into the area from the downtown area. The district offered affordable properties close to work and easily accessible by transit, They also offered the opportunity for homeowners to grow their own food. Some of the newcomers opened snack bars and restaurants, offering familiar tastes of the old country.

Dominion amusement park opened on June 2, 1906 near the Longue Pointe military base, on just over 6 hectares of property on Notre-Dame Street (near Haig Avenue) and the Saint Lawrence River waterfront. General admission was initially 10 cents; 5 cents for children with most rides and attractions being extra charge. The Park was surrounded on three sides by boardwalks and had broad walkways with many trees and benches, many attractions and a central park area. The focal point was the tall tower with a beacon on top near the corner of the main boardwalk. Attractions included The Crystal Maze, Myth City, Ye Olde Mill, The Laundry, a Laughing Gallery, a "Shoot-the-Chutes" ride, a tree-filled grove and The Scenic Railway roller coaster. There was a miniature railway with tracks running between two wooden boardwalks; a carousel, a large restaurant, a dance pavilion and a ferris wheel.

A fire broke out on June 28, 1913 in an attraction that featured the horse act "Mazetta" after a horse knocked over a gasoline-fed torch. The spilled fuel spread the flames quickly and park fire fighters were hampered by inadequate water pressure; even the government tug boat, "Saint-Pierre", helped by using its powerful pumps to boost water pressure. Montreal fire fighters were called in from 10 kilometres away when it was realised that park fire fighters were under-equipped to handle the growing size of the fire. A 50 man strong police force enforced order since the fire had attracted a large number of spectators from the neighbouring community. The fire was brought under control in an hour and a half. During that time the "House of Nonsense" funhouse, "Shipwreck of the Titanic" and the "Mazetta" building were lost. Fortunately, there were no deaths, and minor injuries were related to crowd control, not the fire itself. All animals from the "Wild West" and "Mazetta" attractions were led away safely. The park rebuilt and the horse show was restored.

There was a performance stage located on the North side and also a bandstand. Dominion featured many outside acts on the bandstand over the years although the Park had its own Dominion Park concert band conducted by Henri Delcellier. Even John Sousa, a popular American marching band leader and composer and his orchestra were featured there. The park brought in cowboy acts such as Weadick's Wild West Show to perform for its patrons. The star of the show was silent film cowboy Tom Mix who suffered two injuries at the Park. There were diving and swimming shows and the Park had a diving platform near the edge of the "Chutes" pond. The Jack Delaney - Larry Gaines boxing match was held on

January 22, 1928 at Dominion Park which Canadian fighter Delaney won after 15 rounds. There were two roller coasters during the park's life. The first was the "Scenic Railway" installed in 1906 which included a tunnelled section. This ride ran five-bench cars in trains of two and included a brakeman.

On August 10, 1919 fire started in the "Mystic Rill" dark ride trapping within the ride and killing seven people; three men, three women, and a boy, due to the lack of emergency lighting and exits. Later, an eighth body and the remains of a dog were also found. The fire destroyed the Mystic Rill built of flimsy wood-and-cloth with tar making it watertight, a kind of tunnel of love, with small boats following an enclosed, winding watercourse and part of the Scenic Railway. The darkness and absence of proper emergency exits inside the tunnel made it a firetrap. The fire burned a section of The "Scenic Railway" which then collapsed ending the roller coaster ride. In 1920 a new roller coaster "The Dips" was built which lasted until 1929 when the Park was closed.

Between 1911 to 1922, Boulevard Saint-Joseph was constructed In the Village of Mile-End easing access to the Mile-End town hall and the Saint-Enfant-Jésus Church and the Marie-Jésus Convent and the Monastery of the Most Blessed Sacrament and the Convent of Saint-Basile were built on Mile End road (Mont-Royal Avenue). On March 24, 1911, the Montreal Tramways Company (MTC) acquired and merged all of the other public transit companies on the Island of Montreal. In October 1911 MTC opened its first repair shops in Youville, where the metro's primary maintenance shops are currently located. On November 22, 1919 the Montreal Tramways Company's first buses were put into service on today's Bridge Street. In the early 1920s, the Montreal tramway network comprised over 300 miles (500 km) of tracks and more than 900 vehicles that carried nearly 230 million passengers per year. On January 13, 1924, the first network map was distributed and the tramway cars began indicating the route number.

On February 1, 1924 the first tram cars operated by one employee appeared that passengers had to board at the front of the vehicle. One year later, a huge terminus was opened on Craig Street, today's Saint-Antoine West and a bus division was created. On November 15, 1927 the first traffic light in Montreal underwent testing in front of the Craig terminus. On July 12, 1930 the Mount Royal tramway line was launched followed by a bus service between Montreal, St. Helen's Island and Longueuil the following year. On March 29, 1937 the first modern trolleybus service in Canada was established on Beaubien Street. On August 24, 1950 La Société de Transport de la Communauté Urbaine De Montréal (STCUM) a public body was established replacing the Montreal Tramways Company which in turn was replaced in 2002 by the Société de transport de Montréal (STM) a public transport agency that operates transit bus, and rapid transit services in Montreal. It has grown to comprise four subway lines with a total of 68 stations, as well as over 186 bus routes and 23 night routes.

The Canadian Northern Railway (CNoR) was officially formed in 1899. By 1902 it had over 1,200 miles of track north of the CPR lines extending from Port Arthur, Ontario through the rich agricultural fields of Manitoba to Erwood in northern Saskatchewan and a terminal in Port Arthur taking advantage of Great Lakes shipping. CNoR also had obtained authorization to build as far east as Montreal.

By 1906 it was providing service from Toronto to James Bay Junction on the Georgian Bay. The railway was finally completed coast to coast in 1916 but by then it was in serious financial trouble. In 1917 the CNoR was unable to secure additional government loan funding and was nationalized. In 1923 it became part of the newly formed Canadian National Railway (CNR) and today, large portions of CNoR's network remain in use by CNR.

In 1913 the Canadian Northern Railway (CNoR) had built a 5-km railway tunnel straight through Mount Royal connecting the downtown core with the company's tracks north of the city providing access to downtown Montreal without having to cross the already congested area south of Mount Royal or detouring the railway around the north and east sides of Mount Royal. The tunnel was conceived in 1910 by the Canadian Northern Railway (CNoR) as a means to give the company access to downtown Montreal since the easy routes along the south side of Mount Royal had long been taken by rivals Canadian Pacific Railway (CPR) and Grand Trunk Railway (GTR) and CNoR wanted to avoid crossing their lines. In 1911, the Canadian Northern Montreal Tunnel and Terminal Company, a wholly owned subsidiary of CNoR was incorporated to build the tunnel and terminal. To finance the costly tunnel option, CNoR had planned to develop the low-valued farmland north of Mount Royal into a model community which was named the Town of Mount Royal. CNoR also planned a downtown terminal and associated office and retail developments for low-priced lands at de la Gauchetière Street and McGill College Avenue. Several farms that grew the Montreal melon were bought by the builders to make way for the tracks:

Construction started at the west portal on July 8, 1912. It was dug out by pick and shovel, with horses carrying out the rubble. On December 10, 1913, crews from the east and west portals met beneath Mount Royal; they were out of alignment by 1 inch (2.5 cm). The bore measures approximately 5 kilometres (3.1 mi) and has an ascending grade of 0.6% westbound. There are no fire escapes, ventilation ducts, or water sprinklers. The structure gauge of the Mount Royal Tunnel limits the height of bilevel cars to 14 feet 6 inches (4.42 m). Along some bends the tunnel clearance is barely a few inches on each side. On August 18, 1914 Canada entered World War I and the Canadian Northern Montreal Tunnel and Terminal Company was renamed the Mount Royal Tunnel and Terminal Company. The same year CNoR placed an order with General Electric for 6 boxcab electric-powered locomotives for use in the tunnel; which were delivered in 1916–1917. Lining of the tunnel bore with concrete was completed by 1916 and the 2 parallel standard gauge tracks and 2400 V DC catenary (an overhead wire used to transmit electrical energy to trains) were installed by September 1918 completing the third longest tunnel in Canada.

The cost of the tunnel, along with an expansion to the west coast of Canada, caused CNoR to struggle financially and on September 6, 1918, the insolvent CNoR was nationalized by the federal government. Canadian National Railways (CNR), took over CNoR and several other lines, including the Mount Royal tunnel which had just been completed. The first train ran through the tunnel on October 21, 1918. When the Canadian National Railways (CNR) took over the

Grand Trunk Railway (GTR) in 1923, access to Ottawa and Toronto along GTR lines made the Mount Royal tunnel largely redundant. Commuter trains from the Town of Mount Royal and Via Rail trains to/from Northern Quebec and the northern route to Quebec City (cancelled in 1990) use the tunnel daily. The commuter trains service some 30,000 passengers a day, taking about 10 minutes to be on the other side of the Mountain, downtown central station to Canora, Town of Mont-Royal or vice versa. On weekdays during rush hour there is a train every 15-20 minutes, but on weekends trains are few and far apart.

In 1916 the railway boom drove many rail companies to the brink of bankruptcy. In a series of moves from 1916 to 1923, the federal government nationalized and took control of and merged many railways into the Canadian Government Railway (CGR). On May 20, 1918 several more New Brunswick railways were merged with the CGR. The CGR eventually became part of the Canadian National Railway system together with the Canadian Northern Railway system (CNoR) in 1919. CNR took over CNoR's Mount Royal Tunnel at the time of its completion, along with the empty lands which CNoR had envisioned for real estate development. The Grand Trunk became part of CNR in 1923, giving CNR better routes to Ottawa and Toronto and relegating CNoR's Mount Royal tunnel line to branch-line status. Nevertheless, to this day the tunnel still remains an essential part of Montreal's regional transport system. Central Station begun in 1931, opened on July 14, 1943 consolidating CNR's passenger terminals in the city. It replaced Bonaventure Station which CNR had inherited from GTR. In the late 1950s, the remainder of the CNoR lands acquired in downtown Montreal during the Mount Royal Tunnel project were developed by CNR resulting in Place Ville Marie and Montreal's underground city. The signature Queen Elizabeth Hotel opened in 1958, followed by the CN headquarters building in 1961 and Place Ville-Marie in 1962.

Via Rail, an independent Canadian Crown corporation created in 1978 was mandated to operate both Canadian National (CNR) and Canadian Pacific (CPR) intercity passenger rail services. CP trains that used Windsor Station were consolidated at CN's Central Station. Amtrak headquartered one block west of Union Station in Washington, D.C. continued to use Windsor Station for Amtrak's daily Montreal-New York City train (the Adirondack) until 1986 when it was switched to Central Station. After intercity passenger service was removed, Windsor Station continued to be a commuter rail terminal for the Société de Transport de la Communauté Urbaine De Montréal (STCUM).

Between 1890 and 1910, the face of Sherbrooke Street East was gradually transformed by magnificent, richly furnished homes. Emblems of the rising francophone upper middle class, they belonged to businessmen, lawyers, bankers, doctors and other notables. Some houses were built of Montreal greystone, while others were more modestly dressed in brick. Often, less wealthy owners occupied the ground floor and rented out the upper storeys. Because the City required the builders to set back the buildings from the street, they compensated for the lost space by building exterior staircases, which became a hallmark of Montreal architecture. These new dwellings gave substance to the neighbourhood and defined its character. Between 1910 and 1930, businesses grew in large numbers on Saint-Hubert Street and on Saint-Laurent Boulevard. To the south, near the railway tracks, the quarries De Lorimier and Martineau were exploited. Garages and warehouses for the tramways, construction of railway cars and various industries including the L. Villeneuve & Cie lumberyard (1910), municipal workshops (1910), Catelli factory (1911) and the Coca-Cola plant (1929-30) generated many jobs. Between 1920 and 1950, a wave of immigration from Eastern Europe settled in the Rachel Street market neighbourhood.

The Cartierville route streetcars made their trip from Garland station in Snowden past Bois Franc Road, under the railroad tracks at Val Royal CN Station, past the Blue Bonnets racetrack through what was a trip in the country, occasionally delayed by a cow that got on the tracks then more fields until they reached the station between Grenet and Ranger Streets in Cartierville. There blue and white Laval buses met the streetcars. Streetcar passengers going to Belmont Park disembarked and walked one half block down and one street south to the Park. It was a very busy station on weekends in the summer with thousands of people hoping to get a seat on the streetcar including those with tired kids and babies asleep in their arms. Belmont Park (Parc Belmont) was an amusement park constructed on about 5 hectares of farmland located on the banks of the back river called the Riviere des Prairies which had opened on June 9, 1923 in the Montreal neighborhood of Cartierville. Access to the park was by way of Rivoli Street. Admission initially was 10 cents for adults, 5 cents for children. By 1930 admission prices had gone up. Fortunately, Belmont Park was able to weather the depression, while its competitor, Dominion Park, did not.

In 1931 after paying the 35¢ admission fee, people walked between two towering turret gates, which remained during the life of the Park, to get into Belmont Park and walked past rows of snack bars and concession stands until they reached the ticket booth to buy a strip of 15¢ tickets for access to various attractions and rides. Further in the Park to their left they came to a highly decorated stand with bright banner illustrations of biological rarities and physically unusual humans, dwarfs, giants, Siamese twins, armless and legless people, people with rare skin conditions presented as Alligator Boy, or Lobster Girl, people with excessive hair presented as half human; these were the so-called attractions making up the freak show. Also included were heavily tattooed people, contortionists, fire eating and sword swallowing acts. There was a showman dressed in a red topcoat and black top hat loudly making his pitch of outlandish claims, telling fantastic backstories while inviting people to come in and see the show. Close to the freak show was an act called "Ride of Death" or "Circle of Death" that periodically came to the park involving motorcycle riders who rode in a very large barrel. The viewers stood at the top and watched the riders go around and around the walls for a long period, crossing and just missing a number of times until it was over. That event was always noisy due to the lack of mufflers, and smelly from the exhaust, but it was part of the thrill and sounds of Belmont Park. For years, Belmont Park hosted wrestling matches on Friday nights with wrestling stars in 1958 such as Larry Moquin, Yvon Robert and Don Leo Jonathan attracting large crowds.

The park sported a performance stage, a ballroom or dance hall and a marina situated at the waterfront. The dance hall had a licensed lounge serving beer and wine. Adjacent to the dance pavilion was a wharf and a marina from which canoe and boat rides on the river beside Cartierville's Lachapelle Bridge were offered. The current was very rapid there; and the boat tour took in Paton Island' an island with a beautiful, small river of its own branching off the main river that separated it from the Laval side of the Riviere des Prairies, or the `Back River', as the locals called the St. Lawrence, which ran around the north side of the island. The Carterville Boating Club, started by Hugh Paton in 1904, was located on the river at the bottom of Cousineau Street, one street west of the Lachapelle bridge. They often held regattas and attracted many people who had come to Belmont Park. A number of free acts were featured on the performance stage beside the ballroom. There were entertainers, singers, dancers and orchestras. daredevil, acrobatic and high-flying aerial trapeze shows presented several times a week. One such show was Miss Victory, in 1944, who was a live cannonball, shot out of a cannon into a net. There was a a garish paper-mâché fat Laughing Lady in a red dress at the entrance to the funhouse; housed in her own little oak panelled glass enclosed room with painted-on furniture of a skinny Chippendale style. She was known as "Fou-Rire" in french which translates as insane, silly, or mad laugh. She laughed the same recorded laugh for 50 years, One could hear her laugh track loop from one end of the midway to the other. She had a realistic, albeit extremely bloated face with too much lipstick, and she shook all over in time with her laugh. The park had a band shell, a softball diamond, a running track, a ferris wheel, a roller skating rink, a carousel (merry go round) a "Kiddieland" and picnic grounds.

The Park had a large wooden roller-coaster called the "Cyclone" that took riders to the treetops of the park and was used during the lifetime of the park from 1923 to its closing in 1983. The roller coaster was built of coated British Columbia Douglas fir mounted on concrete footers, with steel cable reinforcement in high stress areas. The lift hill was 110 metres long, 19 metres high, and utilized a 75-horsepower motor. The L-shaped layout was 762 metres long with an 1143 mm track gauge and three block-brake runs. Part of it ran along the Riviere des Prairies. Each train sat 24 riders in 3, four-bench, non-trailered cars with open fronts. Top speed was likely around 65 km/h. Riders boarded the roller coaster train at Cyclone's station staffed by the brakeman who had his hands on large levers that operated the below-track brake shoes to slow and stop the train in the station. Releasing them allowed the train to coast downhill to a point outside of the station where it could engage the lift-hill chain sending it on its journey. Once night had fallen patrons were dazzled by the thousands of lights that illuminated the Park.

Rides included bumper cars, a carousel, the Magic Carpet Ride, or white-knuckle rides on the Wild Mouse. Other adult rides included a "Caracole", "Flying Scooters", "Pirouette", "Rapido", "Safari", "Whirlpool", "Roll-O-Plane", a "Moon Rocket", a "Caterpillar", "Octopus" and "Laff-in-the-Dark". The Cartierville Marina ride was a nautical version of the ever-popular bumper cars. Twenty little two-seat Scoota-Boats bumped around in a fake pool powered by a pole that rubbed against an electrified ceiling. The "Rotor" was a fast moving cylinder in which people got strapped into a space standing against the cylinder wall. The force of the spinning wheel held their body to the wall. The floor they were standing on was then let go and they were spinning pinned to the wall. Entering the `Haunted House' on a two person vehicle, people were plunged into darkness and the scariest thing was the banging of the doors as they progressed from one area to the other. This ruckus was even more frightening than the skeletons that jumped out at them. Added to this there was a strange flowery funeral parlour smell, a lot like sandalwood incense. The ride offered a heart stopping moment called the `caress' by those who experienced it. In a particularly dark part of the ride, there were filaments that hung down from the ceiling and gently swept the rider's face as the car passed through which gave them a very creepy feeling. The Park had a penny arcade in a building known as "Fun Plaza" which housed trick mirrors, pinball machines, coin-operated machines, that claimed to tell a person's fortune or that played mechanical music and arcade games. There were a large variety of carnival games and booths including shooting galleries, a photo gallery, a "Hammer High Striker" and "Guess-Your-Weight" scales where someone tried to guess a person's weight; ring toss and ball-toss games with many prizes of large stuffed animals being won, Kiddieland featured a miniature railroad, turning cars, a merry go round and a pony ride. There was a horse/pony track that wound around the roller coaster structure. People enjoyed the Park grounds and many companies held their annual picnics in the Park. There were always lineups of people buying pink and fluffy cotton candy, bags of pop corn, soft drinks and salted French Fries with vinegar.

The City of Montreal and the Quebec government owned La Ronde and they resented Belmont Park from the time that La Ronde first opened for Expo 67 and they tried to shut it down. Belmont Park continued to operate after La Ronde opened in 1967 as part of the World's Fair, Expo 67. Many people preferred Belmont Park for nostalgic reasons and atmosphere. Changes were made at the Park to compete with La Ronde. A Pay-One-Price policy was started with initial admission being $6 ($2.50 for children), and more stage entertainment was provided. In the late 1970s entrance numbers began to deteriorate as patrons were siphoned off to the newer park and in 1980, the park was sold. The new owners had some different rides erected but after the antique carousel was auctioned off and the quality of park staff began to drop indicating that the Park was on its way out. In 1983, there were accusations about illegal operations at the park and shortly after a police raid motivated by city hall's displeasure at the park, Belmont Park closed permanently on October 13, 1983, never to reopen. The "Cyclone" was torn down starting in the fall of 1983, with the remainder removed in the spring of 1984. After its closing it fell into ruin and was vandalized. The land was then sold to various developers one of whom, Sofitec, built condominiums and the area today is filled with housing. In 1986, three years after the illegal raid, a Quebec Superior Court judge sharply criticized MUC police and ordered the Montreal Urban Community, one of its lawyers and four police officers to pay $90,000 in damages to the park's owners.

Beside fire station number 16 on the north side of Rachel street diagonally across from LaFontaine Park was a three storey house with signs on it proclaiming it as "The Midgets Palace" ("Le Palais des Nains"). The word "midget" is considered to be offensive to people of restrictive growth; and today the proper term would be short statured people. The Palace was a favoured, regular stop for sightseeing tours of Montreal. The signs said that the house was owned by the "King and Queen of All Midgets" who had the "only child born to midgets". The story behind the Palace, began with Philippe Adelard Nicol, who never grew taller than three feet (i.e., one yard). Born to a farm family on September 27, 1881 in Lévis, Quebec, Philippe was the only child in his family born with dwarfism. However he turned his disadvantage into a lucrative opportunity, quitting school at the age of 12 to join a circus. While traveling as part of a circus act throughout North America, Philippe amassed a small fortune selling pictures of himself on the side for a profit that was more than his base salary. With the money he was able to achieve his dream of having a home custom made for little people. During his travels, Philippe met Rose Dufresne, also a little person, in Massachusetts. They got married on November 21, 1913.

Philippe's plan was not only to build his home but in order to earn a living he wanted to turn the home into a tourist attraction. So in 1913, the Midgets Palace was open to the public; with Philippe and Rose calling themselves Count and Countess Nicol, the couple styled themselves as "the world's smallest couple" and "the richest of all dwarfs." The Palace showcased how little people went about their day-to-day life. For an admission charge people went through the nine room house which was like a museum viewing room after room outfitted with furniture, beds, dressers, mirrors, armoires, pictures, clothing all of which were precisely made for the family of short stature. The main attractions to the Palace museum were the rooms and the antique décor. Everything was shrunk to size except the ceilings. The kitchen had a small sink and stove. In the living room stood a miniaturized fully functional piano, with bench only ten inches high. Photos on the walls showed Phillippe and Rose in various places and poses and even in the circus. Several wall plaques told the story of how the couple had worked and earned money in the circus for many years and how through savings and investments, they ended up wealthy at the time buying the house and other properties in Montreal.

They had a son born on September 19, 1926. whom they also named Phillippe. They added a room scaled for his size and added him to the Palace's list of attractions, calling him the "Rare Baby" and the "Prince of all Midgets". One photo on the wall showed father and son at almost equal height. Originally it was thought that the child would be even shorter than the parents. As it turned out, Phillippe Jr. never grew very much taller than his father. He eventually turned to a life of crime. Philippe Nicol Sr. died in Montreal at the age of 58 in 1940, when his son was 13 so he didn't live long enough to be disappointed in his son's fate. Rose passed on in 1964. In 1972, Huguette Rioux, another small person, purchased the property and took over the administration of the Midgets Palace which continued to be a popular tourist destination. The top floors of the Palace were opened up as a hotel for little people visiting Montreal. The Palace closed for good in March 1990.

Frère Marcel telling us about the mountain, LaFontaine Park, Canadian Car & Foundry and Belmont Park brought back great memories for me of attending Can -Car picnics at Belmont Park. My father worked at Can Car back then and the picnics were great fun for the families as was eating french fries with vinegar followed by pink cotton candy at Belmont Park. Memories of visits with my mother to Mount Royal Park, the playground, collecting mushrooms, chokecherries and linden leaves, visits to the zoo at LaFontaine Park, all incredibly memorable times. Both Andre and I thanked Frère Marcel after every one of our many visits for the lessons in history which he so happily conveyed to us.

My friends and I attended college football games and saw the McGill Redmen football team play at The Percival Molson Memorial Stadium whenever officials allowed us to fill empty seats without having to pay admission, Football at McGill University had long been a revered tradition where the first intercollegiate game was played between McGill Redmen and Harvard back in 1874. The Stadium was built and named in honour of Captain Percival Talbot "Percy" Molson, MC (August 14, 1880 – July 5, 1917) a Canadian star athlete and soldier who died fighting in World War I after an outstanding sports career with McGill University. In his will, he donated funds for McGill to build its football stadium which had officially opened on October 25, 1919. Molson Stadium was home field for the Montreal Alouettes Football team of the Canadian Football League (CFL) from 1954 to 1967, in 1972 and in 1998. The Alouettes were first formed in 1946 by CFL hall of famer Lew Hayman. From 1946 to 1953 their home was the Delorimier stadium. They won their first Grey Cup championship in 1949, beating Calgary 28 to15 led by quarterback Frank Filchock and running back Virgil Wagner. The 1950s were a productive decade for the Als, with legendary quarterback Sam Etchevery throwing passes to John "Red" O'Quinn, "Prince" Hal Patterson, and Pat Abbruzzi. In1968 to 1971 and from 1973 to 1976 the Als used the Autostade at the north-west corner of the Cité du Havre sector of the Expo 67 site. In 1976 to 1986 and from 1996 to 1997 the Alouettes used the Olympic Stadium.

In winter no matter how cold it was, we ice skated at the Fletchers Field ice rink, where the soccer field doubled as an ice skating rink. The change rooms used by the soccer players were wooden shacks with a window and benches all around the inside walls of the shack which served to hold the personal belongings and street clothes of the players. These change rooms used for soccer served double duty for the skating crowd in winter. The only difference was that in winter there was a pot bellied wood stove with firewood added to the shacks which kept the place nice and warm. There were no lockers and shoes were often stolen. The shacks were designated as one for the boys and one for the girls as opposed to the different soccer teams. Weekends and evenings were reserved for public skating while hockey games were played in the afternoons during the week. A hot chocolate stand would have been a great money maker if only anyone had the money, so naturally there was no such thing and not even water to be had. People skated, even in very severely cold, crisp weather when you could see a halo around the moon. As soon as people could no longer feel their nose or cheeks or fingers they would go to the change shacks and sit through the pain of having their frost bitten parts return to normal. The warmth was always welcoming, but after a short warm up they went out and skated some more. There were no bathrooms on the premises so a person's skating was usually limited by mother nature as well as the cold temperatures.

Chapter 8 - Time Marches On

It wasn't until the late 1950's that crew cuts and other hairstyles for the teenage set started to creep in from the United States. Brylcreem kept men's hair in place but did little in regard to attracting the girls as the commercials insinuated. Men used Old Spice after shave lotion and girls didn't seem to notice that either. Men's ties after the War became wider and then went back to being more narrow and some had square ends. Striped T shirts for men appeared in the 1950's. Jeans did not become popular until the 1960's. In the 1950's, girls hair was generally worn short and ladies wore calf length skirts or dresses with petticoats and crinolines supporting the skirts to provide a wide hemline. Gloves and nylon stockings were worn on all formal occasions. There were several millinery stores in our area designing and manufacturing ladies and men's hats. Ladies always wore hats and gloves to attend church. In fashion terms, hats were and continue to be a very noticeable accessory because the onlooker's attention is first drawn to the face. A hat is the most noticeable fashion item anyone can wear. There was an old saying that was often quoted that said. "'if you want to get ahead and get noticed, get a hat."

The early 1950's were filled with cold war tensions and spy trials. Less than two weeks after a jury convicted Alger Hiss an American government official of perjury for denying under oath that he had passed secret information to a Communist agent, Klaus Fuchs was arrested. Klaus Fuchs, a German émigré and physicist had worked on the Manhattan Project at the Los Alamos National Laboratory and on January 24 1950 he walked into London's War Office and confessed to being a Soviet spy who for seven years had passed top secret data on U.S. and British nuclear weapons atomic bomb research to the Soviet Union. On January 31, 1950 U.S.A. President Harry S. Truman ordered the development of the hydrogen bomb, in response to the detonation of the Soviet Union's first atomic bomb in 1949. Klaus Fuchs was formally charged on February 2 and sentenced to fourteen years' imprisonment and in December 1950 he was stripped of his British citizenship. He was released on June 23, 1959, after serving nine years and four months of his sentence at Wakefield Prison, and promptly emigrated to the German Democratic Republic (East Germany). The tutorial he gave to Chinese physicists helped them to develop the bomb they tested five years later on October 16, 1964 at the Lop Nur test site. It was a uranium-235 implosion fission device and had a yield of 22 kilotons. With the test, China became the fifth nuclear power.

Klaus Fuchs' arrest, led the Americans to intercept cables (the "Venona Cables") from the Soviet Consulate to the KGB which began a chain of investigations that led authorities to Julius and Ethel Rosenberg and exposed the espionage part that they played in the passing of atomic bomb secrets to the USSR. Calling their crime "worse than murder" and blaming them for 50,000 American deaths in Korea, Judge Irving Kaufman sentenced both Julius and Ethel Rosenberg to death in the electric chair. A two-year long battle followed to save the Rosenbergs' lives. Thousands of Rosenberg supporters paraded on two continents, radio broadcasts were sponsored on their behalf, letters asking for clemency poured into the White House, the Pope asked for mercy. None of it mattered. Julius and Ethel Rosenberg were executed shortly after 8 p.m. in Sing-Sing Prison on June 19, 1953. In the decades that followed the Rosenberg trial, further evidence surfaced following the collapse of the Soviet Union. In 1997, Alexsandr Feklisov, Rosenberg's Soviet control came forward to describe his meetings with Julius in the 1940's. Feklisov credited Rosenberg with providing the information necessary for the Soviets to assemble a proximity fuse that enabled them to shoot down an American U2 spy plane in 1960.

One week after Fuchs' arrest, U.S. Senator Joseph McCarthy from Wisconsin propelled himself into the headlines by charging that the State Department employed over 200 Communist agents. It was a bad time to be a suspected Communist or to be a suspected spy. Senator Joseph McCarthy began his Communist witch hunt and headlines were dominated by his accusations as he relentlessly continued his anticommunist campaign. He conducted scores of hearings, calling hundreds of witnesses in both public and closed sessions. The army hired Boston lawyer Joseph Welch to make its case. At a session on June 9, 1954, McCarthy charged that one of Welch's attorneys had ties to a Communist organization. As an amazed television audience looked on, Welch responded with the immortal lines that ultimately ended McCarthy's career: "Until this moment, Senator, I think I never really gauged your cruelty or your recklessness." When McCarthy tried to continue his attack, Welch angrily interrupted, "Let us not assassinate this lad further, senator. You have done enough. Have you no sense of decency?" Overnight, McCarthy's immense national popularity evaporated. Censured by his Senate colleagues, ostracized by his party, and ignored by the press, McCarthy died three years later, 48 years old and a broken man.

In 1955 tetracycline and optical fiber were invented; Dr. Jonas Salk developed a vaccine for polio. In 1956 the T.V. remote control was Invented. In 1957 Tang, breakfast beverage crystals were introduced by General Foods Corporation and the first aluminum cans were used. In 1958 Fairchild Semiconductor and Texas Instruments submitted patents for integrated circuits; 1958: Hula Hoops were very popular and LEGO toy bricks were first Introduced. In 1959 the first Barbie Doll and the first diet cola soft drink were sold. Columbia Records had released the 33 1/3 rpm 12 inch vinyl LP (Long Playing) in June 1948. RCA Victor released the first 45 rpm, 7 inch record on March 31, 1949 in seven translucent colours. At seven inches it was much smaller than the 10 inch 78 rpm discs. In the 1970s their popularity declined as other portable media players such as boom boxes and portable cassette players took over. There was a lot of news on the world scene that kept the newspapers fed with stories, opinions and editorials. Our neighbours would discuss, rehash, argue and even fight over events that they had no control over and many had proposals and a multitude of solutions for world leaders that never left the neighbours doorsteps. In 1950 the average salary was $2,992 per year and the cost of a loaf of bread was fourteen cents ($0.14) and many things were happening in the world; many inventions and new products appearing on store shelves. At first the Kleenex company had not imagined that there would be a demand for a disposable paper handkerchief, so they initially marketed their product exclusively for make-up removal. It was only after they discovered that people were blowing their noses into the tissues that they began marketing them for this purpose. Support for World War II during the 1940s imposed paper restrictions which limited Kleenex tissue production. During World War II, the same material that was used for Kleenex tissue was used for sterile dressing by field doctors and nurses. After the war cloth handkerchiefs made way for the soft, absorbent, disposable paper facial tissues which took over the market.

On May 29, 1950 the St. Roch a Royal Canadian Mounted Police schooner, became the first vessel to circumnavigate North America and the second sailing vessel to complete a voyage through the Northwest Passage. However it was the first ship to complete the Northwest Passage in the direction west to east, going the same route that Amundsen on the sailing vessel Gjøa went east to west, 38 years earlier. The first modern credit card which was issued by Diner's Club; Kraft introduced packaged sliced process cheese and Cracker Barrel brand natural cheese; sliced bread, prohibited during the war was reintroduced. On January 6, 1950 the United Kingdom recognized the People's Republic of China and in response the Republic of China severed diplomatic relations with Britain. On January 23 the Israeli Knesset passed a resolution establishing Jerusalem as the capital of Israel.

Further to an agreement with the United States, in August 1945, one day after the bombing of Nagasaki, the Soviet Union declared war on Imperial Japan who had ruled Korea since 1910 , and liberated Korea north of the 38th parallel. U.S. forces subsequently moved into the south. By 1948, as a product of the Cold War between the Soviet Union and the United States, Korea was split into two regions, with separate governments. Both claimed to be the legitimate government of all of Korea, and neither accepted the border as permanent. The conflict escalated into open warfare when North Korean forces, supported by the People's Republic of China (PRC), with military material aid from the Soviet Union invaded South Korea on June 25, 1950. The war between North Korea and South Korea lasted from June 25, 1950 to July 27, 1953. Twenty-one countries of the United Nations came to the aid of South Korea. Canada joined a United Nations force and the first Canadian troops arrived in Korea on December 18, 1950. China came to the aid of North Korea, and the Soviet Union also gave some assistance to the North. The United States provided 88% of the UN's military personnel. On September 15 allied troops commanded by Douglas MacArthur landed in Inchon, occupied by North Korea to relieve pressure on the Pusan Perimeter. United States troops launched a counteroffensive at the battle of Inchon and began the U.N. offensive northward. The result was a decisive UN victory. The rapid UN counter-offensive then drove the North Koreans past the 38th Parallel and almost to the Yalu River (the border with China),

On October 19, 1950 the People's Republic of China (PRC) entered the war on the side of the North by sending thousands of soldiers across the Yalu River. The Chinese launched a counter-offensive that pushed the United Nations forces back across the 38th Parallel. MacArthur asked for permission to bomb communist China and use Nationalist Chinese forces from Taiwan against the People's Republic of China which President Truman flatly refused. A very public argument developed between Truman and MacArthur resulting in President Truman firing MacArthur and replacing him with Gen. Matthew Ridgeway. President Truman addressing the nation on April 11, 1951 explained the action he had taken was to limit the war to Korea and to prevent a third world war. The surprise Chinese intervention triggered a retreat of UN forces which continued until mid-1951. Everyone on the street listened to Gen. Douglas MacArthur's speech to Congress on April 19, 1951 after he was fired by President Truman for insubordination. Everyone was on MacArthur's side. North Korea was subjected to a massive bombing campaign. Jet fighters confronted each other in air-to-air combat for the first time in history, and Soviet pilots covertly flew in defense of their communist allies. Seoul changed hands four times, the last two years of fighting became a war of attrition, with the front line close to the 38th parallel. The fighting ended on July 27, 1953, with the signing of an armistice. In total 314 Canadians were killed and 1211 were injured. The agreement created the Korean Demilitarized Zone to separate North and South Korea, and allowed the return of prisoners. However, no peace treaty was ever signed and according to some sources the two Koreas are technically still at war.

An oil pipeline linking Edmonton, Alberta to Sarnia, Ontario was completed in October, 1950. The first oil from Alberta arrived in Sarnia through the new pipeline on January 1954. In 1951 super glue and the first video tape recorder were on the market. In 1952 the first bar code patent was issued; car seat belts and Cheez Whiz pasteurized process cheese spread were introduced and the first diet ginger ale soft drink called the "No-Cal Beverage" was sold by Kirsch. In 1953 DNA was discovered and the radial tire was developed. Prior to 1953, consumer radio sets contained giant, power-guzzling vacuum tubes; the only practical place to put a radio set was on the living room floor. A major change occurred in 1953 when the transistor radio, a small portable radio receiver using transistor-based circuitry, was developed by Texas Instruments. The transistor radio became the most popular electronic communication device in history. The use of transistors instead of vacuum tubes as the amplifier elements meant that the device was much smaller, required far less power to operate than a tube radio, and was more shock-resistant. Powered by batteries coupled with transistors, it allowed "instant-on" operation because there were no filaments to heat up. Most transistor radios included earphone jacks and came with single earphones that provided only mediocre-quality sound reproduction. Listeners sometimes held an entire transistor radio directly against the side of the head, with the speaker against the ear, to minimize the "tinny" sound caused by the high resonant frequency of its small speaker. Their pocket size allowed people for the first time to listen to music anywhere they went and sparked a change in popular music listening habits. Transistor radios gave birth to an explosion of radio stations. Standalone phonographs and vinyl 78 rpm records were very popular also.

My friend Andre's family was the first on the block to get a TV set as soon as the black and white TV sets hit the market. On June 2, 1952 an Indian chief test pattern was broadcast for the very first time from a temporary antenna set up on the roof of the CBC TV building on Mount Royal mountain. The facilities included a master control room, two studios, a telecine system, a 16mm-film kinescope recording machine and a news vehicle. We were glued to watching the test pattern, checking the screen to see if something else was going to be shown. On July 18, 1952 the first televised coverage of a baseball game was broadcast when cameras were set up by Radio-Canada in De Lorimier Stadium. Television arrived in Canada with the official broadcasting launch of CBFT Montreal (bilingual service) on September 6, 1952 at 4 p.m. in the presence of Mayor Camilien Houde and Cardinal Paul Émile Léger. CBFT the flagship station of Télévision de Radio-Canada, the French language television network of the Canadian Broadcasting Corporation CBC broadcasting on channel 2 in Montreal was the first Canadian station to launch Canadian television. The station aired programming in both French (60 percent) and English (40 percent) until January 10, 1954, when CBMT was launched in Montreal. The first program broadcast on CBFT that evening was called "Club d'un soir". CBFT-TV became exclusively French in April 1953 and held a monopoly on French-language television during all of the 1950s. Television quickly became an essential part of the culture of Quebec with most Quebec households owning a television. On September 8, 1952 CBLT (CBC Toronto) started broadcasting. Thanks to a microwave relay system built between Montreal and Toronto, English programming was henceforth broadcast on a CBMT-TV Montreal's English language station. The CN Tower in Toronto opened in 1976, and CBLT started transmitting from it on May 31, 1976 after moving its transmitter to the facility. It currently broadcasts from studios at the Canadian Broadcasting Centre on Front Street. However, it originally broadcast from a series of smaller studios (which now house the National Ballet School) on Jarvis Street next to its old transmitter.

On Wednesday November 4, 1953 we watched La Porte Ouverte, a variety program, followed by La Famille Plouffe, a soap opera based on the novel Les Plouffe, written by Roger Lemelin. It was a chronicle of a working class family just after the Second World War in Quebec City with Guiiliame, Onisim, Cecil and Madame Plouffe among other characters. My friend Andre's family and I as a frequent guest enjoyed watching La Famille Plouffe on Wednesday nights and the weekly hockey broadcast, La Soiree du hockey. La Famille Plouffe included patriarch Théophile, a former provincial cycling champion who had settled into life as a plumber, his wife Joséphine, a naive but kind-hearted mother who doted on her adult children Napoléon, Ovide, Cécile and Guillaume. They faced work problems and dilemmas of a personal nature, and their characters evolved according to the development of the story from show to show and from year to year.

Napoléon, the eldest was the protector of his siblings who mentored his younger brother Guillaume's dream of one day playing professional hockey; Ovide, the intellectual of the family whose education, love of art and music gave him an arrogant demeanour; and Cécile, the only daughter who, like many women in the post-war era, was faced with the choice between the traditional values of marriage, children and security and new aspirations of career independence. Cecile was introduced as thirty-eight and single; although she was interested in love and marriage, and was under pressure to marry, she continued to value her independence. She was courted by Onesime Menard, a bus driver. In spring l955 they married and the whole family moved to another house, with Cecile and Onesime in the downstairs flat and Papa and Maman Plouffe and their three sons upstairs. The youngest Plouffe son, the athlete Guillaume, was under the control of his trainer and older brother, Napoleon, and his dictum that love and sex prevent championships. One season concentrated on Guillaume's refusal to play hockey and be transferred to the Buffalo team, because of his love for Danielle Smith. The third son, Ovide, was the dreamy idealist of the family; an opera fancier, he was also smitten with Rita Toulouse, whose tastes ran more to Crosby than Caruso. The television program was an instant hit, with its skilful combination of sentiment and satire it dominated Quebec on Wednesday evenings, and forced the rescheduling of church services, public meetings, and even hockey playoffs. The program completed its successful run on CBC in 1959, at the end of the Duplessis era.

We got our first television set from Sinclair Radio Store on the "Main" around 1954. All TV sets at the time displayed only black and white programming. Every Sunday night from 8 to 9 p.m. ET we watched the Ed Sullivan Show, an American TV variety show hosted by New York entertainment columnist Ed Sullivan that ran on CBS until Sunday June 6, 1971. The show enjoyed phenomenal popularity in the 1950s and early 1960s. It became a family ritual of gathering around the television set to watch Ed Sullivan. He was regarded as a kingmaker, and performers considered an appearance on his program as a guarantee of stardom. Virtually every type of entertainment appeared on the show; opera singers, popular artists, songwriters, comedians, ballet dancers, dramatic actors performing monologues from plays, and circus acts were regularly featured. The format was the same as vaudeville. Originally the show was titled Toast of the Town, but was widely referred to as The Ed Sullivan Show for years before September 25, 1955, when that became its official name.

On Sunday night September 9, 1956, at 8 p.m., Elvis Presley first appeared on The Ed Sullivan Show and was a major success. Over 60 million people, both young and old, watched the show and many people believe it helped bridge the generation gap for Elvis' acceptance into the mainstream. He had already appeared on other national television shows such as on The Milton Berle Show and The Steve Allen Show. Elvis Presley appeared on three Ed Sullivan shows: September 9, 1956, October 28, 1956, and then on January 6, 1957. The Ed Sullivan Show was especially known to the WWII and "baby boom" generations for airing breakthrough performances not only by Elvis Presley, but by The Beatles, African-American artists, The Rolling Stones, and performances from Broadway shows by their original cast members. Along with the new talent Sullivan booked each week, he also had recurring characters appear many times a season, such as ventriloquist Señor Wences and his "Little Italian Mouse" puppet sidekick Topo Gigio, who first appeared on April 14, 1963. The last show was broadcast on Sunday June 6, 1971 and Ed Sullivan died three years after that last show.

The I Love Lucy Show starring Lucille Ball and Desi Arnaz and the Jackie Gleason Show were very popular with audiences across Canada and the United States in the 1950s. Jackie Gleason portrayed a number of recurring characters, including supercilious, moustachioed "playboy" millionaire Reginald Van Gleason III; friendly Joe the Bartender; loudmouthed braggart Charlie Bratten; mild-mannered Fenwick Babbitt; bombastic Rudy the Repairman; and a put-upon character known only as the Poor Soul, whom Gleason always performed in pantomime. By far the most memorable and popular of Gleason's characters was blowhard Brooklyn bus driver Ralph Kramden, in a series known as "The Honeymooners", with Audrey Meadows as his wife Alice, and Art Carney as his upstairs neighbour Ed Norton. Ralph Kramden portrayed as a bus driver for the fictional Gotham Bus Company was never seen driving a bus but was shown multiple times at the bus depot. Ralph was frustrated by his lack of success, and often developed get-rich-quick schemes. He was very short tempered, frequently resorting to bellowing, insults and hollow threats. Well hidden beneath the many layers of bluster however, was a soft-hearted man who loved his wife and was devoted to his best pal Edward "Ed" Lillywhite Norton, who was portrayed as a New York City sewer worker. Ed described his job as a "Sub-supervisor in the sub-division of the department of subterranean sanitation, I just keep things moving along". He was Ralph's best friend and was considerably more good-natured than Ralph, but nonetheless traded insults with him on a regular basis. Ed typically called "Norton" by Ralph and sometimes by his own wife often got mixed up in Ralph's schemes, and his carefree and rather dimwitted nature usually resulted in raising Ralph's ire, while Ralph often showered him with verbal abuse and threw him out of the apartment when Ed irritated him. Ed and Ralph were both members of the fictional Raccoon Lodge where they held frequent executive meetings, i.e., poker games. Alice Kramden was Ralph's patient but sharp-tongued wife of roughly 15 years. She often found herself bearing the brunt of Ralph's insults, which she returned with biting sarcasm. She was level headed and pointed out the flaws in Ralph's schemes which made him angry. By the end of the episode, her misgivings were always proven to have been well-founded. She had grown accustomed to his empty threats: "...one of these days... POW!!! Right in the kisser! One of these days Alice, straight to the Moon!" These TV episodes were rerun in syndication for many decades later.

Returning from church on Sundays there were multiple posters advertising upcoming wrestling matches that were posted on the outside of the amateur wrestling ring building opposite the streetcar stop on Ontario and Delorimier streets across from the Delorimier Downs baseball stadium. Wrestling was a physical competition involving grappling techniques such as clinch fighting, throws and takedowns, joint locks and pins between two (occasionally more, called a tag team) competitors or sparring partners, who attempted to gain and maintain a superior position. One of Montreal's favourite wrestlers was Yvon "The Lion" Robert (October 8, 1914 - July 12, 1971) a French Canadian wrestler who started wrestling in 1932 at age 17. He won the Montreal International Heavyweight Championship 16 times between 1936 to 1956. During 1943, he won the Montreal British Empire Heavyweight Championship and in 1948, he wrestled Gorgeous George to a draw. In 1953, he formed a successful tag team with Whipper Billy Watson and won the Canadian Tag Team Championship. On November 12, 1953 Watson and Robert defeated Al Mills and Tiny Mills at a wrestling event held in Toronto with boxing champion Joe Louis as the special guest referee. On January 5, 1958, he teamed with Billy Wicks to defeat Corsica Joe and Corsica Jean in Memphis for the Mid-America Tag Team Championship. Yvon Robert died at his home in Laval, Quebec on July 12, 1971.

CBC was the first Canadian television network to broadcast in colour starting on September 1, 1966. CBC was followed within days by the private-sector CTV Television Network. My family and I enjoyed watching variety shows, hockey, the news and wrestling on television. The 1940s and 1950s were described as the First Golden Age of Professional Wrestling and there were many televised wrestling matches. Featured were wrestlers such as Gorgeous George, an American wrestler with an outrageous, flamboyant and charismatic style; Johnny (Jean) Rougeau (June 9, 1929 – May 25, 1983) who feuded with Abdullah the Butcher later was the bodyguard and chauffeur of Québec Premier René Lévesque during the 1960 election. Other wrestlers included the Sheik, Ivan Koloff, Hans Schmidt and Władek (Walter) "Killer" Kowalski (October 13, 1926 – August 30, 2008) a Canadian wrestler who wrestled from 1947 to 1977 and held numerous championships.

"Killer Kowalski" was born in Windsor, Ontario as Edward Władysław Spulnik the son of Polish immigrants Antoni Spulnik and Maria Borowska. Kowalski wrestled as a demonstrative villain and stood out for his larger-than-normal size, and for his faster-paced style in the ring. Other colourful wrestlers that we enjoyed watching were "Nature Boy" Buddy Rogers, Lou Thesz, Gene Kiniski, Verne Gagne, Bobo Brazil, Antonino Rocca, Argentine Apollo, Bobby Managoff, Whipper Billy Watson, Fritz Von Erich, Pat O'Connor, Mr. Moto and the gymnast-turned-wrestling star, Edouard Carpentier born in France to a Russian father and a Polish mother as Édouard Ignacz Weiczorkiewicz (July 17, 1926 - October 30, 2010). He joined the French underground resistance during the period of German occupation during World War II and was subsequently awarded the Croix de Guerre and the Croix des combattant medals by the French government at the close of the war. He moved to Montreal in 1956 and became a Canadian citizen. Carpentier was a crowd favorite who delighted fans with acrobatic leaps from the turnbuckles and a variety of other aerial maneuvers such as the rope-aided twisting head scissors.

Another very colourful wrestler with a strongman in-ring persona we enjoyed watching was Yukon Eric, born Eric Holmback (April 16, 1924 – January 16, 1965). Eric announced as being from Fairbanks, Alaska always wore plaid wool shirts, worn open to show off his 66 inch (170 cm) chest. He was known for whipping his opponent into the ropes so that they would bounce back into his chest. It was during a wrestling match in Montreal between Władek Kowalski and Yukon Eric in 1952 that Kowalski botched a knee drop, and accidentally ripped off a part of Yukon Eric's ear. The mishap fortified Kowalski as being a ruthless villain who gleefully maimed his opponents. Yukon Eric continued to wrestle until his death in 1965.

In April 1956 Grace Patricia Kelly (November 12, 1929 – September 14, 1982) an American actress married Rainier III, Prince of Monaco, to become Princess consort of Monaco, styled as Her Serene Highness The Princess of Monaco, and commonly referred to as Princess Grace. She and Prince Rainier had three children: Caroline, Albert, and Stéphanie. She retained her American roots, maintaining dual US and Monégasque citizenships. She died on September 14, 1982, when she lost control of her automobile and crashed after suffering a stroke. Her daughter Princess Stéphanie, who was in the car with her, survived the accident. From 1956 to 1966 the "Our Pet, Juliette" show was a staple of Saturday night television which followed the NHL hockey game. More than a million Canadians hummed along every week as the buxom blonde with the megawatt smile sang the old favorites. Juliette the daughter of Polish-Ukrainian immigrants became the most glamorous TV star that Canada had ever seen. She had started at age seven, dressed as a boy in top hat and tails, singing at amateur shows where she was a sensation. At 13, Juliette became a nightclub singer, performing with the Dal Richards band at the Hotel Vancouver. By age 15, she had her own CBC Radio program. In 1954, Juliette moved to Toronto and broke into television. In 1956 she had her own show and despite continued high ratings, her show was cancelled in 1966. In the early 1960s, Mitch Miller became a household name with his NBC television show "Sing Along with Mitch", a community-sing along program featuring him and a mixed chorale featuring singer Leslie Uggams and the singing Quinto Sisters. The program was on television from 1961 until it was cancelled in 1964. Mitchell William "Mitch" Miller (July 4, 1911 – July 31, 2010) is best remembered as a conductor, choral director, television performer and recording executive.

In 1953 the newly formed public Montreal Transportation Commission replaced streetcars with buses and proposed a subway line from Boulevard Crémazie to the D'Youville maintenance shops. In 1954 Canada's first subway line in Toronto under Yonge Street was opened. The Avro Canada CF-105 Arrow a delta-winged interceptor aircraft was designed and built by Avro Canada, (A. V. Roe Canada Limited) a subsidiary of the Hawker Siddeley Group, initially handling repair and maintenance work for aircraft at Malton, Ontario Airport, today known as Toronto Pearson International Airport. In 1946 the company began the design of Canada's first jet fighter for the Royal Canadian Air Force (RCAF), the Avro CF-100 Canuck all-weather interceptor. The Arrow was an advanced technical and aerodynamic achievement for the Canadian aviation industry. The CF-105 (Mark 2) held the promise of near-Mach 2 speeds at altitudes of 50,000 feet (15,000 m) and was intended to serve as the Royal Canadian Air Force's (RCAF) primary interceptor in the 1960s and beyond. The Arrow was the culmination of a series of design studies begun in 1953 examining improved versions of the Avro Canada CF-100 Canuck. After considerable study, the RCAF selected a dramatically more powerful design, and serious development began in March 1955. The aircraft was intended to be built directly from the production line, skipping the traditional hand-built prototype phase. The first Arrow Mk. I, RL-201, was rolled out to the public on October 4, 1957, the same day as the launch of Sputnik I.

The Soviet Union launched the world's first artificial satellite (Sputnik 1) from the Baikonur Cosmodrome located in the Republic of Kazakhstan, in the desert steppe city of Baikonur, about 200 kilometres (124 mi) east of the Aral Sea and north of the river Syr Darya near the Tyuratam railway station. The spaceport is leased by the Kazakh Government to Russia until 2050, and is managed jointly by the Roscosmos State Corporation originally known as the Russian Aviation and Space Agency and the Russian Aerospace Forces. Sputnik 1 was launched into an elliptical low Earth orbit (LEO) where it's 65 degree inclination and duration of its orbit made its flight path cover virtually the entire inhabited Earth. The 58 cm (23 in) diameter polished metal sphere, with four external radio antennas broadcasting its radio signal on 20.005 and 40.002 MHz, was easily monitored by radio operators throughout the world. Sputnik 1 orbited the earth for three weeks before its batteries died, then silently for two more months before burning up on January 4, 1958 while re-entering Earth's atmosphere. It had travelled at about 29,000 kilometres per hour (18,000 mph; 8,100 m/s), taking 96.2 minutes to complete each orbit and had completed1440 orbits of the Earth, travelling a distance of about 70 million km (43 million miles).

This surprise success precipitated the American Sputnik crisis and triggered the Space Race, a part of the Cold War. The launch ushered in new political, military, technological, and scientific developments. The United States Congress, alarmed by the perceived threat to national security and technological leadership, urged President Dwight D. Eisenhower to take immediate and swift action. This led to the creation of the National Aeronautics and Space Administration (NASA), a new federal agency to conduct all non-military activity in space which began operations on October 1, 1958. A significant contributor to NASA's entry into the Space Race with the Soviet Union was the technology from the German rocket program led by Wernher von Braun and earlier research efforts within the U.S. including Robert Goddard's earlier works.

Meanwhile in Canada, flight testing of the Arrow began with RL-201 on March 25, 1958, and the design quickly demonstrated excellent handling and overall performance, reaching Mach 1.9 in level flight. Powered by the Pratt & Whitney J75, another three Mk. 1s were completed, RL-202 through -204. The lighter and more powerful Orenda Iroquois engine was soon ready for testing, and the first Mk.II with the Iroquois, RL-206, was ready for taxi testing in preparation for flight and acceptance tests by RCAF pilots by early 1959. In June 1957, when the governing Liberals lost the federal election and a Progressive Conservative government under John Diefenbaker took power, the aircraft's prospects began to noticeably change. From 1953, Canadian military chiefs of staff of the army and navy were strongly opposed to the Arrow, since "substantial funds were being diverted to the air force". In August 1957, the Diefenbaker government signed the NORAD (North American Air Defense) Agreement with the United States, making Canada a partner with American command and control. The USAF was in the process of completely automating their air defence system with the SAGE project, and offered Canada the opportunity to share this sensitive information for the air defence of North America. One aspect of the SAGE system was the Bomarc nuclear-tipped anti-aircraft missile. This led to studies on basing Bomarcs in Canada in order to push the defensive line further north, even though the deployment was found to be extremely costly.

Diefenbaker had campaigned on a platform of reining in what the Conservatives claimed was "rampant Liberal spending". Deploying the missiles alone was expected to cost C$164 million, while SAGE would absorb another C$107 million, not counting the cost of improvements to radar; in all, it was projected to raise Canada's defence spending "as much as 25 to 30%", according to the minister of national defence. Defence against ballistic missiles was becoming a priority. The existence of Sputnik had also raised the possibility of attacks from space, and, as the year progressed, word of a "missile gap" began spreading. It was reported that Canada could not afford the Arrow and the Bomarc/SAGE defensive ballistic missiles. On August 11, 1958, the minister of national defence requested cancellation of the Arrow, but the Cabinet Defence Committee (CDC) refused. The motion was tabled again in September and recommended installation of the Bomarc missile system. The latter was accepted, but again the CDC refused to cancel the entire Arrow program. The CDC wanted to wait until a major review was made on March 31, 1959.

Efforts to continue the program through cost-sharing with other countries were being explored. In 1959, the minister of national defence announced that the ballistic missile was the greater threat, and that Canada had purchased Bomarc "in lieu of more airplanes". On February 20, 1959, the development of the Arrow (and its Iroquois engines) was abruptly halted before the planned project review had taken place. The cancellation was the topic of considerable political controversy at the time. Two months later, the assembly line, tooling, plans, aircraft in production and existing airframes and engines were ordered to be destroyed. The cancellation effectively put Avro out of business and its highly skilled engineering and production personnel scattered. Nonetheless, by 1958, Hawker Siddeley, the parent company of Avro had become Canada's third largest business enterprise and had primary interests in rolling stock, steel and coal, electronics and aviation with 39 different companies under the A. V. Roe Canada banner.

On December 28, 1961 Canada's first BOMARC Missile squadron was formed after the Avro Arrow supersonic manned interceptor aircraft was scrapped. The dispute over whether the missiles should be equipped with nuclear warheads or not led to the collapse of the Diefenbaker government in 1963. The Liberal government of Lester Pearson proceeded to accept nuclear-armed Bomarcs, with the first being deployed on December 31, 1963. The supersonic Bomarc missiles were the first long-range anti-aircraft missiles, rocket boosted and then ramjet powered, capable of carrying conventional or nuclear warheads. The CIM-10 Bomarc was the only surface-to-air missile (SAM) ever deployed by the United States Air Force outside the U.S.A. All other U.S. land-based SAMs were and are under the control of the United States Army. The Bomarcs intended role was defense of North America to prevent intrusion and to destroy enemy bombers before they could drop their payloads on industrial regions. BOMARC and the SAGE guidance system were phased out in the early 1970s.

Queen Elizabeth II and American President Dwight D. Eisenhower formally opened the St Lawrence Seaway (la Voie Maritime du Saint-Laurent), a 2,300-mile-long superhighway for ocean freighters in 1959. The seaway is a system of locks, canals and channels to bypass several rapids and dams along the way that permits ocean-going vessels to travel from the Atlantic Ocean as far inland as the western end of Lake Superior. It extends from Montreal to Lake Erie, and includes the Welland Canal. As part of the construction on July 1, 1958 ten villages in the former townships of Cornwall and Osnabruck (now South Stormont) near Cornwall in Ontario consisting of Aultsville, Dickinson's Landing, Farran's Point. Maple Grove. Mille Roches, Moulinette, Santa Cruz, Sheek's Island, Wales, and Woodlands were permanently submerged.

Prior to 1958 the Place Ville-Marie (PVM) property owned by the Canadian National Railways (CNR) with the exception of the venerable St. James Club at the corner of Dorchester and University was a huge open pit gouged in the flank of Mount Royal between the southern portal of Canadian National Railway's Mount Royal Tunnel and Central Station. It was bounded by Cathcart Street, Dorchester Boulevard (now René Lévesque Boulevard), University Street (now Robert-Bourassa Street) and Mansfield Street. In front of central station, Dorchester Blvd. ran over a bridge built over the hole. Standing on that bridge you could see the Canadian National Railway's tracks between the Mount Royal Tunnel and Central Station. The Tunnel, allowed an efficient and direct northern rail connection to the heart of the city from the Town of Mount Royal which CN's predecessor, The Canadian Northern Railway (CNoR) had built as a model garden suburban city. The rail connection to the city centre being touted as the town's chief advantage.

Construction of PVM with its 47 storey cruciform skyscraper whose address is 1 Place Ville Marie started in 1959 and the complex was inaugurated on September 13, 1962. I was employed by Webb & Knapp Canada, the developers of PVM and attended the topping off ceremony. The building is 188.06 meters (617 feet) high which is only eight meters shorter than Mount Royal. When built it was the highest tower in the Commonwealth and was the third tallest skyscraper on earth outside the United States. The office tower is named the Royal Bank Tower after the structure's largest occupant and anchor tenant the Royal Bank of Canada, the country's largest bank, which moved from its previous location on St James Street (rue St Jacques) in Old Montreal. The tower consists of 47 cantilevered office floors of nearly an acre each. The cruciform shape distributes the volume into four narrow wings in such a way that this very large building actively participates in the space rather than overwhelming it. At the tower's base a monumental sky lit banking hall opens onto the plaza that forms the project's civic heart.

Above ground the three-block plaza enriches the center city with light, open space and a pivotal gathering place for social interaction and public events. Below ground, it shelters a 59,000 square metre innovative retail and entertainment concourse that invigorates downtown well into the night. PVM's 2.5 kilometres of shop-lined promenades gave rise to the underground network that interconnects much of central Montreal. Below the concourse are two levels of parking for 1200 cars and below them, platforms and rail lines to the city's northern and southern suburbs. The direct link to Canadian National's Central Station ensured that 60,000 individuals, or ten percent of those coming into the city's downtown each day, were compelled to pass through the development. Nearly one-half of PVM's 280,000 square metre area lies beneath street level and is protected from Montréal's extreme winter and summer climate. With most of PVM built over railway tracks, the building's structure was built to be more resistant to vibrations than normally required. As a result, PVM is the most earthquake-resistant office tower in Montreal. A rotating beacon on the rooftop (turning counter-clockwise) lights up at night, illuminating the surrounding sky with up to four white horizontal beams that can be seen as far as 50 km away. \

In the early 1950s many of my friends and their families were regularly vacationing with their families in the Laurentians; places like Val David, Val Morin and St Agathe. It was a far cry from the prior decade when they made a visit to Plattsburg once in a blue moon and then talked about it for many tears. In the late 1950s many of my long time neighbours moved away from the neighbourhood to the suburbs; places such as Snowdon, cote des neiges, NDG (notre dame de grace) Outremont, Westmount and Hampstead. Nightly gatherings on the doorsteps still happened but were less frequent but just as informative. Max and Stanislaw and their wives were sitting together as I visited with Yossel, Max's son. Max as usual delighted telling anyone who listened about his last doctor visit. Max had gone to the doctor complaining of a terrible pain in his leg.
"I am afraid it's just old age," replied the doctor, "there is nothing we can do about it."
"That can't be," fumed old Max, "You don't know what you are doing."
"How can you possibly know I am wrong?" countered the doctor.
"Well it's quite obvious," the Max replied, "My other leg is fine, and it's the exact same age!"
Everyone laughed and Stanislaw the plumber, decided to tell everyone about when he had done his friend Witold, the shoemaker, a favor and hired Witold's son Frank, fresh out of high school, to work in his shop. Stan said that Frank reported for his first day of work and Stanislaw greeted him with a warm handshake and a smile, gave him a broom and said, "Your first job will be to sweep out the shop."
"But I'm a high school graduate," Frank replied indignantly.
"Oh, I'm so sorry, so very sorry. I didn't know that," said Stanislaw. "Here, give me the broom – I'll show you how."
They all had a variety of comments about High school, youth in general and Stan laughed and said, " You know that to this day, I don't know if that scared Frank or not but I am very proud of the boy who is now going to McGill University studying to be a lawyer."

The opportunity to talk with the old neighbours and catch up on the gossip slowly dwindled to a trickle as more neighbours left the area. Occasionally we would still meet on the Main or at the Rachel Market when they returned to shop. I think that those who moved and those who remained in the neighbourhood missed the familiar shops and old acquaintances and one another and they certainly had to be missing the exchange of differing points of view and gossip.

In April 1961 a CIA-trained force of Cuban exiles with support and encouragement from the US government invaded southern Cuba at a beach named Playa Girón, located at the mouth of the bay, in an attempt to overthrow the Cuban government of Fidel Castro. The invasion was named after the Bay of Pigs, a modern translation of the Spanish Bahía de Cochinos. In Latin America, the conflict was known as La Batalla de Girón, or just Playa Girón. The invasion was launched less than three months after John F. Kennedy assumed the presidency in the United States. The Cuban armed forces, trained and equipped by Eastern Bloc nations, defeated the invading combatants within three days. The failed invasion severely embarrassed the Kennedy Administration, and made Castro wary of future US intervention in Cuba.

While most Berliners were sleeping during the night of August 12-13, 1961, East German soldiers of the German Democratic Republic (GDR, East Germany) and construction workers built the Berlin Wall, a barrier made of concrete posts and barbed wire along the border between West and East Berlin. The barrier included guard towers placed along large concrete walls, accompanied by a wide area (known as the "death strip") that contained anti-vehicle trenches and other defenses. The Berlin Wall not only cut off West Berlin by land from East Berlin but from all of surrounding East Germany. The Eastern Bloc portrayed the Wall as protecting its population from fascist elements conspiring to prevent the "will of the people" in building a socialist state in East Germany. In practice, the Wall served to prevent the massive emigration and defection that had marked East Germany and the communist Eastern Bloc during the post-World War II period. Before the Wall's erection, 3.5 million East Germans had defected from the GDR by crossing over the border from East Berlin. Once in West Berlin they could travel throughout West Germany and to other Western European countries. Between 1961 and 1989 over 100,000 people attempted to escape and over 5,000 people succeeded in escaping over the Wall, with an estimated death toll ranging from 136 to more than 200 in and around Berlin. In 1989 a series of revolutions in nearby Poland and Hungary caused a chain reaction in East Germany that brought down the wall. ultimately resulted in the demise of the Wall. After several weeks of civil unrest, the East German government announced on November 9, 1989 that all GDR citizens could visit West Germany and West Berlin. Crowds of East Germans crossed and climbed onto the Wall, joined by West Germans on the other side in a celebratory atmosphere. Over the next few weeks, euphoric people and souvenir hunters chipped away parts of the Wall; the governments later used industrial equipment to remove most of what was left. Demolition officially began on June 13, 1990 and was finished in 1992. The "fall of the Berlin Wall" paved the way for German reunification, which formally took place on October 3, 1990.

On April 12, 1961 the Soviets launched Vostok 1 and the first man in space Soviet cosmonaut Yuri Gagarin from the Baikonur Cosmodrome. Gagarin was rocketed into space using an automated system and he completed a single orbit around the Earth. The Vostok 1's top speed reached 28,260 kph (about 17,600 mph). Re-entering the Earth's atmosphere when Vostok 1 was still about 7 km (4.35 miles) from the ground, Gagarin ejected as planned from the spacecraft and used a parachute to land safely near the village of Uzmoriye, near the Volga River. The Vostok 1 flight from launch (at 9:07 a.m.) to touch down on the ground (10:55 a.m.) took 108 minutes. After the space flight, Gagarin helped train future cosmonauts. He died on March 27, 1968 while test-piloting a MiG-15 fighter jet.

The Rachel Street market was considered outdated in the era of new food supermarkets such as the Steinberg's store on St Denis and Mount Royal Streets and was closed in 1961. With Montreal chosen in 1962 as the site of the 1967 World's Fair, Mayor Jean Drapeau ordered a wave of demolitions to clean up the city prior to Expo 67. The St. Jean Baptiste Market (the Rachel Street Market) on the northeast corner of Rachel and St Lawrence, an institution since 1870, was demolished in 1966. The city beside incurring demolition costs also reportedly had to pay the descendants of Come Seraphin Cherrier because the 21,000 square-foot lot (today's Park of the Americas), was given by Cherrier to the city under the condition it be kept as a market in perpetuity. The market site became a parking lot until 1991 when it and Lozeau Street were replaced by parc des Amériques (park of the Americas) in honor of the Latin American community,

The half-hearted Bay of Pigs invasion left Soviet premier Nikita Khrushchev and his advisers with the impression that U.S. President Kennedy was weak, indecisive and not prepared for decision making in crisis situations. Khrushchev's impression of Kennedy's weakness was confirmed by the President's soft response regarding the construction of the Berlin Wall. In August 1962, the Cuban and Soviet governments secretly began to build bases in Cuba for a number of medium-range and intermediate-range ballistic nuclear missiles (MRBMs and IRBMs) with the ability to strike most of the continental United States. This action followed the 1958 deployment of Thor IRBMs in the UK (Project Emily) and Jupiter IRBMs in Italy and Turkey in 1961. More than 100 US-built missiles having the capability to strike Moscow with nuclear warheads were deployed. On October 14, 1962, a United States Air Force U-2 plane on a photo reconnaissance mission captured photographic proof of Soviet missile bases under construction in Cuba. The Americans feared the Soviet expansion of Communism, but for a Latin American country to ally openly with the USSR was regarded as unacceptable, given the Soviet-American enmity since the end of World War II in 1945.

The thirteen days between: October 25 and November 12, 1962 became known as the Cuban Missile Crisis, a confrontation between the Soviet Union and Cuba on one side and the United States on the other during the Cold War. The crisis ranked with the Berlin Blockade, the Suez Crisis and the Yom Kippur War as one of the major confrontations of the Cold War. It is generally regarded as the moment in which the Cold War came closest to turning into a nuclear conflict. The United States considered attacking Cuba via air and sea, but decided on a military blockade instead, calling it a "quarantine" for legal and other reasons. In Canada, Prime Minister Diefenbaker refused to put Canadian forces on alert, angering the U.S. government. The US announced that it would not permit offensive weapons to be delivered to Cuba and demanded that the Soviets dismantle the missile bases already under construction or completed in Cuba and remove all offensive weapons. The Kennedy administration held only a slim hope that the Kremlin would agree to their demands, and expected a military confrontation. On the Soviet side, Premier Nikita Khrushchev wrote in a letter to Kennedy that his blockade of "navigation in international waters and air space" constituted "an act of aggression propelling humankind into the abyss of a world nuclear-missile war". The Soviets publicly balked at the US demands, but in secret back-channel communications initiated a proposal to resolve the crisis. The confrontation ended on October 28, 1962, when President John F. Kennedy and United Nations Secretary-General U Thant reached an agreement with Khrushchev. Publicly, the Soviets would dismantle their offensive weapons in Cuba and return them to the Soviet Union, subject to United Nations verification, in exchange for a US public declaration and agreement never to invade Cuba. The US agreed to dismantle all US-built Jupiter IRBMs deployed in Turkey and Italy. Two weeks after the agreement, the Soviets had removed the missile systems and their support equipment, loading them onto eight Soviet ships from November 5th to the 9th. A month later, on December 5 and 6, the Soviet Il-28 bombers were loaded onto three Soviet ships and shipped back to Russia. The blockade was formally ended at 6:45 pm EDT on November 20, 1962. By September 1963 all American weapons were deactivated. The negotiations also resulted in the creation of the Moscow–Washington hotline, a direct communications link between Moscow and Washington, D.C.

Up until 1962, corporal punishment in the school classroom and capital punishment for crime in society were upheld as the law of the land. Governments, religious leaders, educators, and parents commonly believed that corporal punishment was appropriate to discipline children to maintain and restore order and to prevent inappropriate behaviour. The strap was an important instrument in a teacher's disciplinary arsenal, It was only in 1997 that the Province of Quebec amended its education act banning corporal punishment. Other provinces acted similarly. In January 2004, the Supreme Court of Canada ruled that corporal punishment was an unreasonable application of force in the maintenance of classroom discipline and outlawed corporal punishment in all schools, public or private. Such punishment of students by educators is now illegal throughout Canada. However the Supreme Court upheld the right of Canadian parents to spank or hit their own children between the ages of 2 and 12 by hand only. With this ruling, the strap and other instruments used for disciplinary purposes disappeared from Canadian schools, though certainly not from Canadian families.

Capital punishment, also known as the death penalty, was in full force and effect sanctioning the practice of the government putting a person to death by execution as a punishment for a crime. People still talked about stories that they had heard about public executions in Canada early in the 1900s. At that time reporters were permitted to witness hangings and they painted the scene as compellingly as possible for readers of the newspaper. Stories were retold about the hangmen who apparently were entitled to the clothes off the backs of the men they executed. The stories went on to add that the hangmen made as much money selling the clothes as they did getting paid for the hangings. The last hanging of a man at Montreal's Bordeaux jail was March 11, 1960. The last woman was hanged in Canada on January 9, 1953 and the last two men were hung from the gallows in Toronto's Don Jail on December 11, 1962. Historically, hanging was the only method of execution used in Canada and was in use as punishment for all murders until 1961, when murders were reclassified into capital and non-capital offences. Resistance to capital punishment grew as people begun to question the humanity of capital punishment and its effectiveness as a deterrent. By 1963, it had become de facto policy for the federal government to commute death sentences and, in 1967, a moratorium was placed on capital punishment for all crimes except the murder of on-duty police officers and prison guards. The death penalty was abolished in Canada on July 14, 1976 when the House of Commons voted to strike capital punishment from the Canadian Criminal Code. Meanwhile in the U.S.A. although capital punishment laws are being challenged Americans continue to hand out death sentences in all but 14 states.

The Place Ville-Marie (PVM) complex with an underground shopping mall is at the center of Montreal's underground city with tunnels extending all over downtown interconnecting office towers, hotels, shopping centres, residential and commercial complexes, convention halls, universities and performing arts venues. The network forms the heart of Downtown Montreal; is largely climate controlled, well-lit and is integrated with the city's entirely underground rapid transit system, the Montreal Metro, the CN Central train station and the Queen Elizabeth Hotel. An estimated half a million people use it every day and it is particularly useful during Montreal's long winters. The Trans-Canada Highway, a federal-provincial highway system that travels through all ten provinces of Canada, was officially opened on July 30, 1962, although not fully completed. Construction of the highway had started in 1950 and was completed in 1971. It is one of the world's longest national highways, with the main route spanning 8,030 km (4,990 mi) and is recognizable by its distinctive white-on-green maple leaf route markers.

In 1962 audio cassette tapes were developed for recording and playback; the first person was killed trying to cross the Berlin Wall and Marilyn Monroe was found dead. The Champlain bridge and Montreal's first underground tunnel between Place Ville-Marie and the Central Station were opened. On March 21, 1962 the birth-defect-causing drug thalidomide sold from 1957 until 1961 to treat morning sickness was banned. On May 2, 1962 the Canadian dollar was pegged to the U.S. currency. On September 29, 1962 Alouette 1, Canada's first satellite was launched into orbit around the earth by NASA from the Pacific Missile Range at Vandenberg AFB, California. Alouette was used to study the ionosphere, an area of the upper atmosphere where many future satellites were to be placed into orbit. Alouette's mission lasted for 10 years before the unit was deliberately switched off. Alouette 1 remains in orbit and is estimated to remain in orbit for 1000 years.

At the start of the 1960s, Montreal was Canada's business capital. It was Canada's leader in the clothing, textiles, leather and shoe industries. It was home to a thriving financial industry, the head offices of the Bank of Montreal, the Royal Bank of Canada, Sun Life insurance, the Montreal Stock Exchange, the Canadian Stock Exchange, a large community of brokerage and investment firms and head offices in Quebec's natural resource industry and headquarters for both Canadian National and Canadian Pacific Railways. At the same time, Montreal was in the midst of a series of infrastructure projects spurred on by Jean Drapeau who served as mayor of Montreal from 1954 to 1957 and 1960 to 1986. Drapeau oversaw the expansion of Dorval airport (now Montreal-Pierre Elliott Trudeau International Airport), the opening of the Champlain bridge, the construction and inauguration of Place Ville Marie and Place des Arts, the construction of the Montreal metro system that had started on May 23, 1962. Under Drapeau, Montreal was awarded the 1967 International and Universal Exposition (Expo 67), whose construction he oversaw; a franchise from the National Baseball League for the now-defunct Montreal Expos Baseball team; and the 1976 Summer Olympics.

Construction of the Montreal subway called the Metro was inaugurated on October 14, 1966. It started with two lines and was expanded to four lines serving the north, east and centre of the Island of Montreal with connections to Longueuil and to Laval. The service was opened gradually after October 1966 as the stations were completed. The main line, number 1 (Green Line - Ligne verte) runs on a northeast to southwest axis under De Maisonneuve Boulevard which is between Sainte-Catherine and Sherbrooke streets; originally from the English-speaking west at Atwater station to the French-speaking east at Frontenac. The line was extended to Honoré-Beaugrand in 1976 to provide easy access to the 1976 Summer Olympics sites and it was extended again to Angrignon in 1978. There is a connection to the Orange and Yellow Lines at Berri-UQAM station, and with the Orange Line west of downtown at the Lionel-Groulx station located on Atwater street. The Berri-UQAM station is on Berri street and UQAM signifies it as a stop for the french speaking public university, the Université du Québec à Montréal (UQAM).

Line 2 (Orange Line - Ligne orange) runs in a north south axis and initially ran from Crémazie station in the north to the business district at Place-d'Armes station in the south. In 1963 the line was extended adding the Sauvé and Henri-

Bourassa stations in the north. From 1980 to 1986 it was further extended to Square-Victoria-OACI and Bonaventure stations in the south. and on its way to Lionel-Groulx and then north to Côte-Vertu and the line now runs in a U-shape from Côte-Vertu in northwestern Montreal to Montmorency in Laval, northeast of Montreal. Line 3 (Red Line - Ligne rouge) a proposed line that never made it past its planning stage was supposed to have 15 stations and end at Bordeaux-Cartierville using the CN tracks and the Mount Royal Tunnel under Mount Royal. Line 4 (Yellow Line - Ligne jaune) is the first Metro line to leave the island of Montreal which runs from Berri-de Montigny (Berri-UQAM) under the St. Lawrence River to Longueuil with a stop at St Helen's Island (Île Sainte-Hélène). The St Helen's Island stop was used for Expo 67 and La Ronde and has since been renamed as has the island to Parc Jean Drapeau. The Longueuil station is now called Longueuil - Université-de-Sherbrooke. Line 5 (Blue Line - Ligne Bleue) runs between Snowdon and St Michel with further expansions planned..

Montreal's winter conditions influenced the design of the Metro which was inspired by the Paris Métro. The entire system runs underground with some stations directly connected to buildings, making the Metro an integral part of Montreal's underground city. Most of the station entrances are set back from the sidewalk and are completely enclosed and many of the stations are decorated with over one hundred works of public art, such as sculpture, stained glass, and murals by noted Quebec artists. Montreal's Metro trains are 2.5 m (8 ft 2 $\frac{3}{8}$ in) wide, narrower than most other subway trains and are made of low-alloy high-tensile steel, painted blue with a thick white stripe running lengthwise. Metro subway cars use rubber tires which transmit minimal vibration helping cars negotiate turns at high speeds and more easily to go uphill. Trains draw electrical current from two sets of 750-volt direct current third rails on either side of each motor car and the trains use electromagnetic brakes, generated by the train's kinetic energy until they slow down to about 10 km/h (6.2 mph). The trains then use composite brake blocks made of yellow birch injected with peanut oil to bring them to a complete stop. Hard braking produces a characteristic burnt popcorn scent.

During Metro construction tunnels were created to join metro stations on the orange line with buildings such as Bonaventure Metro station connected to the Château Champlain hotel, the Place du Canada office tower, Place Bonaventure, Central Station, Windsor Station and the Square-Victoria-OACI Metro station connected to the Tour de la Bourse, Montreal's stock exchange building added to Montreal's Underground City. The Transit Commission had a policy of offering emphyteutic leases for the aerial rights above Metro station entrances enabling the construction of buildings over the entrances. Emphyteutic leases basically leased the aerial rights to the property for an extended period of time for little if any compensation and at the expiry of the lease term the building s ownership transfers from the lessee to the owner of the land. When the Metro ran in 1966, there were ten buildings connected directly to Metro stations. The construction of the Complexe Desjardins office tower complex in 1974 resulted in a second downtown underground city segment between Place-des-Arts and Place-d'Armes station, via Place des Arts, Complexe Desjardins, the Complexe Guy

Favreau federal government building, and the Palais des Congrès convention centre. Between 1984 and 1992, the underground city expanded further with the construction of three major linked shopping centres in the Peel and McGill Metro station areas: Cours Mont-Royal, Place Montréal-Trust, and the Promenades Cathédrale built underneath Christ Church Cathedral. McGill Metro station was already linked with The Bay, Eaton's (now the Complexe Les Ailes), Centre Eaton, and two other office/mall complexes. Between 1984 and 1989, the underground city grew from 12 km (7 mi) of passages to almost 22 km (14 mi).

The 1967 International and Universal Exposition or Expo 67 was held in Montreal from April 27 to October 29, 1967. Expo 67 was Canada's main celebration during its centennial year and 62 nations participated making it the most successful World's Fair of the 20th century setting the single-day attendance record for a world's fair, with 569,500 visitors on its third day. The theme of Expo67 was Man and his World (Terre des Hommes) meant to encapsulate the world's progress in industry, science, and culture. It was Mayor Drapeau's idea to have the site of Expo on new artificial islands in the St Lawrence River and to enlarge the existing Saint Helen's Island. The small Ronde Island was joined to the north eastern tip of Saint Helen's Island and was enlarged to 146 acres (59.1 ha) to host La Ronde amusement park as the entertainment complex for Expo 67. Notre Dame Island (Île Notre-Dame) is an artificial (man made) island in the Saint Lawrence River east of Saint Helen's Island and west of the Saint Lawrence Seaway and the city of Longueil on the south shore. The choice required a lot of technical expertise but it overcame opposition from Montreal's surrounding municipalities and prevented land speculation. Construction of the artificial island of Notre Dame Island, enlarging Saint Helen's Island and lengthening and enlarging the Mackay Pier which became the Cité du Havre started on August 13, 1963. Some 25 million tons of fill was needed to construct the islands, 10-12% came from the Montreal Metro's excavations that was under construction. The remainder of the fill came from dredging the river and from quarries on Montreal and the South Shore. The newly created grounds rising out of Montreal harbour to hold the fair were officially transferred from the City of Montreal to the Expo Corporation on June 20, 1964. Colonel Churchill in charge of the project had only 1042 days to have everything built and functioning for opening day. The critical path method (CPM), a new project management tool at the time was used to get Expo built in time and everything was ready on opening day. Aside from building and enlarging the islands, a new Concorde Bridge was built connecting the site with the Montreal harbour to accommodate the Expo Express a site specific monorail mass transit system. The Turcot Interchange and the Bonaventure and Decarie Expressways all opened on time for Expo67 as did the newly built Metro, helping to provide many transportation options for visitors, including the Expo-Express, a monorail that allowed visitors to see the pavilions from above; the cable cars at La Ronde (the on-site amusement park); the vaporetto, which navigated across the canal; and even a hovercraft. None of these innovations, ever spread to the mainland after Expo closed.

Expo 67 opened to the public on the morning of Friday, April 28, 1967, with a capacity crowd estimated at 335,000 visitors at the Expo gates at Place d'Accueil participating in a space age-style atomic clock-controlled countdown. 90 pavilions representing Man and His World themes were featured. The Soviet Union's pavilion attracted the most visitors estimated at about 13 million; next were the Canadian Pavilion at 11 million visitors, the United States pavilion, a geodesic dome designed by Buckminster Fuller at 9 million visitors, France at 8.5 million, and Czechoslovakia at 8 million. Expo 67 featured the ten-storey Habitat 67 modular housing complex on the Marc Drouin Quay on the Saint Lawrence River designed by architect Moshe Safdie for his thesis project at McGill's School of Architecture as a solution to affordable urban housing providing an efficient and innovative way to house a large number of families as an alternative to the standard apartment complex. His creation looked like enormous concrete Lego pieces stacked unevenly on top of each other with external walkways (pedestrian streets) providing direct access to each of the 158 units of residence with each house having a terrace on top of the unit below, Habitat 67 is probably the only standing legacy of Expo 67 that is currently used as a residential space after the units were purchased by private individuals from the Canada Mortgage and Housing Corporation in 1985 and are still being occupied.

After Expo 67 ended in October 1967, the city tried to keep the spirit of Expo alive. The site and most of the pavilions continued on as a permanent exhibition called Man and His World, open during the summer months from 1968 until 1984. As attendance declined, the physical condition of the site deteriorated, and less and less of it was open to the public.

As the largest Canadian cities grew in the 1950s and 1960s, the volume of mail passing through the country's postal system also grew, to billions of items by the 1950s and tens of billions of items by the mid-1960s. It became progressively more difficult for employees who hand sorted mail to memorize and keep track of all the individual letter-carrier routes within each city. New technology that allowed mail to be delivered faster also contributed to the pressure for these employees to properly sort the mail. Due to this necessity Canada implemented a six-character alphanumeric code or string that forms part of a postal address from 1972 to 1974 allowing Canada Post to use sorting machines to simplify and speed up the flow of mail.

After the 1971 season, the entire Notre Dame Island site closed and was completely rebuilt opening three years later with a new rowing basin for Montreal's 1976 Summer Olympics for canoe sprint and flatwater canoeing events. Many of the former pavilions were demolished to make space for the basin, the boathouses, the changing rooms and other buildings. In 1976, a fire destroyed the acrylic outer skin of Buckminster Fuller's dome, and the previous year the Ontario pavilion was lost due to a major fire.

On May 12, 1970 after being awarded the 1976 Summer Olympics, officially called the Games of the XXI Olympiad, an international multi-sport event; the Organizing Committee for the Olympic Games (OCOG) had six years to plan the financing and operation of the Games and to oversee the construction of Olympic facilities including the Olympic Stadium, the Swimming Pool, the Olympic Basin, the Velodrome, the Olympic Village, the Claude Robillard Centre and the Étienne Desmarteau Centre. Montréal hosted the first Olympic Games held in Canada from July 17 to August 1, 1976 starting with the opening ceremony at which Elizabeth II, as Queen of Canada, opened the games with several members of the Royal Family attending the opening ceremonies, held at the Olympic Stadium in front of an audience of some 73,000 in the stadium, and an estimated half billion watching on television. This was particularly significant since the Queen's daughter, Princess Anne, competed in the games as part of the British riding team. The Montreal ceremony was the last of its kind, as future Olympic ceremonies, beginning with the 1980 Moscow Games, were more focused on theatrical, cultural and artistic presentations and less on formality and protocol.

In 1980 the Notre Dame Island site was reopened to hold the outdoor gardens for the Floralies Internationales de Montréal, the 8th international horticultural exposition recognized by the Bureau of International Expositions. The Floralies outdoor garden exhibition by 12 countries made both islands simultaneously accessible again, albeit only for a brief time. The outdoor gardens opened to the public on May 31 and ran until September 1, 1980. After the 1981 season, the Saint Helen's Island site permanently closed, shutting out the majority of attractions.

The former site for Expo 67 on Saint Helen's Island and Notre Dame Island was incorporated into a municipal park run by the city of Montreal, named Parc Jean-Drapeau, after Mayor Jean Drapeau. Today very little remains of Expo; the American pavilion's metal-lattice skeleton from its Buckminster Fuller dome, now encloses an environmental sciences museum called the Montreal Biosphere; The French pavilion was inaugurated as the Casino de Montreal in 1993; and Habitat 67 is now a condominium residence. La Ronde survives, and since 2001 it has been leased to the New York amusement park company Six Flags. The Alcan Aquarium built for the Expo remained in operation for a number of decades until its closure in 1991. Notre Dame Island today is the site of the Circuit Gilles Villeneuve race track that is used for the Canadian Grand Prix. The Olympic basin is used by many local rowing clubs. A beach was built on the shores of the remaining artificial lake. There are many acres of parkland and cycle paths on both Saint Helen's Island and the western tip of Notre Dame Island. The young trees and shrubs planted for Expo 67 are now mature and the plants introduced during the botanical events have flourished making the islands ideal for recreational purposes and parkland.

In the early 1960s Quebec underwent what it called a Quiet Revolution (Révolution tranquille), a period of intense change initiated by the Liberal governments of Jean Lesage (elected in 1960) and Robert Bourassa (elected in 1970). The provincial government took control over health care and education from the Roman Catholic Church; allowed unionization of the civil service; nationalized electricity production and distribution; took over the administration of the Canada/Quebec Pension Plan and witnessed renewed Quebecois nationalism. Prior to the 1960s, the government of Quebec was controlled by conservative Maurice Duplessis, leader of the Union Nationale party supported by the bulk of small-town and rural Catholic clergy. Some quoted the Union Nationale slogan Le ciel est bleu, l'enfer est rouge (The sky (Heaven) is blue, Hell is red) as a reference to the colours of the Union Nationale (blue) and the Liberals (red), Within a year of Duplessis's death, the Liberal Party won the election, led by Jean Lesage who campaigned under the slogans Il faut que ça change ("Things have to change") and Maîtres chez nous ("Masters of our own house").

Quebec in 1960 was not what it was in 1940. The population had grown from just over 3 million to 5.3 million, and the movement of people off the land and into urban areas rendered Duplessis' agrarian focus obsolete. The very rapid abrupt shift from being the greatest bastion of piety to secularism in Quebec was exceptional. Quebec's anti-clerical upheaval and resentment felt by many French Canadians over the church's perceived abuse of power diminished the influence of the Catholic church. The church lost its power over schools and hospitals, and the French language replaced Catholicism as the province's badge of distinction. Montreal today is a non-religious place where Catholic practice is plummeting with cheerful indifference to Catholic morals; church and civil marriages are unusual and Mass attendance is at its lowest. Sprawling, metropolitan Montreal in 1961 contained 2.1 million people, 40% of the province's total population. It was in the politically powerful urban areas that support for substantial social and economic change and modernization was most in demand. It was there that Improved educational and social welfare programs were a first priority, as was the nationalization of the entire hydroelectric sector under Hydro-Québec allowed the government to ensure that Quebecers had first call on construction-related jobs and that highly skilled francophones would not be denied management and technical positions as they arose. The crown corporation functioned in French first and was the centrepiece of a suite of policies aimed to achieve the goal of Maîtres chez nous (masters of our own house).

The Hydro-Québec project grew to become an important symbol in Quebec. It demonstrated the strength and initiative of the Quebec government ushering in an era of "megaprojects" that continued until 1984. The provincial government thereafter applied similar nationalizing models to other areas of their resource sector, increasing jobs and government revenue at the same time. More public institutions were created to follow through with the desire to increase the province's economic autonomy. The public companies SIDBEC (iron and steel), SOQUEM (mining), REXFOR (forestry) and SOQUIP (petroleum) were created to exploit the province's natural resources. The Société générale de financement (General financing corporation) was created in 1962 to encourage Québécois to invest in their economic future and to increase the profitability of small companies. In 1963, in conjunction with the Canada Pension Plan the government of Canada authorized the province to create its own Régie des Rentes du Québec (RRQ, Quebec Pension Plan); universal contributions came into effect in 1966. The Caisse de dépôt et placement du Québec (CDPQ, Quebec Deposit and Investment Fund) was created in 1965 to manage the considerable revenues generated by the Régie des Rentes du Québec (RRQ, Quebec Pension Plan). The RRQ was authorized by the government of Canada and spun off from the Canada Pension Plan to provide the capital necessary for various projects in the public and private sectors.

In 1964 a Ministry of Education was established and schools became secular institutions. According to the Canadian Constitution of 1867 education was a provincial responsibility. Quebec had set up a Ministry of Public Instruction in 1868 but abolished it in 1875 under pressure from the Catholic Church. The clergy believed that they could provide appropriate teaching to young people. However until the Quiet Revolution, higher education was accessible to only a minority of French Canadians because of the generally low level of formal education and the expense involved. The Ministry introduced several reforms; raising the age for compulsory schooling from 14 to 16, providing free schooling until the 11th grade. They reorganized school boards, standardized school curricula and replaced classical colleges with CEGEPs (publicly funded pre university colleges). Classical colleges had provided a classical and general education. The curriculum was focused almost entirely on the humanities rather than meeting postwar needs for science, technology and commerce and they depended on voluntary religious teachers. The timing of education reform was significant. Removing the Catholic Church from its dominant position in education coincided roughly with the Second Vatican Council (Vatican II) reforms where the possibility of careers for nuns and priests as educators and health professionals was in retreat. The Provincial government took over the nuns' traditional role as provider of educational and social services. All of these changes ensured that authority increasingly resided with the state, not the Church.

The societal and economic innovations of the Quiet Revolution empowered Quebec society and emboldened certain nationalists to push for political independence. In 1968, the sovereigntist Parti Québécois was created, with René Lévesque as its leader. A small faction of Marxist sovereignists began terrorist actions as the Front de libération du Québec, (FLQ), resulting in the 1970 October Crisis in Montreal. Members of the Front de libération du Québec (FLQ) kidnapped the provincial cabinet minister Pierre Laporte and the British diplomat James Cross. In response, Prime Minister Pierre Trudeau invoked the only peacetime use of the War Measures Act. The kidnappers murdered Laporte, and negotiations led to Cross's release and the kidnappers' exile to Cuba. The War Measures Act limited civil liberties and granted the police far-reaching powers. The Quebec government also requested military aid to support the local police, and Canadian Forces were deployed throughout Quebec; acting in a support role to the Quebec civil authorities. 497 individuals were arrested and detained, without bail; all but 62 of whom were later released without charges. The events of October 1970 galvanized support against the use of violence in efforts to gain Quebec sovereignty and accelerated support for the sovereigntist Parti Québécois (PQ), which formed the provincial government in 1976.

René Lévesque (August 24, 1922 – November 1, 1987) had been a reporter and a minister of the Liberal government of Quebec (1960–1966). He left the Liberal Party and founded the Mouvement Souveraineté-Association which later merged with the Quebec sovereignty movement, the Ralliement National of Gilles Grégoire, to create the Parti Québécois (PQ) in 1973. Lévesque became the 23rd Premier of Quebec (November 25, 1976 – October 3, 1985) after winning a landslide victory at the 1976 election, with 41.1 per cent of the popular vote and 71 seats out of 110. In 1977, during their first term in office, the Parti Québécois enacted the Charter of the French Language, known in English as Bill 101, whose goal was to protect the French language by making it the normal and everyday language of work, instruction, communication, commerce and business. Bill 101 also made it illegal for businesses to put up exterior commercial signs in a language other than French at a time when English dominated as a commercial and business language in Quebec. The bill also restricted the eligibility for elementary and high school students to attend school in English, allowing this only for children of parents who had studied in English in Quebec. All other children were required to attend French schools in order to encourage immigrants to integrate themselves into the majority French culture. On May 20, 1980, the PQ held, as promised before the elections, the 1980 Quebec referendum on its sovereignty-association plan. The result of the vote was 40.44% in favour and 59.56% opposed (with 86% turnout). Lévesque conceded defeat in the referendum by announcing that, as he had understood the verdict, he had been told "until next time." This was understood to mean that the fight was not over and more attempts would be made. Lévesque was the first Quebec political leader since Confederation to attempt, through a referendum, to negotiate the political independence of Quebec.

Lévesque led the PQ to victory in the 1981 election, increasing the party's majority in the National Assembly and increasing its share of the popular vote from 41 to 49 per cent. With the turmoil generated by nationalization, prohibition of English signs, language of work legislation, the threat of violence, the murder of Pierre Laporte, the exploding mailboxes and the general reaction of the populace at large; where neighbours overnight suddenly refused to speak or understand English saying 'Je ne comprends pas" where the day before they had no problem with English, made Anglophones generally feel unwelcomed and people and business started to move away. Political tensions over language and the issue of Quebec sovereignty hurt private investment and drove some of the wealthiest and best educated people out of the province. The number of head offices that called Montreal home declined sharply. Head offices supported a range of activities like legal, financial, accounting and advertising services. They maintained high-quality, high-income jobs and provided the city with a measure of economic influence and they were gone. Sun Life left in 1978 after the Parti Québécois took power for the first time. The head office operations of the Bank of Montreal and the Royal Bank gradually shifted to Toronto. The Parti Québécois had twice led Quebecers through unsuccessful referendums, the first in 1980 on the question of political sovereignty with economic association to Canada, and the second in 1995 on full sovereignty. The Canadian Stock Exchange closed its doors in 1974. The Montreal Exchange lost increasing trading volumes to its Toronto rival and switched to financial derivatives. The fancy new airport built in Mirabel had to be abandoned, while Toronto became the hub for Canadian air travel. In the mid 1980s the company that I was working for transferred me and my immediate family to Toronto. Except for two or three of my friends and less than a handful of neighbours remaining in the district I said farewell to them and to family. We had all witnessed neighbours who had moved previously to more affluent suburbs of Montreal, but this was different, we were moving away from the city of my youth and joining the 1980s exodus migration mostly to Toronto and surrounding areas. Times were changing, our meeting place, the Rachel Street Market was gone as were many of our friends and neighbours. Je me souviens, the official motto of Quebec carved in stone below the coat of arms of Quebec above the Quebec Parliament Building's main entrance door, acquired a more personal meaning in our collective memories which I have chosen to record mine before they fade and become forgotten. It was time to say Adieu to my youth and to embrace the future walking in step with the march of time.

FIN   END

ABOUT THE AUTHOR

Roman Susel, born and raised in the ethnically diverse neighbourhood of Le Plateau Mont Royal district of Montreal, Quebec near the Rachel Street Market, is retired and now resides with his wife, Wanda in Ontario. He is a graduate of Concordia University having earned an associate in Science diploma, B.Comm (major in Accountancy), C.M.A., C.G.A., CPA, A.C.I.S., P.Adm. and is a winner of the prestigious 1965 E.G. Hardman Prize from the Council of the Chartered Institute of Secretaries (U.K.). Roman specialized in applying financial accounting business solutions for clients in a broad range of industries, government and healthcare in Canada, the U.S. and the Caribbean. He authored several articles and courses in finance and was guest speaker at various events. Roman was awarded The 2004 Teaching Excellence Award from George Brown College Centre for Continuous Learning where he was a professor whom students called "the best teacher". Roman is a proud father of four sons and treasures his nine grandchildren. Find out more about Roman at romansemporium.com

www.ingramcontent.com/pod-product-compliance
Lightning Source LLC
Chambersburg PA
CBHW061430040426
42450CB00007B/979